MW00850961

CULTIVATING CAPSTONES

SERIES ON **ENGAGED LEARNING** AND **TEACHING**

Series Editors: Jessie L. Moore and Peter Felten

Mind the Gap
Global Learning at Home and Abroad
Edited by Nina Namaste and Amanda Sturgill, with Neal Sobania and Michael Vande Berg

Promoting Equity and Inclusion Through Pedagogical Partnership
Alise de Bie, Elizabeth Marquis, Alison Cook-Sather, and Leslie Patricia Luqueño

Key Practices for Fostering Engaged Learning
A Guide for Faculty and Staff
Jessie L. Moore

The Faculty Factor
Developing Faculty Engagement With Living–Learning Communities
Edited by Jennifer E. Eidum and Lara L. Lomicka

Cultivating Capstones
Designing High-Quality Culminating Experiences for Student Learning
Edited by Caroline J. Ketcham, Anthony G. Weaver, and Jessie L. Moore

CULTIVATING CAPSTONES

Designing High-Quality Culminating Experiences
for Student Learning

Edited by Caroline J. Ketcham,
Anthony G. Weaver, and Jessie L. Moore

Series Foreword by Jessie L. Moore and Peter Felten

Series on Engaged Learning and Teaching

Copublished in association with

STERLING, VIRGINIA

COPYRIGHT © 2023 BY STYLUS PUBLISHING, LLC.

Published by Stylus Publishing, LLC.
22883 Quicksilver Drive
Sterling, Virginia 20166-2019

All rights reserved. No part of this book may be reprinted or reproduced in any form or by any electronic, mechanical, or other means, now known or hereafter invented, including photocopying, recording, and information storage and retrieval, without permission in writing from the publisher.

Library of Congress Cataloging-in-Publication-Data

Names: Ketcham, Caroline J., editor. | Weaver, Anthony G., editor. | Moore, Jessie L., editor.
Title: Cultivating capstones : designing high-quality culminating experiences for student learning / edited by Caroline J. Ketcham, Anthony G. Weaver, and Jessie L. Moore ; series foreword by Jessie L. Moore and Peter Felten.
Description: First Edition. | Sterling, Virginia : Copublished in association with Elon University Center for Engaged Learning | Stylus Publishing, LLC, [2023] | Series: Series on Engaged Learning and Teaching / series editors, Jessie L. Moore and Peter Felten | Includes bibliographical references and index. | Summary: "Capstones have been a part of higher education curriculum for over two centuries, with the goal of integrating student learning to cap off their undergraduate experience. This edited collection draws on multi-year, multi-institutional, and mixed-methods studies to inform the development of best practices for cultivating capstones at a variety of higher education institutions"-- Provided by publisher.
Identifiers: LCCN 2022061837 (print) | LCCN 2022061838 (ebook) | ISBN 9781642674170 (Paperback : acid-free paper) | ISBN 9781642674163 (Cloth : acid-free paper) | ISBN 9781642674170 (Paperback : acid-free paper) | ISBN 9781642674187 (library networkable e-edition) | ISBN 9781642674194 (consumer e-edition)
Subjects: LCSH: Independent study--United States--Handbooks, manuals, etc. | Project method in teaching--Handbooks, manuals, etc. | Undergraduates--Research--Handbooks, manuals, etc. | Internship programs--United States. | Mentoring in education--United States.
Classification: LCC LB1620 .C85 2023 (print) | LCC LB1620 (ebook) | DDC 378.1/7943--dc23/eng/20230118
LC record available at https://lccn.loc.gov/2022061837
LC ebook record available at https://lccn.loc.gov/2022061838

13-digit ISBN: 978-1-64267-416-3 (cloth)
13-digit ISBN: 978-1-64267-417-0 (paperback)
13-digit ISBN: 978-1-64267-418-7 (library networkable e-edition)
13-digit ISBN: 978-1-64267-419-4 (consumer e-edition)

Printed in the United States of America

All first editions printed on acid free paper
that meets the American National Standards Institute
Z39-48 Standard.

Bulk Purchases

Quantity discounts are available for use in workshops and for staff development.

Call 1-800-232-0223

First Edition, 2023

CONTENTS

SERIES FOREWORD

*C*ultivating Capstones: Designing High-Quality Culminating Experiences *for Student Learning* is part of the Series on Engaged Learning and Teaching, published by Stylus in partnership with the Center for Engaged Learning at Elon University. The series is designed for a multidisciplinary audience of higher education faculty, staff, graduate students, educational developers, administrators, and policymakers interested in research-informed engaged learning practices. Although individual books in the series might most appeal to those interested in a specific topic, each volume concisely synthesizes research for nonexperts and addresses the broader implications of this particular work for higher education, including effective practices for teaching, curriculum design, and educational policies. All books in the series are supplemented by open-access resources hosted on the Center for Engaged Learning's website.

Cultivating Capstones features new international and multi-institutional research as well as concrete strategies for designing high-quality culminating experiences in diverse higher education institutions. This book introduces an ecological model for situating this high-impact practice within individual, organizational, and cultural contexts, thereby providing a practical and equity-oriented tool for understanding—and for reimagining—culminating student experiences. Chapters explore topics including the defining characteristics of capstones, case studies of novel culminating experiences, and evidence-informed strategies for professional development to support high-quality capstone teaching and learning. Supplemental resources for *Cultivating Capstones*—including additional examples, discussion questions for reading groups, and more—are available at www.centerforengagedlearning .org/books/cultivating-capstones.

We extend our thanks to Caroline J. Ketcham, Anthony G. Weaver, and the collection's contributing authors for writing this significant text for the series. Their research, practical advice, and strategic guidance will help faculty and institutions cultivate integrative, equitable, inspiring, and transformational culminating experiences for students across the United States and around the world.

To learn more about the Series on Engaged Learning and Teaching, including how to propose a book, please visit www.centerforengagedlearning.org/publications/.

Series Editors, Jessie L. Moore and Peter Felten
Center for Engaged Learning
Elon University

INTRODUCTION

Capstone Experiences in Undergraduate Education

Jillian Kinzie, Caroline J. Ketcham, Anthony G. Weaver, and Jessie L. Moore

Capstones are a classic feature of undergraduate education. Typically designed as an integrating project or a culminating educational experience for students at the end of their undergraduate program, they can also foster transition to work or further education beyond the bachelor's degree (Gardner et al., 1998; Hunter et al., 2012; Lee & Loton, 2019). Although capstones have existed since the late 1800s, interest in the experience grew beginning in the 1990s corresponding to a renewed focus on reinventing undergraduate education (Boyer Commission on Educating Undergraduates in the Research University, 1998). Boyer championed the capstone experience as a core component of a "new model of educating at the undergraduate research universities" (p. 16).

In the mid-2000s, capstones garnered new attention as an identified "high-impact practice" (HIP) due to their positive association with student engagement, learning, and retention (Brownell & Swaner, 2010; Kuh, 2008; National Survey of Student Engagement, 2018). Capstones have also garnered attention internationally; for example, in 2013, the Australian Government Office for Learning and Teaching funded a National Senior Teaching Fellowship on the topic of capstone curriculum across disciplines (Lee & Loton, 2015a). More recently, growing critiques about the fragmented nature of learning in college, equity of opportunity, and students' career readiness (Abel & Deitz, 2014; Greenstein, 2017; Hovland et al., 2015; Strada-Gallup, 2017) focused attention on capstones as an opportunity to pull key ideas together at the end of senior year and to ensure that students experience a crowning achievement in their educational journey.

As pressure mounts for higher education to assure high-quality educational experiences for all students while expanding access and increasing completion rates, educators should examine the value of long-standing educational practices to achieve these aims. Renewed attention to capstones as part of an educational reinvention strategy, and among the currently popular

1

HIPs, makes it important to explore what capstones contribute to addressing current pressures and goals for higher education and to examine what is fueling interest. Even more, as colleges and universities embark on the difficult work of improvement and change in a context of increased skepticism about the value of a college degree, it is helpful to have models to account for and offer new ways of looking at the complex challenges that come with adopting and refining educational practices.

The widespread popularity of HIPs, paired with interest from colleges and universities in adopting capstones as a strategy for broadening, deepening, and integrating the totality of the undergraduate experience and preparing students postcollege, provides an important occasion to consider the current landscape of capstones. This chapter first offers a brief overview of capstone experiences, history, and scholarship. It then applies Bronfenbrenner's (1977) human ecology theory as a framework for examining higher education reform, capstones, and the interacting forces of ideology and culture, social and organizational structure, time, and individuals. Bronfenbrenner's socioecological framework provides an analytical tool to map the capstone landscape, to identify gaps, and to point to possible levers for enhanced educational practice, policy, and research. The framework suggests a comprehensive approach for examining the complex environment for understanding capstones as an educational strategy to assure quality learning and to improve the conditions for student success. The chapter closes with a discussion of four contemporary pressures in higher education relevant to capstone implementation: assurance of student learning, career outcomes and students' transitions to the 21st-century workplace, relationship-rich education, and equitable design and implementation of courses to foster learning.

Capstones History and Promise

Since their beginnings in the 1800s as senior seminars to discuss the connection between philosophy and religion, capstones served the goal of fostering integration at the end of students' educational journey. Levine (1998) described four purposes of capstones:

- integration (connecting ideas through all years of college)
- breadth (moving students beyond specialization in the major to a broad general education experience)
- application (applying expert knowledge to examine real-world issues and produce a substantial product)
- transition (preparing students to move from college to the world beyond)

These purposes continue to animate most current-day capstones, as Part One, "Understanding the Landscape of Capstone Experiences," explores.

The idea of offering students an opportunity to create a "crowning achievement" is a consistent theme of capstone descriptions. As a result, most capstones are defined by substantive qualities, including student-initiated, time-intensive, inquiry-based, integrative, and real-world application. Capstones have been associated with the opportunity for *signature work*, a term the Association of American Colleges and Universities (AAC&U) has used to describe a student's use of their cumulative learning to pursue a significant project related to a problem defined with guidance from faculty and mentors, and as a multifaceted investigative project that culminates in a final product, presentation, exhibit or performance, or a portfolio of best work (AAC&U, 2015; Kinzie, 2018). Capstones ask students, for example, to select a topic or social problem that interests them, conduct research on the subject, maintain a portfolio of findings or results, create a final product demonstrating their learning or conclusions, and publicly present the project to an audience who evaluates its quality. Ultimately, a capstone project represents new work and ideas, and gives students the opportunity to demonstrate the expertise, knowledge, and skills gained during their college career.

The availability of capstones in institutions of higher education has ebbed and flowed over time, with the offering estimated to occur in one of 20 institutions in the 1990s (Levine, 1998) and more recently, at up to 60% of all institutions (Hauhart & Grahe, 2015). Interest in quantifying capstones has shifted to classifying types and purposes across disciplines (Lee & Loton, 2019) or, in the case of *U.S News & World Report*, to rank stellar examples of senior capstones. Capstones have been formally profiled across several iterations of the National Survey of Senior Capstone Experience. Surveys conducted in 1999, 2011, and 2016 provide institution-level information to identify practices and characteristics of senior capstone experiences (Young et al., 2017). These profiles demonstrate that among institutions that claim a capstone or culminating experience, discipline-based courses are the predominant form of culminating senior experience. Independent research papers, internships, arts exhibitions/performances, and student teaching are just slightly less popular forms of culminating experiences. Cocurricular culminating experiences, notably honors and service-learning or community-based senior experiences, have increased as important venues for capstones. Part Two, "Exploring Capstone Experience Models," highlights seven contemporary venues and implementations for capstones.

Student access to culminating experiences and capstones and faculty perceptions about the importance of capstones have been tracked for almost

2 decades via the National Survey of Student Engagement (NSSE) and the companion survey, the Faculty Survey of Student Engagement. Since 2000, NSSE has asked students at 1,600 bachelor's-granting institutions to report participation in culminating experiences, senior projects, or capstones, and annual results between 2013 and 2020 show about 45% of seniors report a culminating experience (NSSE, 2020a). Faculty members consistently agree that it is important for students to do a capstone, with 86% identifying capstones as "very important" or "important" (NSSE, 2020b). Perhaps not surprisingly, there is a strong positive association between students' participation in capstones and faculty belief in the importance of capstones (NSSE, 2007).

Faculty who design and teach capstones have favorable impressions about their value and find them rewarding (Paris & Ferren, 2013; Laye et al., 2020). Yet capstones are demanding for faculty who teach them (Hauhart & Grahe, 2015; Laye et al., 2020). Facilitating integrative learning, a significant undertaking, requires faculty to create intentional settings, projects, and occasions, and the expectations for tailored guidance, personalized feedback, and mentoring are demanding. Designing and delivering a high-quality capstone experience creates unique faculty challenges that require institutional and administrative support, including funds for faculty development to host workshops and informal meetings about the elements that lead to high-quality capstones—curricular design, sequenced assignments, attention to research methods, supervision and mentoring, and applied work, among others. Part Three, "Supporting Capstone Faculty and Staff," shares strategies for bolstering this work.

Capstones are significant, integrative, and reflective learning experiences. They are considered educationally enriching, transformative, and high impact given their positive association with significant outcomes for student learning and development (NSSE, 2007). Students who participate in capstones are more likely to report gains in personal and practical educational outcomes (thinking critically, working with others, solving complex problems in a globally networked world, etc.) than students who do not have the experience (Kinzie, 2013; Kuh, 2008; NSSE, 2018).

Another role of capstones is to provide a bridge between college and the workplace. This objective is typically expressed in capstone experiences or assignments that allow students to demonstrate mastery in the context of an authentic learning experience, usually a simulated or real-life problem or project situated in the field of practice (Devine et al., 2020; Lee & Loton, 2015b). The benefit of this intentional connection between learning in the academic program and application to the field is demonstrated in NSSE 2018 results that show a large difference between seniors who had a capstone compared to those who did not on two educational gains items: institutional contribution to knowledge, skill, and personal development in solving complex real-world problems (67% vs. 53% "substantial") and acquiring job or work-related knowledge and skills (69% vs. 56% "substantial"). Capstones can also help students synthesize their plans postcollege. Again, NSSE results show that taking part in a culminating experience was positively related to seniors' perceptions of preparation for their postgraduation plans, and seniors who had participated in a culminating experience were more likely to believe that coursework in their academic programs prepared them for their postgraduation plans (NSSE, 2018). Research on capstone course goals and professional transition (Appleby et al., 2016; Chorazy & Klinedinst, 2019) shows that capstones that connect professional dispositions and skills with content learning and knowledge help students understand and choose a profession that is a good personal and professional fit. These results suggest capstones may expose students to authentic field-based opportunities and provide relevant experiences related to students' future plans that prepare them for work and life beyond college.

Capstones can also serve various functions in the undergraduate curriculum, including as the culminating experience in general education, the major, or as an interdisciplinary requirement (Coker & Gatti, 2017; Lee & Loton, 2019). For example, a capstone course for history majors may be the site for students to fully engage in the practice of history, pose a significant historical question, apply disciplinary skills by executing original historical research, and produce a substantial paper, while gaining broad, translatable skills for the workplace (Schroer, 2009). In another example, Schroetter and Wendler (2008) described a nursing curriculum capstone that provided field-based experience and affirmation of professional competence at graduation. In a similar way, a capstone in general education may invite students to connect across disciplines, link theories to practice, and to engage their own lived experiences in the context of what they have learned in general education. Other capstones more broadly invite students to bring everything they have learned—from the major, general education, experiential learning, clubs, jobs, and friends—and pull it all together in a culminating project. Such a project allows students to explore their passions and demonstrate well-roundedness and what they have mastered in earning their degree. Capstones that are intentionally designed into the curriculum can connect prior coursework and educational activities to interdisciplinary, disciplinary, and professional skills.

Capstones have also served an important assessment function in higher education, providing data on student attainment (Berheide, 2007) and the effectiveness of the academic program (Black & Hundley, 2004).

Culminating projects provide a learning artifact that can be evaluated to determine if learners have mastered expected competencies and skills, particularly for accredited academic programs. Apgar (2019) described how a capstone assignment can provide an effective means of program assessment in social work education if it showcases students' mastery of program competencies. The assessment of student work in the capstone can reveal the extent to which the program is ensuring graduates attain expected outcomes while also shining a light on weaknesses in student learning that the program might need to address. Quite simply, capstones can function as the formal site for determining if students have achieved learning outcomes in the major or general education and to gauge the effectiveness of curriculum to prepare students for desired outcomes.

In summary, this overview of capstones describes the long-standing historical purpose of providing integration, breadth, application, and transition at the culmination of the undergraduate program. Surveys about the purpose and availability of capstones indicate that the experience is valued, yet participation statistics from NSSE indicate fewer than half of all undergraduates have done the experience. The groundswell of interest in capstones as a HIP, their connection to sharpening graduates' work-related knowledge and skills, and their potential for assessment further suggest a strong endorsement for expanding and improving this crowning experience and the value in understanding the changing landscape of capstones. Finally, while the integrative purpose of capstone experiences hasn't changed much since the 1800s, the who, why, and what of capstones has, and institutions have an opportunity to respond in unique and innovative ways aligning their mission to the culmination of an undergraduate education. In the next section we discuss a framework for examining the current pressures in the higher education landscape with the greatest implications for capstones.

Framework for Considering the Changing Landscape of Capstones

The history and purpose of the capstone influences the current landscape. To further consider the role of capstones to foster student learning and development, and to create high-quality experiences for more students, we draw on an ecological systems theory. Bronfenbrenner's (1977) human ecology theory offers a framework for examining capstones in relation to reform efforts and the interacting forces of ideology and culture, social and organizational structure, time, and individuals.

Bronfenbrenner's socioecological framework (1977) has both evolved and been adapted over the past 3 decades to describe the direct and indirect environmental influences on the development of an individual. The value of this framework is to provide a structure to examine the reciprocal nature of an individual and their environment. While the context both directly and indirectly influences the individual, the characteristics and experiences of the individual also matter. In the context of higher education, assessing the layers of the environment and the impact/influence on student experience can be a useful exercise for institutions to consider as they make intentional decisions around strategic planning and resourcing. This exercise can be applied to the overall student experience or specific components that are integral to the unique institutional experience—in this case, the capstone experience (Figure I.1).

The most peripheral layer of the environmental context of the student experience is the *chronosystem*, referring to changes over time and including influential drivers on our educational system from a historical or generational perspective. The next layer is the *macrosystem*, which is consideration of the culture and ideology that shape social structures, opportunities, and expectations. Specifically, our society has been engaged in ideological conversations around the value of a college degree feeding both negatively and positively to the perception of higher education. This conversation often inappropriately

Figure I.1. Bronfenbrenner's socioecological framework, with examples in higher education.

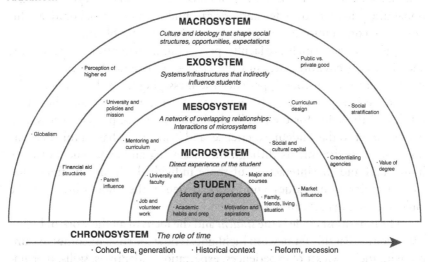

pits the values of the academy (thoughtful, evidence-based discourse) against the needs of the working world (job skills and career competencies). This artificial polarization should highlight the role higher education has in articulating the value of a college education with clarity. The goals of higher education institutions directly align with the needs of the "working world." The potential of utilizing this framework and defining the characteristics of the macrosystem is to both recognize the current cultural and ideological landscape that may influence the systems and policies in place as well as allow institutions to directly address these societal concerns in the messaging of their programs.

The next layer of environmental influence is the *exosystem*. This layer is institution-specific and includes the systems and policies in place that impact the educational experiences of students, such as whether a capstone experience is required at an institution as part of the curriculum or if it is an optional experience. If the capstone experience is an institutional priority, then within this level it is important to spend time and resources on, and potentially highlight in messaging, the unique institutional context and intentional alignment to the university mission. Additionally, policies and infrastructure should support development and implementation of these capstone experiences in the institution's unique context, supporting the microsystem and mesosystem layers focusing on the student experience and outcomes in these resourcing decisions. This also connects to the macrosystem and the need to link how the institution's programs and policies address societal concerns. Institutions have a responsibility to articulate how their capstone experience matches students with community-oriented projects that integrate foundational disciplinary knowledge and critical thinking using collaborative solutions with community stakeholders to solve tangible problems.

The *microsystem* includes faculty, peers, alumni, parents, majors, courses, and the living environment, and the *mesosystem* is how these components interact. For the capstone experience the messaging from the people in the student's microsystem directly influences their experience and their perception of the value for their individual growth. These people, spaces, and places matter to the student experience, and institutions have a role in creating positive environments through the messaging and experiences of these individuals and the interaction of those individuals. It also matters what characteristics, skills, values, and lived experiences the student brings to the table, creating dynamism in the system.

The innermost circle is the *student* and the focus of all the work of higher education. What this framework highlights is how the student comes to campus with their own set of experiences, expectations, identities, skills, preparation, and motivations. What the student brings to the ecosystem and how that interacts and intersects surrounding environmental influences affects their experience. While we know students are key to the higher education ecosystem, we ignore their individuality by referring to a monolithic description of the "student population." This can lead to curricular structures that do not consider what the student brings and who they are, *all* of them, in our classrooms and on our campus; this matters. Considering the student as instrumental to curricular design and campus climate, and simultaneously appreciating the dynamic strengths and needs they bring, challenges us to be forward-thinking, innovative, and responsive—creating a campus where *all* belong.

As we dive deeper into discussion of the current context of capstones and undergraduate reform, we encourage readers to consider how this framework can be utilized in a way that supports institutions to leverage their strengths, align their mission, and identify challenges that should be addressed to more holistically impact student experiences and outcomes. We include a figure at the beginning of each chapter to help readers orient the content into the socioecological model.

Current Context of Capstones and Undergraduate Reform

As a final component in undergraduate education, the capstone or culminating experience is something to build to and cap off the graduates' educational journey. The framework of an ecological systems theory and metaphor of crowning achievement convey the importance of capstones for student learning and their contribution to educational quality. As a result, it is essential to consider how capstones connect to current issues in undergraduate education reform. In this section we discuss four issues in undergraduate education relevant to capstones: (a) assurance of learning, (b) career outcomes and transition to the workplace, (c) interpersonal relationships as a key student–faculty interaction, and (d) holistic, equitable curricula. We then consider how these reform issues influence capstone design and improvement.

Assurance of Learning

Quality assurance in higher education is a top priority. The current context of higher education reform has been shaped by a multidimensional definition of *quality*, influenced by an underlying philosophical shift emphasizing the demonstration of what students know and can do, and more explicitly, the role of developing specific job-related skills and capabilities (Bridgstock, 2009; Gilbert et al., 2004; Hammer et al., 2009). This philosophical shift is prompted by a combination of external, macrosystem pressures from accreditors and the labor market, along with evolving student needs and an increasing accountability to demonstrate the "return on investment."

Despite the historical and current interest in using the capstone experience to demonstrate student learning, studies have documented the challenges associated with using the capstone for such assessment. For instance, Schmidt and Clark (2017) felt that students often struggle with the open-ended nature of their capstone. Other scholars noted that despite the recognized potential of capstone courses to deepen learning, many students underperform due to lack of preparation (Hinckley et al., 2019). Kilgo et al. (2015) encouraged future research to explore how effective this high-impact practice truly is in educating students.

The specification of explicit learning outcomes and work-related knowledge and skills for the capstone experience, combined with the need to assure the experience contributes to these outcomes, are critical emphases for colleges and universities to address at the exosystem level and to align at the microlevel. Ensuring that capstone experiences are designed with an explicit purpose and stated learning outcomes, and are delivering on these goals, are key issues for capstones.

Career Outcomes and Transition to the Workforce

There is a growing macrosystem belief that the main purpose of a college education is to teach work-related skills and knowledge. Higher education has often been scrutinized for not meeting current workforce demands. Research has shown that college graduates are not prepared to achieve important learning outcomes such as written and oral communication skills, teamwork skills, ethical decision-making, critical thinking, and the ability to apply knowledge (Hart Research Associates, 2013). More recently, a 2017 Strada-Gallup poll found that two thirds of students felt unprepared for success in their careers.

To address these demands, it seems natural for colleges and universities to turn to culminating experiences aimed at assisting students to successfully transition from undergraduate education to work (Holdsworth et al., 2009; Julien et al., 2012; van Acker & Bailey, 2011). In fact, Martin (2018) suggested that as we look at the current and future generation of students, the pressure to prepare the next generation of students may place greater emphasis on career preparation in the capstone experience. The call to address constantly evolving industry needs is, and will continue to be, one of the academy's greatest challenges. However, placing this responsibility solely at the feet of the capstone is worrisome.

Interpersonal Relationships and Faculty/Mentor Involvement

The perspective of the "student-as-customer" model of higher education has put increased pressure on faculty to move away from teacher-focused pedagogies to innovative, student-centered pedagogy (Furedi, 2011). This transition to learner-focused pedagogies places more emphasis on skill development and colearning (Judson & Taylor, 2014) and corresponds with increased attention to research on student learning (Ambrose et al., 2010; National Academies of Sciences, Engineering, and Medicine, 2018; National Research Council, 1999). However, the transition comes with a need for more resources devoted to faculty development. Specifically, faculty face the expansion of pedagogical tasks; increased tension in balancing scholarship, teaching, and service; and the challenges and affordances of working with students who have varied preparations for their capstone experiences. Faculty, now more than ever, devote significant time to their teaching and student mentoring in this learner-focused style of education, particularly as it relates to HIPs, including the capstone. Given these tensions, universities should support faculty to participate fully in the capstone experience through recognition in evaluation processes and provision of necessary resources.

The delivery of a successful capstone experience can be dependent on several relationships, but perhaps none more important than that of the microlevel student–faculty relationship (Felten & Lambert, 2020). In many cases, faculty must learn to develop a different relationship with students throughout the capstone. The professor should be a mentor and guide, helping students integrate the various goals of their total education, including lessons from major and nonmajor courses (Smith, 1998). Faculty who lead these experiences have to provide the freedom for students to take on projects that might not be associated with faculty expertise, leading to a sometimes uncomfortable dynamic. The freedom given to students can generate questions that are difficult to answer and projects that have uncertain outcomes. Faculty who have not been trained to address these questions or to be comfortable with the uncertainty of the capstone project can impede the quality of the experience. In addition, faculty might find their unfamiliar role in the capstone unappealing, which could have a detrimental effect on the quality of the experience.

Holistic, Inclusive Curriculum

Carey (2015) offered a critical analysis of current-day higher education, centering on the lack of an interconnected curriculum that allows for intentional student learning and development. Poor design can play out in two specific areas: lack of a commitment to student access and inclusivity, as students do not have equal access to these experiences, and if and when they do, their experience is not validated, and failures in the curriculum, when prior coursework does not sufficiently prepare students to undertake the higher-level thinking associated with a successful capstone. Lagging graduation rates and outcome gaps by income and race have prompted scrutiny about inequitable experiences, including questions about whether all students are getting what they need. In response, colleges and universities have adopted a more holistic approach that focuses on student well-being, aims to deepen connections among students' college experiences, and attempts to eliminate barriers that prevent some populations of students from thriving (Lipka, 2020). A holistic approach means the creation of an environment and experiences in which all students are welcomed, supported, and respected, with an emphasis on social justice.

The more specific construct of critical race theory in education explores how to disrupt race and racism in educational theory and practice (Ladson-Billings, 2013). Race must be a prominent variable in discussions about educational equity and in creating spaces of racial inclusion that include community-building, high expectations for all students, validation of students' identities, and content reflective of their backgrounds, histories, and experiences. For instance, how does the curriculum provide space for students to represent their identities and their interests? Or how does the capstone integrate student identities? Attending to the insights, concerns, and questions that historically underrepresented minority students have about capstone experiences is a critical issue for equity and inclusion.

A holistic approach also addresses students where they are, "rebundling" their curricular and cocurricular experiences to facilitate integration. Macrosystem pressures to "unbundle" education so that students can "purchase educational services *a la carte*—low budget, cafeteria-style education" privilege narrow views of career readiness (Bass & Eynon, 2017, p. 10), often excluding the communication, critical thinking, and teamwork competencies that employers would like to see more of. Even when colleges commit to a comprehensive core curriculum, exosystem practices may lead to "unbundled" course sequences, with little attention to how individual classes are intended to prepare students for subsequent coursework. Intentional instructional scaffolding is essential if students are to acquire skills that will help them integrate prior coursework and produce meaningful capstone products.

About This Book: Pulling It All Together to Frame Capstones and Current Issues

In response to both the popularity of HIPs and the potential of capstones for broadening, deepening, and integrating the totality of students' undergraduate experiences, this collection contextualizes new research on capstones within the landscapes influencing their development. In each of the collection's three sections, Bronfenbrenner's (1977) system theory frames current-day concerns about delivering high-quality capstone experiences. Considering capstones in this socioecological framework provides institutions strategies to address the issues facing higher education and to manage change.

Bronfenbrenner's theory does not promote a one-size-fits-all solution; instead, it offers a framework for colleges and universities to leverage their strengths and unique contexts and to target resources to support meaningful learning experiences for the students and communities they serve. For example, considering the social issues of the time, university mission, and students' strengths and needs, what policies, training, resources, or scaffolding in curriculum design are needed to implement a high-quality capstone? And, depending on the student identities and community context, what needs to be in place through the layers of the socioecological framework to support capstone experiences that are equitably accessible? As an important reminder, the capstone should engage students in integrating and reflecting on their individual experiences, helping them articulate how their experiences translate to their postgraduate goals (i.e., career, graduate programs).

As a framework for examining capstone development and reform and the interacting forces of ideology and culture, social and organizational structure, time, and individuals, Bronfenbrenner's theory encourages educators to consider the complex environment in which capstones fit in undergraduate education. For example, consideration of the macrosystem layer points to the influence that employers and society have in terms of articulating students' skills and outcomes and the role that capstones play in signaling a place in the curriculum that intentionally integrates students' interests with the graduate outcomes. The outcomes associated with capstones must be explicit and transparent to students, and if the capstone is in the major, aligned with outcomes desired by employers. Upon completing the experiences, students must be able to demonstrate their competence and articulate learning gains and outcomes. Capstones' potential as a site to assure learning must be strengthened.

Bronfenbrenner's framework also helps identify gaps and possible levers for educational practice, policy, and research. For instance, the microsystem and mesosystem draw attention to faculty and alumni and their interactions in the environment. This level aligns with current attention to the power of mentoring relationships for student development and learning and suggests that institutions developing or enhancing capstones must explore their commitment to faculty members' capacity for mentoring, effective integrative pedagogy, and culturally responsive teaching. Faculty development must be in place to ensure strong mentoring models for teaching capstones. Even more, student–faculty relationships have a strong influence on students' sense of cultural identity and capacity for achieving the significant demands of the capstone. Faculty teaching capstones must positively act on their authority to validate students for their unique and cultural ways of knowing.

Most important to contemporary capstone design is the attention to students and their identities. The inner circle of Bronfenbrenner's model focuses on the student, highlighting what the student brings to the campus and how curriculum can either fail to consider what the student brings or lift up and integrate students' prior experiences, knowledge, and identities. At the most basic level of access, colleges and universities must study their participation data to identify who participates in capstones and how to make the experience possible for more students. This important layer of the model also connects with the contemporary issue of holistic and inclusive curriculum.

The multi-institutional studies that follow—many of which were facilitated by the Elon University Center for Engaged Learning's 2018–2020 research seminar on capstone experiences—add depth to our understanding of capstones within universities' environmental systems and allow readers to reflect on how capstones address the four higher education reform issues introduced previously. Part One offers multi-institutional typographies of capstones, illustrating the diversity of experiences included in this HIP while also identifying essential characteristics that contribute to high-quality culminating experiences for students. Janet Bean (University of Akron), Christina Beaudoin (Grand Valley State University), Tania von der Heidt (Southern Cross University, Australia), David I. Lewis (University of Leeds, UK), and Carol Van Zile-Tamsen (University at Buffalo) examine "Frames, Definitions, and Drivers: A Multinational Study of Institutionally Required Undergraduate Capstones," to understand exosystem definitions and goals for capstones and macrosystem forces that motivate institutions to embrace this labor-intensive practice. Next, "Capstone Influences and Purposes" by Russell Kirkscey (Penn State Harrisburg), David I. Lewis (University of Leeds, UK), and Julie Vale (University of Guelph, Canada), discusses institutional (exosystem) decisions about capstones, such as disciplinary or nondisciplinary, required or elective, and comments on the drivers or influences on capstone purposes, including macrosystem disciplinary or accrediting body requirements. Finally, in "Institutional Considerations for Capstones on Campus: Perspectives Based on National Data on Senior Culminating Experiences," Dallin George Young (University of Georgia), Tracy L. Skipper (University of South Carolina), and Rico R. Reed (University of South Carolina) highlight the various forms that capstone experiences take on campuses across the United States and examine the exosystem, institutional concerns for students' senior years.

Part Two examines specific culminating experiences, with examples from multiple institutions and strategies for adapting them for readers' own campus contexts. The first three chapters in this section are case study examples from the Center for Engaged Learning research seminar, exploring how institutional context and mission (exosystem) interact with the curriculum, programs, and people in their particular contexts (meso- and microsystem). In "Where There's a Will, There's a Way: Implementing a Capstone Experience for General Education," Van Zile-Tamsen, Bean, Beaudoin, Lewis, and von der Heidt provide a case study analysis of a universally required general education capstone at the University at Buffalo in the United States. In "Preparing Students for the Fourth Industrial Revolution," this same research team led by Lewis details a 20-year journey of taking a discipline-specific capstone course and evolving it into a course with a focus on personal and professional development and preparation for the workplace. Next, led by von der Heidt in "How Two Australian Universities Achieved 'Capstones for All': A Change Management Perspective," the team describes the evolution of the capstone requirement at two Melbourne-based universities amid macro- and exosystem influences. This section then moves into "Adapting a Capstone: Projects and Portfolios Across Four Courses and Three Institutions" by Sandra Bell (University of New Brunswick, Saint John, Canada), Frederick T. Evers (University of Guelph, Canada), Shannon Murray (University of PEI, Canada), and Margaret Anne Smith (St. Stephen's University, Canada), which shares how they adopted and adapted a capstone course to be responsive to exo- and microsystem expectations. Matthew Park (Bard High School Early College, Newark), Paul Hansen (Bard High School Early College, Cleveland), Guy Risko (Bard High School Early College, Cleveland), and Joshua Walker (Bard High School Early College, Cleveland), in "Just a Few Minutes of Your Time: Using Qualitative Survey Data to Evaluate and Revise a Capstone Project at an Early College Network," describe the capstone research project at Bard High School Early College and illustrate exo- and microsystem decisions about course design that help maintain courses that are both inclusive and equitable.

The last two chapters of this section center the student and the student experience as integral to the capstone. In "Students-as-Partners and Engaged Scholarship: Complementary Frameworks," Andrew J. Pearl (University of North Georgia), Joanna C. Rankin (University of Calgary, Canada), Moriah McSharry McGrath (Portland State University), Sarah Dyer (University of Exeter, UK), and Trina Jorre de St Jorre (Deakin University, Australia) explore how the complementary macrosystem frameworks of students-as-partners and community-engaged scholarship can inform exosystem and microsystem design of capstones. Finally, in "Designing Democratic

Spaces: Public-Facing Civic Capstone Courses," Cindy Koenig Richards (Willamette University), Nicholas V. Longo (Providence College), and Caryn McTighe Musil (AAC&U) show how capstones in a variety of disciplines and institutions can develop civic competencies through collaborative learning, reflective practice, and publicly engaged research.

The book's final section offers research-informed strategies for professional development to support implementation of high-quality student learning experiences across a variety of campus contexts. In "Understanding Faculty Needs in Capstone Experiences," Morgan Gresham (University of South Florida St. Petersburg), Caroline Boswell (University of Louisville), Olivia S. Anderson (University of Michigan), Matthew J. Laye (Idaho College of Osteopathic Medicine), and Dawn Smith-Sherwood (Indiana University of Pennsylvania) examine which faculty teach capstone experiences, their intrinsic and extrinsic motivations, and the type of support they receive at their institutions. The team also offers resources to support professional development for faculty teaching capstones. In "The Development of Capstone Assignments Using a Faculty Community of Practice Model," Silvia Reyes, Nelson Nunez Rodriguez, and Sarah Brennan (all of Hostos Community College of the City University of New York) share how an exo-system-level faculty development initiative enhanced capstone experiences at the community college. Michelle J. Eady (University of Wollongong, Australia) and Simon Bedford (Western Sydney University, Australia)—in "Peer Reviewing to Support Quality Assurance of Capstone Experiences: A View From Australia"—explore how a macrosystem quality assurance effort can promote faculty confidence and improve the quality of capstones within participating institutions' exosystems. In "Positionality and Identity in Capstones: Renegotiating the Self Through Teaching and Learning," McSharry McGrath, Dyer, Rankin, and Jorre de St Jorre identify salient and hidden aspects of diversity and identity that affect capstones and offer recommendations to improve capstone quality through more inclusive approaches to teaching. Finally, in the conclusion, "Committing to Equitable, High-Quality Capstone Experiences," editors Ketcham, Moore, and Weaver offer four significant and thoughtful takeaways for readers to consider in their context. Readers are also left with a sincere challenge to carry forward in their personal and professional development journey. As lifelong learners and higher education leaders, we have and will have platforms and opportunities to implement meaningful change. Let equity, access, and resource allocation drive the learning landscapes moving forward.

Across these sections and chapters, authors share explicit implications for faculty who teach or direct capstone experiences and for administrators and institutions who support them. Section introductions help readers frame their exploration within the ecological system model; the collection's conclusion challenges readers to apply this research to creating or redesigning equitable, high-quality capstone experiences for all students; and supplemental resources on the book's website (www.centerforengagedlearning.org/books/cultivating-capstones) support this application and adaptation in readers' contexts. With these goals in mind, we invite you to reflect on four sets of questions as you continue reading:

- How are the macrosystem pressures we've described—and others unique to your sociocultural context—shaping exo- and microsystem decisions about capstones and students' experiences?
- What exosystem infrastructures, policies, and practices function as affordances or constraints for (re)designing your college's capstones to foster equitable, high-quality learning experiences?
- What meso- and microsystem characteristics can you tap to deepen capstone experiences?
- And, most importantly, who are your students? How will their identities, experiences, and goals inform your capstone design?

References

Abel, J. R., & Deitz, R. (2014). Do the benefits of college still outweigh the costs? *Current Issues in Economics and Finance, 20*(3), 1–9.

Ambrose, S. A., Bridges, M. W., DiPietro, M., Lovett, M. C., & Norman, M. K. (2010). *How learning works: Seven research-based principles for smart teaching.* Jossey-Bass.

Apgar, D. (2019). Conceptualization of capstone experiences: Examining their role in social work education. *Social Work Education, 38*(2), 143–158. https://doi.org/10.1080/02615479.2018.1512963

Appleby, K. M., Foster, E., & Kamusoko, S. (2016). Full speed ahead: Using a senior capstone course to facilitate students' professional transition. *JOPERD: The Journal of Physical Education, Recreation & Dance, 87*(3), 16–21. https://doi.org/10.1080/07303084.2015.1131214

Association of American Colleges and Universities. (2015). *The LEAP challenge: Education for a world of unscripted problems.* (EJ1094941). ERIC. https://eric.ed.gov/?id=EJ1094941

Bass, R., & Eynon, B. (2017). From unbundling to rebundling: Design principles for transforming institutions in the new digital ecosystem. *Change: The Magazine of Higher Learning, 49*(2), 8–17. https://doi.org/10.1080/00091383.2017.1286211

Berheide, C. W. (2007). Doing less work, collecting better data: Using capstone courses to assess learning. *Peer Review, 9*(2), 27–30.

Black, K. E., & Hundley, S. P. (2004). Capping off the curriculum. *Assessment Update, 16*(1), 3.

Boyer Commission on Educating Undergraduates in the Research University. (1998). *Reinventing undergraduate education: A blueprint for America's research universities.* http://naples.cc.sunysb.edu/Pres/boyer.nsf/673918d46fbf653e8525 65ec0056ff3e/d955b61ffddd590a852565ec005717ae/$FILE/boyer.pdf

Bridgstock, R. (2009). The graduate attributes we've overlooked: Enhancing graduate employability through career management skills. *Higher Education Research & Development, 28*(1), 31–44. https://doi.org/10.1080/07294360802444347

Bronfenbrenner, U. (1977). Towards an experimental ecology of human development. *American Psychologist, 32*(7), 513–531. https://doi.org/10.1037/0003-066X.32 .7.513

Brownell, J. E., & Swaner, L. E. (2010). *Five high-impact practices: Research on learning outcomes, completion, and quality.* Association of American Colleges and Universities.

Carey, M. (2015). The limits of cultural competence: An indigenous studies perspective. *Higher Education Research & Development, 34*(5), 828–840. https://doi.org/ 10.1080/07294360.2015.1011097

Chorazy, M. L., & Klinedinst, K. S. (2019). Learn by doing: A model for incorporating high-impact experiential learning into an undergraduate public health curriculum. *Frontiers in Public Health, 7*(31), 1–6. https://doi.org/10.3389/fpubh.2019.00031

Coker, J. S., & Gatti, E. A. (2017). Interdisciplinary capstones for all students. *Journal of Interdisciplinary Studies in Education, 5*(2), 1–10.

Devine, J. L., Bourgault, K. S., & Schwartz, R. N. (2020). Using the online capstone experience to support authentic learning. *TechTrends, 64*, 606–615. https://doi .org/10.1007/s11528-020-00516-1

Felten, P., & Lambert, L. M. (2020). *Relationship-rich education: How human connections drive success in college.* JHU Press.

Furedi, F. (2011). Introduction to the marketisation of higher education and the student as consumer. In M. Molesworth, R. Scullion, & E. Nixon (Eds.), *The marketisation of higher education and the student as consumer* (pp. 1–8). Routledge.

Gardner, J., Van der Veer, G., and Associates. (1998). *The senior year experience: Facilitating integration, reflection, closure and transition.* Jossey-Bass.

Gilbert, R., Balatti, J., Turner, P., & Whitehouse, H. (2004). The generic skills debate in research higher degrees. *Higher Education Research and Development, 23*, 375–388. https://doi.org/10.1080/0729436042000235454

Greenstein, L. M. (2017). *Restorative assessment: Strength-based practices that support all learners.* Corwin Press.

Hammer, S., Star, C., & Green, W. (2009). Facing up to the challenge: Why is it so hard to develop graduate attributes. *Higher Education Research and Development, 28*, 17–29. https://doi.org/10.1080/07294360802444339

Hart Research Associates. (2013). It takes more than a major: Employer priorities for college learning and student success. *Liberal Education, 99*(2), 1–8.

Hauhart, R. C., & Grahe, J. E. (2015). *Designing and teaching undergraduate capstone courses.* Wiley.

Hinckley, R. A., McGuire, J., & Danforth, T. L. (2019). Improving student success in the capstone seminar: The importance of a prior research intensive experience. *Journal of Political Science Education, 18*(3), 362–378. https://doi.org/10.1080/15512169.2019.1608831

Holdsworth, A., Watty, K., & Davies, M. (2009). *Developing capstone experiences.* Centre for the Study of Higher Education, University of Melbourne.

Hovland, K., Anderson, C., & Ferren, A. (2015). Interrogating integrative learning. *Peer Review, 16*(4)/*17*(1), 2014–2015.

Hunter, M., Keup, J., Kinzie, J., & Maietta, H. (2012). *The senior year: Culminating experiences and transitions.* University of South Carolina, National Resource Center for the First Year Experience and Students in Transition.

Judson, K. M., & Taylor, S. A. (2014). Moving from marketization to marketing of higher education: The co-creation of value in higher education. *Higher Education Studies, 4*(1), 51–67. https://doi.org/10.5539/hes.v4n1p51

Julien, B. L., Lexis, L., Schuijers, J., Samiric, T., & McDonald, S. (2012). Using capstones to develop research skills and graduate capabilities: A case study from physiology. *Journal of University Teaching & Learning Practice, 9*(3), 6. https://ro.uow.edu.au/jutlp/vol9/iss3/6/

Kilgo, C. A., Sheets, J. K. E., & Pascarella, E. T. (2015). The link between high-impact practices and student learning: Some longitudinal evidence. *Higher Education, 69*(4), 509–525. https://doi.org/10.1007/s10734-014-9788-z

Kinzie, J. (2013). Taking stock of capstones and integrated learning. *Peer Review, 15*(4), 27–30.

Kinzie, J. (2018). Assessing quality and equity: Observations about the state of signature work. *Peer Review, 20*(2), 29–31.

Kuh, G. D. (2008). *High-impact educational practices: What they are, who has access to them, and why they matter.* Association of American Colleges and Universities.

Ladson-Billings, G. (2013). Critical race theory—What it is not! In M. Lynn & A. Dixson (Eds.), *The handbook of critical race theory in education* (pp. 34–47). Routledge.

Laye, M. J., Boswell, C., Gresham, M., Smith-Sherwood, D., & Anderson, O. S. (2020). Multi-institutional survey of faculty experiences teaching capstones. *College Teaching, 68*(4), 201–213. https://doi.org/10.1080/87567555.2020.1786663

Lee, N., & Loton, D. (2015a). *Capstone curriculum across disciplines: Synthesising theory, practice and policy to provide practical tools for curriculum design.* Australian Government Office for Learning and Teaching. http://www.capstonecurriculum.com.au/wp/wp-content/uploads/2019/06/Lee_N_NSTF_report_20152-1.pdf

Lee, N., & Loton, D. (2015b). Integrating research and professional learning—Australian capstones. *Council on Undergraduate Research Quarterly, 35*(4), 28–35.

Lee, N., & Loton, D. (2019). Capstone purposes across disciplines. *Studies in Higher Education, 44*(1), 134–150. https://doi.org/10.1080/03075079.2017.1347155

Levine, A. (1998). A president's personal and historical perspective. In J. Gardner, G. Van der Veer, & Associates (Eds.), *The senior year experience: Facilitating integration, reflection, closure, and transition* (pp. 51–59). Jossey-Bass.

Lipka, S. (Ed). (2020). *What a "holistic" student experience actually means*. Oracle.

Martin, J. M. (2018). Culminating capstone courses. In M. G. Strawser (Ed.), *Transformative student experiences in higher education: Meeting the needs of the twenty-first century student and modern workplace* (pp. 41–56). Rowman & Littlefield.

National Academies of Sciences, Engineering, and Medicine. (2018). *How people learn II: Learners, contexts, and cultures*. The National Academies Press. https://doi.org/10.17226/24783.

National Research Council. (1999). *How people learn: Brain, mind, experience, and school* (Expanded ed.). The National Academies Press. https://doi.org/10.17226/9853.

National Survey of Student Engagement. (2007). *Experiences that matter: Enhancing student learning and success—Annual report 2007*. http://nsse.iub.edu/NSSE_2007_ Annual_Report/

National Survey of Student Engagement. (2018). *Engagement insights: Survey findings on the quality of undergraduate education—Annual results 2018*. Indiana University Center for Postsecondary Research.

National Survey of Student Engagement. (2020a). *Our research: Projects, publications, and more*. Indiana University Center for Postsecondary Research. https://nsse.indiana.edu/research/annual-results/index.html

National Survey of Student Engagement. (2020b). *Faculty survey of student engagement. FSSE 2020 frequencies*. Indiana University Center for Postsecondary Research. https://go.iu.edu/3qOe

Paris, D., & Ferren, A. (2013). How students, faculty, and institutions can fulfill the promise of capstones. *Peer Review, 15*(4). https://www.aacu.org/publications-research/periodicals/how-students-faculty-and-institutions-can-fulfill-promise

Schmidt, D., & Clark, R. (2017). *Improving student capstone experience by early exposure and engagement*. American Society for Engineering Education.

Schroer, T. (2009, April 1). Placing the senior capstone course within the history program. *Perspective on History*. https://www.historians.org/research-and-publications/perspectives-on-history/april-2009/placing-the-senior-capstone-course-within-the-history-program

Schroetter, S. A., & Wendler, M. C. (2008). Capstone experience: Analysis of an educational concept of nursing. *Journal of Professional Nursing, 24*(2), 71–79. https://doi.org/10.1016/j.profnurs.2007.06.019

Smith, B. L. (1998). Curricular structures for cumulative learning. In J. N. Gardner & G. Van der Veer (Eds.), *The senior year experience: Facilitating integration, reflection, closure, and transition* (pp. 81–94). Jossey-Bass.

Strada-Gallup. (2017). *2017 college student survey: A nationally representative survey of currently enrolled students*. http://www.stradaeducation.org/consumer-insights/strada-gallup-college-student-survey/

van Acker, L., & Bailey, J. (2011). Embedding graduate skills in capstone courses. *Asian Social Science, 7*(4), 69. https://doi.org/10.5539/ass.v7n4p69

Young, D. G., Chung, J. K., Hoffman, D. E., & Bronkema, R. (2017). *2016 National Survey of Senior Capstone Experiences: Expanding our understanding of culminating experiences* (Research Report No. 8). University of South Carolina, National Resource Center for the First-Year Experience and Students in Transition.

PART 1

**Understanding the Landscape
of Capstone Experiences**

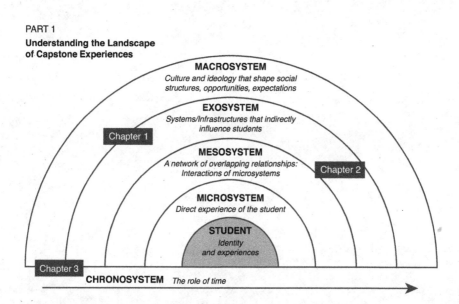

UNDERSTANDING THE LANDSCAPE OF CAPSTONE EXPERIENCES

Anthony G. Weaver, Caroline J. Ketcham, and Jessie L. Moore

This section presents a current view of the capstone landscape both from U.S. and international perspectives, highlighted by multi-institutional studies that address the broader context in which capstone decisions are made. In the first chapter, "Frames, Definitions, and Drivers: A Multinational Study of Institutionally Required Undergraduate Capstones," the authors examine the frequency of and drivers for capstone offerings across an international sample of campuses. The chapter describes the varied exosystem and macrosystem frameworks utilized in developing capstone experiences, helping readers identify and reflect on the driving factors, frames, and definitions that could inform the planning, implementation, and assessment of capstones in their contexts.

Chapter 2, "Capstone Influences and Purposes," also provides a global perspective on the landscape of the capstone experience, with specific emphasis on the importance of understanding the integration of stakeholder influence, programmatic goals, and a clear articulation of capstone learning outcomes. With three examples of capstones—and their socioecologies—from Canada, the United States, and the United Kingdom, the chapter highlights the meso-, exo-, and macrosystem impacts on capstones and prompts readers to consider how these example programs could be adapted for other postsecondary contexts.

The final chapter in Part One, "Institutional Considerations for Capstones on Campus: Perspectives Based on National Data on Senior Culminating Experiences," shares data from a national survey to describe the various capstone offerings on U.S. campuses. This look at the macrosystem and exosystem impacts on capstones also facilitates a chronosystem analysis when reading the chapter's report of a 2016 survey alongside the 2018–2020 mappings in chapters 1 and 2.

These chapters address the driving motivations for and development of university capstones. The uniqueness of this section is that it underscores the importance of the chrono-, exo-, and macrosystem influences on capstone experiences, while also touching on the impacts of the mesosystem. By introducing readers to the complexities of implementing a successful capstone experience, each chapter offers recommendations on how to address these challenges that exist due to multiple influences, with an eye toward improving the delivery of and access to the capstone.

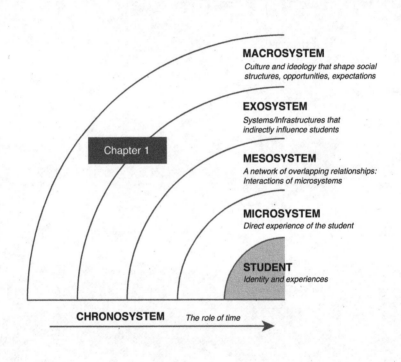

MACROSYSTEM
Culture and ideology that shape social structures, opportunities, expectations

EXOSYSTEM
Systems/Infrastructures that indirectly influence students

Chapter 1

MESOSYSTEM
A network of overlapping relationships: Interactions of microsystems

MICROSYSTEM
Direct experience of the student

STUDENT
Identity and experiences

CHRONOSYSTEM   *The role of time*

FRAMES, DEFINITIONS, AND DRIVERS

A Multinational Study of Institutionally Required Undergraduate Capstones

Janet Bean, Christina Beaudoin, Tania von der Heidt,
David I. Lewis, and Carol Van Zile-Tamsen

More than 20 years ago, the Boyer Commission's *Reinventing Undergraduate Education: A Blueprint for America's Research Universities* (1998) recommended that all undergraduate programs include a capstone experience. Capstones enhance student learning by filling a gap in the undergraduate curriculum, which can seem fragmented without a culminating experience. They add value and, like all valuable things in a democratic society, should be subject to questions of equity and access. While almost all institutions of higher education offer capstone experiences in some form to some students, it is less clear how many meet the Boyer Commission's goal of capstones for *all* undergraduate students. Required baccalaureate capstones ensure equal access to a high-impact learning experience—but how widespread is this practice? How do institutions with required capstones define the culminating experience and its goals? What drives their commitment to this labor-intensive practice?

Our research team set out to determine the prevalence of required capstones in three countries: Australia, the United Kingdom, and the United States. By studying required capstones from a multinational perspective, we hoped to better understand the range of this high-impact practice in a variety of contexts. After identifying 55 institutions that require baccalaureate capstones, we analyzed the language in public-facing documents to better understand how institutions define and frame capstone work. The themes that emerged provide insight into what institutions value about capstones and what drives their commitment. Our findings also suggest that there are many viable approaches to achieving universal access to capstones for undergraduates.

How Many Institutions Require Capstones?

To determine the prevalence of required undergraduate capstones, we conducted a systematic review of higher education institutions in Australia, the United Kingdom, and the United States. Our data set included all 42 public and private baccalaureate-granting institutions in Australia and all 126 public, baccalaureate-granting institutions in the United Kingdom. Because the United States has more than 2,000 colleges and universities that grant 4-year degrees, we used a random stratified sampling procedure to select a subset of 319 institutions. For each institution in our sample, we systematically reviewed public-facing documents available online (academic catalogs, bulletins, and programs of study) to determine if the institution requires a capstone for all bachelor's degrees (see Table 1.1).

How Do Institutions Define and Frame Their Required Capstones?

Clear definitions and effective framing can help institutions establish coherence for their culminating experiences. The language used to describe capstones can also impact buy-in from stakeholders, including students who must engage in capstone work, faculty who must design and teach the capstone, and administrators who must allocate resources (Budwig & Jessen-Marshall, 2018). From the 55 institutions with a required capstone, we collected all public-facing statements regarding this requirement. This included material written for a faculty audience as well as information geared to students. Using grounded theory, our research team identified

TABLE 1.1
Percentage of Institutions in Sample With Required Capstone

Country	Institutions Reviewed	Institutions With Required Undergraduate Capstone	Percentage
Australia	42	2	5%
United Kingdom	126	5	4%
United States	319	48	15%

themes that emerged from the data and employed a consensus model for coding.

Defining the Capstone

More than 90% of the institutionally required capstones in our data set are major capstones. A few U.S. institutions with project-based capstones allow or encourage interdisciplinary work. A minority of U.S. capstones—five of the 48 institutions—require a general education or core curriculum capstone that operates completely outside of the major. Most often, the general education capstone is a topic-based, multidisciplinary course. (For a different model of a general education capstone, see chapter 6.) One U.S. institution in our study requires students to complete both a general education capstone and a capstone in the major, which illustrates the distinct function of these two culminating experiences.

Most of the institutions in our study defined capstones as a wide range of experiences, which we have compiled and grouped here by similarity:

- senior seminar, capstone course, culminating course
- practicum, internship, co-op, clinical setting, student teaching, consultancy, applied activities
- research project, design project, scholarly inquiry, semester project, original project, independent study project, self-guided study, enquiry-based independent study, autonomous piece of research work, participation in a faculty-generated research project, construction project, engagement in an industry-driven project, investigations undertaken as part of preprofessional internship
- creative project, exhibition, performance, show, recital, artistic expression of some sort
- experiential learning, fieldwork, service-learning course/project, study abroad, immersion experience, intensive experience in the major or interdisciplinary field, integrative experience designed for the major
- signature work, signature project
- senior thesis, research paper, extended essay, dissertation, piece of academic writing, senior integration paper
- professional portfolio, reflection portfolio, portfolio of best work
- public presentation, participation in student symposium
- comprehensive exam, senior integration assessment

Several institutions maximize flexibility by adding terms like "any other appropriate mode," "any other approved activity," or "a similar product" to their list of acceptable capstone experiences.

In contrast to institutions that emphasize multiple options for fulfilling the capstone requirement, a smaller number of colleges and universities promote the capstone as a shared experience for all students. These include institutions that require all students to complete an independent scholarly project as well as those that require a general education capstone in the form of a common, interdisciplinary course.

Some institutions appear to be balancing the need for flexible options with the need for consistency for all undergraduates. One institution stipulates that each capstone must include a writing and reflective component. Several institutions require applied experiences such as internships, co-ops, and other preprofessional experiences to include inquiry projects or written reports that require analysis, evaluation, or reflection. Because institutionally required capstones are often implemented in a variety of contexts, clear definitions are essential. Through brief statements or more expansive descriptions, all but three of the 55 institutions in our study set out the parameters of the capstone experience to establish a shared understanding of this requirement.

Framing the Capstone

Ten themes emerged from the institutional statements, each providing a different way of framing the required capstone. These themes suggest capstone purposes and goals as well as institutional values (see Figure 1.1).

Figure 1.1. Frequency of capstone themes by country.

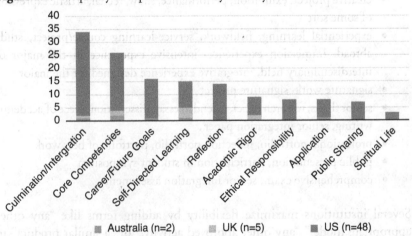

Integration and Culmination

Almost two thirds of institutions with required capstones defined them as an integrative experience that requires students to draw together multiple aspects of their education, as is evident in statements such as these:

> The senior year . . . represents the culmination of students' curricular experience. Seniors use this time to draw together and synthesize the various threads of study and experience through a variety of intellectual activities: senior seminars, comprehensive exams, theses, projects, performances and/or exhibitions.
>
> A capstone experience is a high-impact educational practice in which students integrate and evaluate the knowledge and skills gained in both the General Education and major curricula.

Institutions with integrative capstones ask their students to "synthesize theory, knowledge, and experience" and to place disciplinary learning "in a larger social, intellectual, and professional context." Some institutions frame the capstone as the culmination of the major, while others ask students to draw together elements of the entire undergraduate experience in their capstone work.

Core Competencies

About half of the institutions explicitly connect capstones to core competencies such as communication and critical thinking. Capstones can serve as a site of assessment, as is clear in these descriptions:

> Each program of study will also use a capstone course or experience to provide both further application of higher order thinking and an assessable product to document achievement of the learning outcomes at the summation of the undergraduate experience.
>
> These courses are designed to allow students to demonstrate their mastery of institution-wide learning outcomes as well as their achievement of competency in their chosen area of concentration.

By requiring the capstone to address broad undergraduate learning goals, these institutions have created a pathway for accountability. Academic programs must design their capstones to address core competencies, which ensures that all students demonstrate these skills before graduation.

Career and Future Goals

Many universities and colleges see the capstone as a way to connect undergraduate learning with what comes next—whether that is a career or further study. Career and future goals appear in almost a third of institutional descriptions of required capstones. Capstones are called "a bridge from college to career/postgraduate success" and an experience that will "prepare students for the intellectual, ethical, interpersonal, and professional challenges that lie ahead after graduation."

Several universities promote capstones directly to students, emphasizing the role they can play in postgraduate aspirations. As one university puts it, the capstone is a way to "signal to professors, employers, and graduate programs that you are ready to make extraordinary contributions in your discipline, workplace, and community." Another institution emphasizes that employers value the kinds of skills that capstones develop. Several emphasize the capstone as a customized experience, as this statement shows: "Each student's unique capstone experience is completely tailored to their personal academic and career goals." With increasing societal emphasis on career readiness and employability, many colleges and universities view capstones as a critical bridge between the undergraduate experience and postgraduate success.

Self-Directed Learning

More than a quarter of institutions define capstones as an opportunity for students to take control of their own learning and see a project through to completion. Self-directed learning has long been a goal of higher education. The American Association of Colleges and Universities identifies agency and self-direction as one of the design principles for effective general education (AAC&U, 2015). In Australia and the United Kingdom, the emphasis on employability has shown the need for institutions to address skills like personal initiative, self-motivation, and the ability to work independently. It is not surprising, then, that institutions would see the required capstone as a means for promoting self-directed learning. Project-based or thesis capstones are more likely to emphasize student agency and self-direction, with the experience described in terms such as "an autonomous piece of research" or "a self-directed final production or product carried out under faculty direction." One institution describes its capstone as a

> complex individual or group project that is substantially defined and carried forward by the student under the guidance of a faculty mentor. It can take the form of a thesis or project; in consultation with a faculty adviser, you will define and carry forward the project on your own initiative.

Several institutions framed their capstone to emphasize the role of individual agency and personal interest:

> Student inquiry and *personal interest* drive every original project.
> All undergraduate students are required to plan, undertake and report on a scholarly project in *an area of their own choosing.* (emphasis added)

Our data show some national differences in this theme. While about a quarter of all the institutions in our data set emphasized self-directed learning, this theme was found in four of five UK institutions, a frequency that reflects the project-based nature of UK required capstones.

Reflection

Reflection requires students to create connections among their learning experiences and to become aware of intellectual and personal growth. About a quarter of the institutions in our study defined the capstone in terms of reflection. Given that reflection is not a typical part of most disciplinary writing, the number of institutions in our study that include it confirms the importance of this activity to the unique goals of the capstone experience. There are national differences in this theme, as it is only found in U.S. institutions, perhaps a reflection of cultural norms that emphasize individualism and personal expression.

Fourteen institutions emphasize the reflective nature of their required capstone. One university designates reflection, along with application and synthesis, as core learning objectives. Another requires students to demonstrate writing competence and "reflect upon their intellectual development and the nature of knowledge in their domain of study." Reflection supports program coherence, transition, and personal growth, as these statements illustrate:

> The capstone experience invites students to reflect on the entire undergraduate experience with emphasis on the chosen major and future career.
> By combining major capstone experiences with an opportunity to reflect on their educational experience and growth, the Core helps students identify and "own" portions of their educational experience that are particularly meaningful to them.
> This writing intensive course invites students to reflect and analyze how their General Education Program has impacted their understanding of themselves in the world, as well as how their world view has developed.

Several institutions set up structures to support reflection in the capstone experience, including required components and the use of portfolios.

Academic Rigor

As the culmination of the undergraduate experience, capstones afford students the opportunity to do their best academic work. This theme appeared in nine institutions' capstone descriptions. Some institutions promote capstones directly to students and encourage them to think big: "This endeavor will involve advanced work that addresses a significant issue, problem, or theme in your field—or in the world." Students are encouraged to see capstone work as meaningful:

> [The capstone] is your chance to make change. Do the research no one's ever done, present it and publish your thesis. Launch a tech start-up, or a social entrepreneur venture. Build and program a robot. Write a textbook that revolutionizes how Modern Standard Arabic, or middle-school science, is taught. Write a novel. Develop original curriculum. Produce a feature documentary, or your own choreographed dance performance. Design and distribute new software or apps. Create and present a portfolio of original works. Design and curate an interactive art exhibit.

Institutions set a high bar for end products as well. One university asks students to view the final year project

> as the pinnacle of their academic achievement, not only because of the academic rigor that is imposed on it by the University, but also because of the control they have to design, carry out and evaluate what they do. It is often seen to represent the point at which students become truly members of a disciplinary group.

Academic rigor was often described in terms of disciplinary contribution, as original scholarly or creative work that may be presented and published.

Ethical Responsibility

Ethical responsibility appears in eight U.S. capstone descriptions. Some institutions define *ethical responsibility* in terms of academic inquiry, requiring students to "adhere to discipline-specific norms of academic integrity and ethical practices" and "reflect on the ethical issues that are implicit in their project." Another requires attention to consider "personal and professional values" as part of capstone work. Several institutions describe ethics in terms of civic responsibility, including several U.S. Roman Catholic institutions with general education capstones that emphasize social justice. One capstone asks students to engage in "envisioning the future and humankind's responsibility in helping to shape that future."

Application

Applied learning appears in eight institutional capstone descriptions. These institutions want students to "connect knowing with doing" through "experiential learning," "hands on practice," or "applied, real-world experiences." Some institutions that emphasize applied learning include experiences that take students off campus as appropriate capstone work, including internships, clinicals, and fieldwork, while others emphasize applied learning within capstone courses and projects.

Public Sharing

Seven institutions in the United States link the capstone experience to public sharing of academic work. Public dissemination of student work occurs through institutionally sponsored events such as poster presentations, performances, readings, and displays. Institutions host annual conferences, student symposiums, senior capstone celebrations, and award ceremonies. Institutions use public sharing of capstone experiences to promote the value of the undergraduate degree and to create a sense of institutional distinctiveness. The capstone is presented to students as an exciting milestone and a time for celebration:

> In your final year . . . , it's time to show the world how far you've come. You'll complete your major with a capstone course or other advanced academic experience, then present your intellectual achievements through a thesis, recital, performance, or other public presentation.

Another university sets aside a day in spring for a campus-wide celebration of senior student capstone work. Many institutes publish samples or snapshots of student capstone projects on their websites, and several institutions publish all capstone work in digital repositories. One university's website includes a world map that tracks downloads of student work, with a message to students that "researchers and employers from across the globe can read, download, and share what you have accomplished." One institution views public sharing of capstone work in a broader context:

> Just as we expect scholars and artists to move beyond their fields of expertise and participate in collective activities that help to invigorate intellectual life, students are expected to engage in activities concurrent with [their capstone project] that broaden the scope of their intellectual endeavor and make their skills and viewpoints available to the College and the community at large.

Public sharing sends a message to students that the work they do in their capstone projects is a not just a classroom assignment—it connects them with a broader community. Public demonstration and dissemination of student work has been designated a high-impact practice in the United States (Kuh, 2008) and one of the six principles of capstones in Australia (Lee & Loton, 2020).

Spiritual Life
Three U.S. institutions describe their capstones in terms of students' faith journey and alignment with the affiliated church's values. One institution's capstone course engages an interdisciplinary approach to a local or global problem that "presents a test-case for this integrative experience and personal faith." Students at another institution must "demonstrate understanding of explicit and implicit connections between biblical perspectives and the discipline" as part of their capstone work.

What Drives "Capstones for All"?

The institutional discourse surrounding capstones suggests a range of motivations: attention to student learning, assessment and accreditation, institutional mission, and enhancement of institutional distinctiveness. The pressure for accountability—whether this takes the form of academic program assessment or data on postgraduate employment—influences how institutions talk about their capstones and provides some insight into what motivates them to make the commitment to institution-wide requirements. For institutions in all three countries, capstones are a site for demonstration of the institution's undergraduate core competencies or learning goals. Institutions of higher education in Australia, the United Kingdom, and the United States also face the pressure to attract and retain students. Capstone experiences can enhance institutional distinctiveness, whether the goal is to market a university's research prestige, a college's attention to career preparation, or the customized experience a student will get.

In U.S. institutions, general education has had a large impact on institutionally required capstones. Many institutions have revised their general education or core curriculum in terms of key undergraduate learning outcomes, aligning general education and baccalaureate learning outcomes. The Association of American College and Universities LEAP initiative (Liberal Education & America's Promise) established an influential set of essential learning outcomes, including one that aligns with the goals of capstones:

> Integrative and applied learning, including synthesis and advanced accomplishment across general and specialized studies, demonstrated through the application of knowledge, skills, and responsibilities to new settings and complex problems. (National Leadership Council, 2007, p. 3)

Fourteen states in the United States have joined the LEAP States Initiative, a set of formal collaboratives that promote large-scale implementation of high-impact practices like capstones. Similarly, the Lumina Foundation's Degree Qualifications Profile (Adelman et al., 2014) emphasizes applied and collaborative learning through activities that require students to address unstructured problems, conduct scholarly inquiry, and apply knowledge and skills in and outside the classroom—the kinds of learning that often happen in capstones. Our data shows many institutional statements on capstones include language that echoes either the AAC&U's essential learning outcomes or the Lumina Foundation's Degree Qualifications Profile. As institutions revise their general education and core curriculum programs to focus on core learning outcomes, many see senior-level capstones as an effective way to include integrative learning in the undergraduate curriculum.

General education plays a large role in how U.S. institutions in our study implement their required capstone: 43% require the capstone through their baccalaureate requirements, while 57% house this requirement in the general education or core curriculum program. (Higher education in Australia and the United Kingdom does not have a general education component, so all capstones are a component of the major.) Even when an institution houses the capstone within disciplinary majors, it fulfills a general education or core curriculum requirement. In terms of implementing change, it can be easier to revise the general education program rather than to implement a new baccalaureate requirement. Locating the institutional requirement within a general education program also provides a structure for accountability and a site for assessment.

There is alignment between the institutional statements we studied and scholarly literature about capstones. Institutions have clearly drawn on higher education literature as they have developed required capstones, just as scholarship often describes best practices at institutions like those in our study. Whatever the synergy between theory and practice, the result is alignment in the language used to describe capstones.

Implications for Faculty Who Teach or Direct Capstones

This study provides insights into the landscape of required capstones, including institutional strategies for defining and implementing this requirement, common themes used to frame goals and purposes, and possible drivers that motivate institutions to provide "capstones for all." Our findings can benefit faculty who teach or direct capstones by providing a broader context for reflection:

- *Drivers.* How does your capstone support your institution's mission? Do your capstone learning goals align with your institution's undergraduate student learning goals? How might your capstone contribute to the creation of a distinctive learning experience that will attract new students? How does your capstone prepare students for career or further study?
- *Frames.* How do you frame the capstone in your syllabus, assignments, and discussion with students? Have you explicitly stated the purpose and value of the capstone? Do your learning outcomes align with any of the themes in this study? Which additional themes might enhance the capstone experience for your students?
- *Definitions.* What are the parameters of the capstone that you teach or direct? Would students benefit from having more options for types, formats, and products? Would students benefit from more clearly communicated expectations about process and product?

Implications for Administrators and Institutions

Institutions planning to implement a required capstone or expand their capstone offerings can benefit from considering these questions:

- *Drivers.* What factors are driving our institution's interest in capstones? How will the capstone fit into the institutional structure? Will the capstone address broad undergraduate learning goals as well as disciplinary learning goals? For U.S. institutions, will the capstone be a baccalaureate requirement or a general education/core curriculum requirement?
- *Frames.* What is the purpose of capstones at our institution? Broadly speaking, what do you want students to do and demonstrate in the capstone? Which frames from this study might best serve our institution? Which frames will be most persuasive to stakeholders, particularly faculty and students?
- *Definitions.* What kinds of learning experiences will qualify as a capstone at your institution? What essential elements must each capstone include? How can you build on the existing capstones in our programs?

References

Adelman, C., Ewell, P., Gaston, P., & Schneider, C. (2014). *Degree Qualifications Profile*. Lumina Foundation. https://www.luminafoundation.org/files/resources/dqp.pdf

American Association of Colleges and Universities. (2015). *General education maps and markers: Designing meaningful pathways to student achievement.*

Boyer Commission on Educating Undergraduates in the Research University. (1998). *Reinventing undergraduate education: A blueprint for America's research universities*. State University of New York–Stony Brook.

Budwig, N., & Jessen-Marshall, A. (2018). Making the case for capstones and signature work. *Peer Review, 20*(2). https://www.aacu.org/peerreview/2018/Spring

Kuh, G. D. (2008). *High impact practices: What they are, who has access to them, and why they matter*. Association of American Colleges and Universities.

Lee, N., & Loton, D. (2020). *The capstone principles*. Australian Government Office of Learning and Teaching. https://www.capstonecurriculum.com.au/the-capstone-principles/

National Leadership Council for Liberal Education & America's Promise. (2007). *College learning for the new global century*. Association of American Colleges and Universities. https://www.aacu.org/sites/default/files/files/LEAP/GlobalCentury_final.pdf

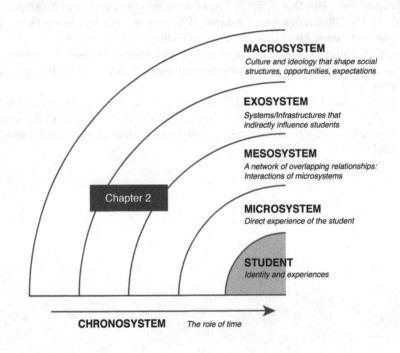

MACROSYSTEM
Culture and ideology that shape social structures, opportunities, expectations

EXOSYSTEM
Systems/Infrastructures that indirectly influence students

MESOSYSTEM
A network of overlapping relationships: Interactions of microsystems

Chapter 2

MICROSYSTEM
Direct experience of the student

STUDENT
Identity and experiences

CHRONOSYSTEM   *The role of time*

CAPSTONE INFLUENCES
AND PURPOSES

Russell Kirkscey, David I. Lewis, and Julie Vale

Capstone experiences (CEs) have arisen over time to satisfy a diverse set of purposes and to respond to a variety of influences. This chapter explores the dynamics and functions of CEs and is directed at colleagues seeking to introduce CEs, to modify existing programs considering current best practices, and to innovate as they develop their own capstone courses or programs.

In this chapter, we address this evolving strategy by providing an overview of dynamics affecting CEs, a short list of curriculum design goals derived from the dynamics, a menu of possible capstone purposes, three illustrative examples of existing capstone programs, and suggestions for how interested faculty can incorporate these learning outcomes into their own CEs. Our findings and recommendations stem from international, empirical studies of course outlines (Kirkscey et al., 2021), college and university mission statements (Bean et al., 2021), faculty interviews (personal communication), and faculty and student feedback to surveys (Vale et al., 2020).

Dynamics Affecting Capstone Experiences

CEs exist in an ecology of many stakeholders (see Figure 2.1). This ecology aligns with the socioecological framework highlighted in the Introduction; the context here frames these by institutional and noninstitutional stakeholders. While student learning is the ostensible goal, it should be supported by institutional and noninstitutional representatives. This transactional, reciprocal association among disparate actors should seek to balance curricular goals with the mission of the institution. However, the relationships should

Figure 2.1. Ecology of capstone experience stakeholders.

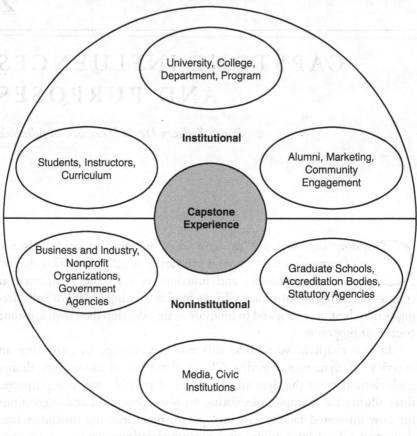

also address the needs, goals, and abilities of noninstitutional organizations to support and extend the institution's mission and curricular goals.

Institutional Stakeholders

Within the institution, the CE may align vertically with an integrated approach to learning throughout the 3 or 4 years of undergraduate education. Some institutions have addressed this need by creating a first-year experience for students and linking it to the objectives of a CE. While this approach can succeed with nondisciplinary/general education CEs, the strategy may be more difficult to accomplish with disciplinary CEs since, apart from highly structured programs such as engineering or pharmacology, students may not immediately declare a major in their first year. Thus, departments and programs should find ways to identify and support those students in appropriately preparing them for a CE. Moreover, since the purposes of CEs may involve outward-facing educational opportunities such as client-oriented, service-learning, or civic engagement components, CE designers and directors should also involve representatives in these areas in planning and decision-making. Additionally, CE goals of transition from undergraduate to prepared member of society also often entail communication with alumni as guest speakers and institutional advocates. Institutional media organizations can also assist the CE through press releases and online presence.

Noninstitutional Stakeholders

Noninstitutional stakeholders can also play a large role in affecting the creation of a CE curriculum. Business, industry, government agencies, and non-profit organizations in the institution's region may rely on graduates with workplace competencies to contribute to the economy. These entities, then, can benefit from the relationship with institutional partners by creating opportunities to engage with CE participants. Additionally, graduate programs need strong relationships with undergraduate CE programs, especially for disciplinary CEs whose goals include preparation for advanced education. Accreditation bodies also affect curriculum and assessment choices for all CEs. Lastly, CE designers should develop relationships with noninstitutional media to advertise programs and disseminate success stories.

Curriculum Design Choices: Programmatic Goals

Guided by an understanding of the dynamics of institutional and noninstitutional stakeholders, developers should consider at least four programmatic goals as they design CEs: individual student versus team participation, disciplinary versus nondisciplinary course content, elective versus required course credit, and learning outcomes based on professional versus personal needs (see Figure 2.2). We perceive these choices not as binary or mutually exclusive, but as elements on a spectrum of emphases that may be addressed according to the dispositions of various stakeholders. For example, instructors in a disciplinary CE may choose to give individual assignments that scaffold a final team project required by the mandates of professional licensure and guided by a professional organization's standards. In another scenario, course designers, guided by the institutional mission, may choose to emphasize personal growth and transition in a nondisciplinary CE; however, they may still require assignments that address the individual student's choice of vocation.

Furthermore, these choices may also inform other decisions about CE curriculum development. For example, course designers who must meet the criteria of a disciplinary CE in a profession that requires refined

Figure 2.2. Curriculum design choices spectra for programmatic goals.

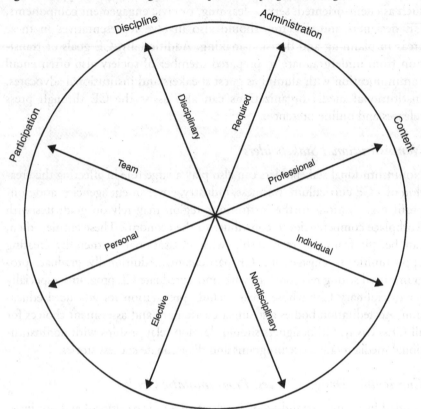

communication skills may need to emphasize oral and written communi-cation exercises that lead to a final project presentation. Or, in a CE that emphasizes personal growth, the curriculum may foreground reflection on a service-learning project. However, emphasizing one programmatic goal over another may have detrimental outcomes for a CE, which could very well meet disciplinary guidelines but fall well short of supporting the mission of an institution. For example, a CE in education may meet the guidelines of an accreditation agency without addressing a university mission of interdiscipli-nary research. We suggest that curriculum designers consider both program-matic and societal goals to balance the purposes in a curriculum and address as many stakeholders as possible.

Capstone Experience Purposes

CEs can and should be formed and revised to reflect the dynamics of insti-tutional and noninstitutional conditions according to the mission of the institution. While a large research university may value preparing professionals for their careers, a small liberal arts college may value graduate school preparation. For example, the curriculum of a CE at a large teaching university may need to emphasize the requirements of discipline-level, noninstitutional stakeholders such as accreditation agencies or business and industry, while a small religious college might value its relationship with its regional nonprofit partners. Thus, a CE's curriculum may address many or few purposes according to an institution's objectives, which are often reflected in its mission statements and its relationships with noninstitutional partners.

To assist with intentional integration and planning, we have assembled a list of CE purposes drawn empirically from disciplinary, interdisciplinary, and nondisciplinary programs across the globe. Methods of the studies included content analysis of syllabi and course calendars (Kirkscey et al., in press), mission statements (Bean et al., 2021), surveys of faculty and student perceptions (Vale et al., 2020), and a review of literature (J. Weiss, personal communication, August 21, 2020). While this list is not exhaustive, it should assist CE developers in considering curricular goals in their programs. Furthermore, we reiterate that these purposes do not exist in a vacuum and are affected by both institutional and noninstitutional forces that drive social, economic, and political change (see Figure 2.1).

To address the breadth of purposes that we have substantiated, in Figure 2.3, we roughly categorize them into the four categories as outlined in the Introduction and collapsed categories of Breadth and Application, acknowledging the overlap:

- integration (connecting ideas through all years of college)
- breadth (moving students beyond specialization in the major to a broad general education experience)
- application (applying expert knowledge to examine real-world issue and produce a substantial product)
- transition (preparing students to move from college to the world beyond)

We encourage readers to review this menu, their institution's mission, and their disciplinary guidelines before identifying the specific learning outcomes of their CE. We hope that readers will be inspired to include purposes they may not have previously considered (e.g., including a service-learning component in a science CE).

Furthermore, genuine assessment of some of the listed objectives is difficult (e.g., ethical behavior). Therefore, for those instructors who adopt a constructive alignment philosophy for course design, listing such learning outcomes at a course level may be challenging. We encourage instructors to consider that dynamics within the CE stakeholders ecology

Figure 2.3. Capstone purposes.

Integration
Coherent Academic Experience • Reflection • Integrative Learning • Core Competencies
Breadth and Application of Academic Skills
Inquiry and Analysis • Written Communication • Reading • Critical Thinking • Oral Communication Problem-Solving • Creative Thinking • Quantitative Literacy Institutional Resources • Study Skills Academic Rigor • Civic Engagement/Service-Learning
Transition
Teamwork • Career Planning • Independence • Ethical Reasoning • Support Networks Intercultural Knowledge • Spiritual/Religious Knowledge Global Learning • Information Literacy • Leadership • Alumni Development • Preparation for Graduate School • Lifelong Learning Financial Literacy • Public Sharing of Knowledge

(see Figure 2.1) may affect final choices of purposes and the means of measuring those goals.

Exemplar Capstone Experiences

In this section, we present three different examples of CEs from three countries and illustrate how they navigate the dynamics of their own CE ecologies. The designers of each curriculum have considered not only the ecologies of their CEs but also the spectra of curriculum design decisions illustrated in Figure 2.2.

Accreditation Required, Disciplinary Capstone Experience (Canada)

Design is a central tenet of engineering practice, and many engineering programs around the world culminate in a design experience. Indeed, the Canadian Engineering Accreditation Board (CEAB) requires all accredited engineering programs to

> culminate in a significant design experience conducted under the professional responsibility of faculty licensed to practice engineering in Canada, preferably in the jurisdiction in which the institution is located.

> The significant design experience is based on the knowledge and skills acquired in earlier work and it preferably gives students an involvement in team work and project management. (Engineers Canada, 2021, p. 22).

The University of Guelph (Canada), a medium-size, research-intensive, public university, has a long history of integrating design experiences in a "design spine," a model of vertical alignment that spans the curriculum from first to fourth year, following a cornerstone-keystone-capstone philosophy. Indeed, when a capstone design course became a mandatory part of Canadian engineering accreditation in 2001, the Guelph Engineering Department became the model upon which many other Canadian engineering programs built their design CEs. More recently, many of these other institutions have adopted the idea of the design spine.

The culmination of the Guelph engineering 4-year honors program is a double-weight course comprising a team-based, self-directed design project (75%) and a lecture-based grounding in principles of engineering ethics and law (25%). As a culminating experience, the Guelph engineering design capstone is positioned to assess all 12 engineering graduate attributes (i.e., learning outcomes) as defined by the CEAB (Engineers Canada, 2021). This list includes knowledge, communication, professionalism, and lifelong learning, among others.

A purpose of the ethics and law component is to prepare students for the Professional Practice Exam, a required component to obtain professional engineering licensure, while simultaneously preparing students for uncomfortable situations that they may encounter in the workplace (e.g., conflict of interest and whistleblowing). This component is assessed through a series of low-weight reflections and a final exam.

The project-based component of the course is highly experiential and modeled after an actual engineering work environment. Student teams identify a problem, define the criteria and constraints, develop and assess multiple solution ideas, then implement the solution, typically via a prototype or a thorough simulation. Student groups are guided in this process by a self-selected faculty advisor who must be a licensed professional engineer.

Guelph is unusual in offering the course simultaneously to all engineering subdisciplines; for example, a group may include a water resources engineer, a biomedical engineer, a mechanical engineer, and a computer engineer. Most other Canadian engineering CEs are housed within a single engineering subdiscipline, and therefore teams are composed entirely (for example) of mechanical engineers.

The focus of the project is integration of technical knowledge and professional communication. Assessment is via a series of technical reports and a design symposium that includes a poster presentation. Reports are graded by the faculty advisor and require the student groups to discuss the design process and analyze the final design using a variety of lenses including economic cost, social impacts, and environmental effects. The final presentation is focused on design justification, assessed by industry professionals, and open to the public.

The design symposium provides a crucial avenue of multimodal communication among graduating students, alumni, and industry professionals. It is regularly praised as being one of the most rewarding experiences in the curriculum and is a key avenue for students and career advisors to connect with possible employers and for the alumni office to reconnect with potential donors.

Institutionally Required, Nondisciplinary Capstone Course Housed Within a Discipline (UK)

Bioscience students in the United Kingdom have historically undertaken a research or honors CE in the final year of their undergraduate education, a requirement of the UK Quality Assurance Agency for Higher Education Biosciences Benchmark Statement (Quality Assurance Agency, 2019) and the two biosciences/biomedical sciences degree accrediting bodies (Institute of Biomedical Sciences, 2017; Royal Society of Biology, 2020). Traditionally, projects were individual and constituted laboratory work, fieldwork, or literature reviews. Purposes included gaining research, experimental, and technical skills, with a focus on preparing students for careers in research or analytical laboratories.

Because fewer than 10% of graduates will go into research careers and half will leave science altogether (Lewis, 2020), institutions that grant bioscience degrees have begun to introduce nontraditional inquiry rather than research-based project opportunities into their programs. Indeed, the Biosciences Benchmark Statement now permits nontraditional project opportunities: "Students may work outside of the laboratory or field environment, for example, in education or in the public understanding of science" (Quality Assurance Agency, 2019, p. 14).

The University of Leeds (UK), a large, research-intensive, public university, requires all undergraduates to undertake a significant research project in their final year of study. Undergraduate students in the Leeds School of Biomedical Sciences programs—human physiology, medical sciences, pharmacology, and neuroscience—all take a single CE course, within which they can select one of 15 different formats. These formats encompass both traditional (e.g., laboratory, computer modeling) and nontraditional (e.g., educational development and service-learning) options (University of Leeds, 2014). The CE combines an inquiry-based experience with personal and professional development, 21st-century workplace preparation, and career leadership training. Given that most people work in teams in the workplace, most CEs are team-based or multiteam-based (i.e., multiple subteams all working on the same inquiry-based problem).

The learning outcomes for the CE reflect its ethos and purpose:

- apply knowledge, understanding, and skills gained in earlier years of their program to a problem relevant to the biomedical sciences
- gather or generate information, critically analyzing this information to address this problem
- gain new knowledge, understanding, and skills in creating a solution to, or output for, this problem
- develop and apply skills required in employment, including 21st-century skills
- effectively communicate the outcomes and outputs of this inquiry-based learning experience
- recognize health, safety, and ethical considerations where appropriate

The assessments for the CE reflect tasks that would be undertaken at the workplace: an academic paper (science, public engagement, or educational), a commercial/technical report, or a reflective portfolio comprising digital examples and critical reflection. Students, in consultation with their mentor, decide the most appropriate assessment for their capstone. In addition, all students deliver (and defend) an oral presentation.

The impact of this innovative CE has been substantial. It better addresses the needs and aspirations of students and provides them with the work experience and skills required for their career paths. Indeed, the program has inspired most UK bioscience degree providers to introduce nontraditional capstone projects into their courses. As a result of the work at Leeds, the two UK bioscience/biomedical sciences accrediting bodies have changed their project accreditation criteria, broadening the range and scope of what is permitted (Institute of Biomedical Sciences [IBMS], 2020; Royal Society of Biology, 2020).

Elective, Nondisciplinary, Personal Growth–Focused Capstone (U.S.)

Boston College (U.S.) is a private, Jesuit, Tier 1 research institution. Founded in 1990, the Boston College Capstone Program is nondisciplinary and focuses on personal development. The capstone seminars deliberately move away from knowledge specialization toward assisting students to integrate the many components of their 4 years of academic and personal growth. These CEs provide seniors an elective opportunity to holistically assess their education.

The program comprises approximately 25 seminar CE courses per year. Almost one fifth of the senior class elects to participate in one of these courses. Course instructors are drawn from all four undergraduate colleges: Arts and Sciences, Education, Management, and Nursing.

Every CE seminar emphasizes educational formation and later life commitments, following a philosophy of review and preview. Students review their educations as a series of personal choices within the framework of their required core, majors, and minors, as well as the university's extensive program of retreats, volunteering programs, foreign study options, and extra-curricular opportunities. They also preview the process of making long-term life and work commitments.

Within this framework, instructors are free to design their own CE, with seminars ranging from courses that use literature and history to help first-generation students expand their voice and agency to courses in "adulting" that blend developmental psychology, career construction, and basic tasks like budgeting, life-partner selection, and consumer goals. Typically, instructors draw on materials from their areas of specialization. While this is easier for instructors in the social sciences, faculty members in physical and natural sciences also value the opportunity to leverage their years of attentive mentoring and their own wider reading, enabling them to create syllabi and share wisdom they could not feasibly use in a departmental elective.

The program is carefully managed. New seminars are vetted by the program director and by current CE instructors. All instructors also participate in an annual retreat, which includes reflection and reporting on new seminars, student feedback, and faculty development. Because each seminar is different, this collegial interaction ensures the program's coherence around it and the institution's common goals.

The faculty members believe that the measurable academic skills of reading, interpreting, application, discussion, and analytical or creative writing should play a role in discerning a student's life purpose and significance. Learning outcomes are aligned in the "Capstone Quadrilateral": (a) personal relationships, friendships, life-partnerships, and family; (b) work and career; (c) citizenship and efficacy in issues affecting one's local community, the nation, and the world; and (d) spirituality, defined broadly as the search for an encompassing framework of meaning. While assignments vary from course to course, they all contribute to the traditional liberal arts and Jesuit pedagogy of personal formation. Specific outcomes often involve class leadership, interviews with established older adults, mindfulness practices, goal setting, creating budgets, and team service-learning projects. Additionally, every seminar is required to have a final written project as part of the assessment.

The program has received external funding for development from the Lilly Foundation and other sources and has continued to provide institutional funding for assessment and curriculum building. CEs in the program are now vertically linked to two first-year courses: the Cornerstone Seminar, a one-credit course that focuses on goal setting, and Courage to Know, a three-credit course that supports personal and academic growth. Enrollment in these courses has also remained popular and expanding. CE assessment reflects the success of the program in end-of-semester student surveys that evaluate student perceptions of the courses' effects on educational and personal development, the nature of thinking about long-term commitments to work and career, creating meaningful relationships, and views of spirituality.

Implications: Future Directions for Capstone Experiences

There is increasing global recognition of the benefits to students, institutions, employers, and society of appropriately crafted opportunities for students to participate in a meaningful final experience that reflects academic preparation and provides a transition to life after graduation. The nature and format of a CE will vary among programs and institutions depending on identified purpose(s); accrediting, regulatory, or professional bodies; institutional mission statements; and other influences (see Figure 2.1). Given the diverse range of career pathways available to students, educators should incorporate as broad a range of identified purposes as possible. For example, in engineering, students often undertake a "design and build" project, a narrow interpretation of accrediting bodies' requirement for a design experience. Rather than design another widget, the project or prototype could provide social and economic benefits (e.g., "Engineers Without Borders"). Such a project could develop skills and attributes not traditionally forefronted in engineering capstones (e.g., interdisciplinary effort, dialogue with key stakeholders, and increased awareness of societal issues).

However, one size doesn't fit all. Ideally, institutions should offer a broad range of CEs, from individual opportunities to team-oriented interdisciplinary opportunities. Either mode should still focus on a breadth of goals, including personal and professional development, work experience, and global citizenship. Furthermore, programs should provide appropriate scaffolding and support for students from the moment they begin the curriculum, developing and preparing them for their CEs and the transition to life after university.

Finally, administrators and instructors need to consider their assessment of CEs to extend past formulaic undergraduate essays or multiple-choice exams to more real-world, authentic assessments, undertaken during the CE, that better reflect the desired purpose or outcome of the CE. A critical step in advancing CE purposes is for educators to move beyond their disciplinary comfort zones. To accomplish this goal, colleagues in higher education need a widespread distribution of good practices and ideas among disciplines, institutions, and nations—and a willingness to learn from each other, to adapt practices for their own programs and students, and to revise untenable established practices.

References

Bean, J., Beaudoin, C., Lewis, D. I., van Zile-Tamson, C., & von der Heidt, T. (2021, July 11–13). *The landscape of required baccalaureate capstones: A multinational study*. Conference on Engaged Learning, Elon University, Elon, North Carolina.

Engineers Canada. (2021). *Report of the visiting team on the accreditation visit*. https://engineerscanada.ca/sites/default/files/2021-11/EN_VT_Report_Template_2022-2023.doc

Institute of Biomedical Sciences. (2017). *Criteria and requirements for the accreditation and re-accreditation of BSc (Hons) in biomedical science*. https://www.ibms.org/resources/ documents/criteria-and-requirements-for-the-accreditation-and-re/

Institute of Biomedical Sciences. (2020). *Final year research or capstone projects*. https://82b1248a-8d51-4814-ab1c-ba8f72828534.filesusr.com/ugd/4b6beb_402a92c0f60344cc 92c1c20e91ecbae3.pdf

Kirkscey, R., Vale, J., Hill, J., & Weiss, J. (2021). Capstone experience purposes: An international, multidisciplinary study. *Teaching and Learning Inquiry*, *9*(2), 1–21. https://doi.org/10.20343/teachlearninqu.9.2.19

Lewis, D. I. (2020). Final year undergraduate research project or a "Capstone Experience"? Time for a re-think. *British Journal of Clinical Pharmacology*, *86*(6), 1227–1228. https://doi.org/10.1111/bcp.14266

Quality Assurance Agency. (2019). *Biosciences benchmark statement*. https://www.qaa.ac.uk/ docs/qaa/subject-benchmark-statements/subject-benchmark-statement-biosciences.pdf

Royal Society of Biology. (2020). *Accreditation handbook*. https://www.rsb.org.uk/images/accreditation_home/RSB_Overall_Handbook_Sept_2019_September_2020_Implementation.pdf

University of Leeds. (2014). *Leeds curriculum.* https://ses.leeds.ac.uk/leedscurriculum

Vale, J., Gordon, K., Kirkscey, R., & Hill, J. (2020). Student and faculty perceptions of capstone purposes: What can engineering learn from other disciplines? *Proceedings of the Canadian Engineering Education Association.* https://doi.org/10.24908/pceea.vi0.1414

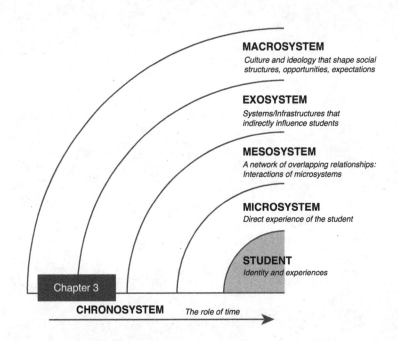

3

INSTITUTIONAL CONSIDERATIONS FOR CAPSTONES ON CAMPUS

Perspectives Based on National Data on Senior Culminating Experiences

Dallin George Young, Tracy L. Skipper, and Rico R. Reed

For postsecondary institutions and the professionals who work in them, the final year of undergraduate education represents the last opportunity to prepare students for demands that lie ahead (Gardner et al., 1998). Capstone experiences deliver on multiple fronts (Brownell & Swaner, 2010; Henscheid, 2000), providing a rite of passage to the world of work and a distinct scholarly or professional community while integrating the knowledge, skills, and experiences of the undergraduate years (Henscheid, 2000). Achieving these twin aims is fraught with challenges because multiple models of the senior capstone exist on college campuses (Kuh, 2008; National Survey of Student Engagement [NSSE], 2013; Young et al., 2017). To capitalize on the opportunities and obligations of providing meaningful and high-impact culminating experiences, institutions must design and intentionally weave a host of reflective and integrative learning experiences throughout a student's undergraduate education (Boyer Commission, 1998; Henscheid et al., 2019).

Drawing on data from the National Survey of Senior Capstone Experiences, this chapter will highlight the various forms of culminating experiences on U.S. campuses. The chapter will also interrogate the national landscape, highlighting concerns for institutions and faculty who teach and direct capstones.

Institutional Landscape

The 2016 National Survey of Senior Capstone Experiences (NSSCE), conducted by the National Resource Center for the First-Year Experience and Students in Transition, was administered to produce a national profile of campus efforts to support student success in the final year of baccalaureate study. This chapter contains data previously reported elsewhere (see Young et al., 2017, for a complete description of the research methods and an in-depth discussion of the results).

This section uses results from the NSSCE to describe the state of practice in U.S. colleges and universities by answering two primary questions:

1. What types of senior capstone experiences are offered?
2. How are capstones situated to achieve objectives for the senior year?

Types of Senior Capstone Experiences

Previous studies on the senior capstone highlighted the many forms that it might take (see Henscheid, 2000; NSSE, 2013; Padgett & Kilgo, 2012). In preparation for the 2016 administration of the NSSCE, Young et al. (2017) reviewed the diversity of capstones described in this scholarship. They generated a typology of culminating experiences, containing five main categories: (a) courses (e.g., credit-bearing courses offered in specific disciplines, courses emphasizing integrative learning offered outside specific disciplines), (b) exams, (c) performances and exhibitions, (d) projects, and (e) experiential learning (see Young et al., 2017, for an expanded description of the typology of culminating experiences). Additionally, based on their review of the literature and previous administrations of the NSSCE, Young et al. (2017) classified capstone experiences as one of three administrative types: (a) academic department or discipline-based, (b) cocurricular, or (c) campus-wide. The most prevalent administrative home of capstone experiences is in academic departments or disciplines; nearly all (98.7%) of the participating institutions reported at least one discipline-based capstone experience on their campus. Slightly more than half of the respondents reported offering cocurricular capstones (51.5%), and more than a third reported having a campus-wide capstone experience (37.8%).

Academic departments or programs reported using a variety of capstone experiences. Discipline-based capstone courses (96.6%) were the most frequently reported of the 13 types. In addition, about two thirds of institutions reported offering thesis or independent research (69.4%), internships (68.7%), art exhibitions (66.3%), and student teaching (66.3%). Figure 3.1 provides additional frequencies.

Figure 3.1. Discrete capstone experiences based in academic departments (n = 291).

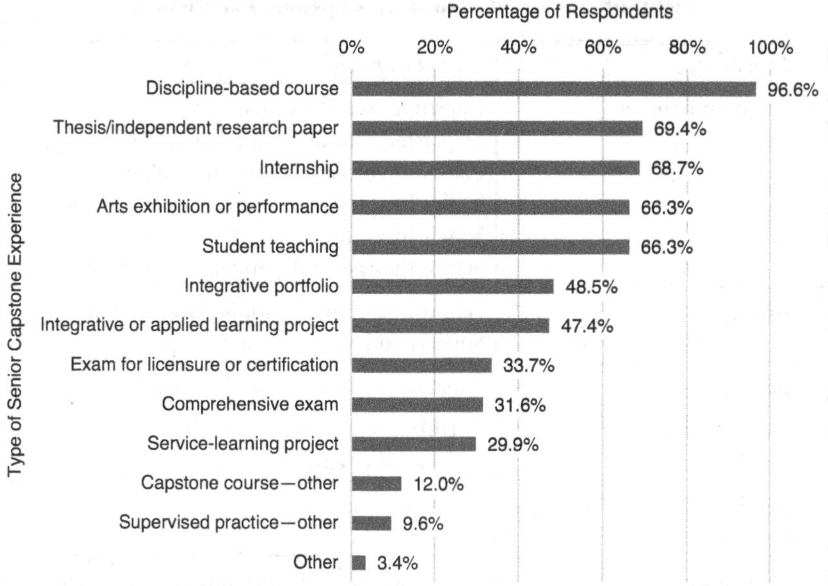

Percentage of Respondents

Type of Senior Capstone Experience	Percentage
Discipline-based course	96.6%
Thesis/independent research paper	69.4%
Internship	68.7%
Arts exhibition or performance	66.3%
Student teaching	66.3%
Integrative portfolio	48.5%
Integrative or applied learning project	47.4%
Exam for licensure or certification	33.7%
Comprehensive exam	31.6%
Service-learning project	29.9%
Capstone course—other	12.0%
Supervised practice—other	9.6%
Other	3.4%

Note. Percentages will add up to more than 100% due to participants' ability to select all options that applied.

Source. 2016 National Survey of Senior Capstone Experiences (Young et al., 2017). Reprinted with permission.

Situating Capstones to Achieve Objectives

When colleges and universities create culminating experiences, they should be concerned with aligning the form of the initiative and its objectives, which occur both at the departmental and institutional levels. Data from the 2016 NSSCE provide valuable context for how capstone experiences might align with the overall institutional approach to the senior year and how different capstone types might meet departmental goals for students. For example, one primary method is to align capstone type with the ways of doing and knowing in the field of study. Table 3.1 lists the capstone types associated with fields of study. Arts and humanities was identified as the field of study using the broadest range of capstone experiences—perhaps not surprising, given the diversity of majors that fall under that heading. Three types of capstone experiences had strong correspondences with specific fields of study. First, almost all (95.7%) institutions offering one or more performance-based capstones did so within arts and humanities. Second, nearly every campus (97.9%) offering student teaching did so in education-related majors. Finally, a majority of institutions used exams leading to professional licensure in education (e.g., the Praxis, 64.2%) and health-related fields (e.g., the National Council Licensure Examination for nursing, 55.8%).

TABLE 3.1
Fields of Study and Associated Capstone Experiences

Field of Study	Type of Capstone
Arts and humanities	Capstone course—other Department or discipline-based course Exhibition of performing, musical, or visual arts Senior integrative or applied learning project Senior integrative portfolio Senior thesis or independent research project
Business	Senior integrative or applied learning project Supervised practice—internship
Education	Supervised practice—student teaching
Health professions	Certification or professional licensure exam Supervised practice—other
Physical sciences, mathematics, and computer science	Exam—comprehensive
Social sciences	Service-learning or community-based learning project

Note. This table reports the most frequent field of study for each capstone type offered by campuses responding to the 2016 NSSCE. Associations presented here should not be interpreted that the types of capstones listed are the most frequently used types of capstones by any specific field of study.

Data source. 2016 National Survey of Senior Capstone Experiences (Young et al., 2017).

Participants in the NSSCE reported the campus-wide objectives, if any, their institutions had developed specifically for the senior year. The most frequently named objectives included the following:

- career preparation (71.1%)
- employment or job placement (62.6%)
- graduation (61.3%)
- graduate or professional school enrollment (50.5%)
- critical thinking skills (43.3%)

A small but substantial (10.8%) percentage of participants reported that their campuses had not identified objectives for the senior year. Table 3.2 presents a breakdown of the most frequently identified institution-level goals for the senior year based on the type of department-based senior capstone experience offered.

TABLE 3.2
Most Frequently Identified Senior Year Objectives by Type of Department-Based Senior Capstone Experience Offered

Type of Capstone	Institutional Objective for Senior Year				
	Career Preparation	Employment or Job Placement	Graduation	Graduate School Enrollment	Critical Thinking Skills
Department or discipline-based course	72.5%	63.9%	61.4%	50.7%	44.6%
Capstone course—other	85.7%	77.1%	74.3%	60.0%	68.6%
Exam—comprehensive	78.3%	72.8%	70.7%	57.6%	44.6%
Certification or professional licensure exam	79.6%	72.4%	70.4%	51.0%	44.9%
Exhibition of performing, musical, or visual arts	73.6%	64.8%	64.2%	56.5%	44.0%
Senior integrative portfolio	75.9%	68.8%	63.8%	53.2%	46.1%
Senior integrative or applied learning project	74.6%	61.6%	62.3%	48.6%	47.8%
Senior thesis or independent research paper	76.2%	64.4%	62.4%	56.4%	47.5%
Service-learning or community-based learning project	72.4%	60.9%	67.8%	48.3%	47.1%
Supervised practice—internship	82.0%	72.5%	69.0%	54.5%	48.0%
Supervised practice—student teaching	78.8%	69.9%	66.8%	56.0%	47.2%
Supervised practice—other	69.2%	65.4%	61.5%	57.7%	38.5%

Source. 2016 National Survey of Senior Capstone Experiences (Young et al., 2017). Reprinted with permission.

With a few minor exceptions, the rank order and relative percentage of institutional objectives identified by institutions do not differ by capstone type. The findings suggest institutions frequently use different forms of the capstone to achieve similar aims, namely preparation for what follows graduation, such as employment or postgraduate education. Overall, the results from the 2016 NSSCE signal that administrators, faculty, and staff responsible for capstones more frequently take up a career or vocational approach to culminating experiences than one foregrounding metacognitive development, such as reflection, critical thinking, or integrative learning (Henscheid et al., 2019).

Implications for Administrators and Institutions

While capstones are common on U.S. college campuses, student access to them may be uneven. Among college seniors participating in the 2016 NSSE, only 45% had completed (or were completing) a capstone. Finley and McNair (2013) asked students to identify barriers to participating in high-impact practices (HIPs), including senior capstones. These barriers included a lack of advising about the importance of such experiences, competing priorities such as needing to work for pay while in college, and not seeing the connection to academic work. Those who were least likely to participate in capstones were first-generation college students, part-time students, those living off campus, and students of color (NSSE, 2016b). Transfer students are also much less likely to report participating in culminating experiences (NSSE, 2016a).

Such disparities are concerning, as Finley and McNair (2013) found that students who participated in a senior capstone reported levels of engagement in deep learning and perceived learning gains on average 6.1 points higher than students who did not participate in such experiences. Evidence also suggests that first-generation students, transfer students, and students of color may experience larger gains than their counterparts, especially when they have exposure to multiple HIPs (Finley & McNair, 2013).

The challenge facing postsecondary institutions is twofold: (a) scaling up culminating experiences so that more students, especially those who have been historically marginalized and have the most to gain from participating, have access to them and (b) ensuring access to a high-quality capstone experience regardless of form or administrative home. These challenges can be addressed through more intentional collaboration within individual academic units and across the institution. Such collaborations need not result in a single capstone model, nor is this desirable. Grounding the capstone requirement in institution-wide learning outcomes, Indiana University–Purdue University Indianapolis implemented a flexible approach to capstones with three different models: (a) interdisciplinary, team-based projects; (b) discipline-specific capstones; and (c) licensure or certification mandates (Rowles et al., 2004). Portland State University aligned disparate capstones through a common assignment where students reflected on how the capstone helped them gain experience related to one of the University Studies goals (Rhodes & Agre-Kippenhan, 2004).

Faculty learning communities or working groups focused on senior capstones (see McGill, 2012; Rowles et al., 2004) can identify strategies for ensuring high-quality learning experiences across different contexts, examine methods for assessing capstone experiences or using them as programmatic assessment, share resources and effective pedagogies, and provide a peer review structure for teaching in the capstone. Strategic mapping of the learning environment (see Wawrzynski & Baldwin, 2014) would allow committees to identify both the formal and informal curricula students experience, providing opportunities to align activities across the institution and discover potential partnerships for reinforcing student learning. It is also important to acknowledge the role of external partners in mapping the learning environment, especially for capstone experiences involving licensure or certification or those defined by internships, practica, or work with community partners.

Implications for Faculty Who Teach or Direct Capstone Experiences

A 2020 study assessing quality and equity in HIPs (Kinzie et al., 2020) suggested that students participating in capstone experiences may be less satisfied with those experiences than other HIPs common in the senior year (i.e., internships and undergraduate research experiences). McGill's (2012) study of student perceptions of the capstone revealed four primary concerns that point to possible sources of dissatisfaction: (a) preparation for the capstone, (b) communication about the capstone, (c) structure of the experience, and (d) support. These concerns also highlight ongoing challenges to delivering high-quality culminating experiences and remain relevant for faculty who teach or direct capstones.

Preparation for the Capstone

Successful completion of capstone experiences requires students to engage in a set of advanced academic or professional skills that may include writing, working as part of a team, making presentations, communicating with clients or community members, networking, and time management, among others. Henscheid and colleagues (2019) suggested that acquisition of these skills derives from "educational experiences [that] have been intentionally and logically sequenced so that earlier experiences provide the knowledge and skills for later, more challenging experiences" (p. 96). They observed that preparing students for the capstone required a backward-design approach: introducing the reflection, integration, and application of learning essential in a culminating experience early in college. This *vertical alignment* or sequenced and sustained support has implications for capstone experiences and learning structures throughout the undergraduate experience. If integration and application are important outcomes, these skills are more likely to be fully realized in the capstone if they are included in general education courses, first-year seminars, advising, and other cocurricular experiences designed for beginning college students. As Henscheid et al. opined, "if the culminating experience is the first time a student is exposed to applied or integrative learning, it is too late" (p. 96).

Mills and Beliveau (1999) described a "vertically integrated" capstone experience at Virginia Tech that involved integrating upper- and lower-division undergraduates into a student-directed enterprise designed to foster critical thinking, "out-of-the-box" problem-solving, and improved decision-making. A series of "home courses" corresponding to the sophomore, junior, and senior years in a construction management major met simultaneously, allowing the faculty to create cohort-based teams. The senior cohort led the completion of the project, with sophomore and junior teams having progressively more challenging roles and responsibilities within the project.

Communication

For both students and faculty, clarity about the purpose and goals of the capstone is critical for success. Faculty and administrators need to be transparent about the specific learning outcomes for the culminating experience, lest students dismiss it as merely a hoop to jump through on the way to graduation. Moreover, linking capstones to shared learning outcomes for the undergraduate curriculum, principles, or institutional values gives students, faculty, and administrators a common language to describe and understand the purpose of capstone experiences (see Wawrzynski & Baldwin, 2014). When multiple faculty members are involved in the design, delivery, supervision, or assessment of departmental capstone experiences, students expect faculty to operate with a "shared set of criteria and standards to assess capstone projects" (McGill, 2012, p. 498). For capstones involving internships, practica, fieldwork, or service, ensuring that supervising faculty, students, and external partners have a set of shared expectations is critical.

In addition to understanding the purpose and goals for capstones, students need to understand the requirements, options available to them, and parameters for designing a project (McGill, 2012). Having a sense of what the culminating experience entails upon entering the major ensures that students can develop an educational plan with the senior capstone in mind. As such, professional and faculty advisors should be well versed in capstone requirements so they can initiate conversations about culminating experiences and guide students in their planning.

Structure

Faculty feedback to students bridges concerns related to communication and structure. Students want frequent, high-quality feedback from faculty directing capstone experiences to ensure that they remain on track. Kinzie (2013) reported that more frequent meetings with the supervising faculty member, clear expectations, and helpful feedback were among the factors making the most significant contributions to learning gains for capstone participants. One strategy is having a series of deliverables, with opportunities for feedback on each, rather than a single deliverable with more limited feedback. When designing capstone experiences, faculty should consider the discrete tasks that contribute to the final project and create structures that allow students to move through tasks in a logical sequence, receiving feedback on their performance at critical junctures.

Capstone experience structure varies widely, with some students completing projects during a single academic term and others engaging in multiterm projects. One-term projects requiring students to deliver a product for an external partner or conduct an independent research study can be incredibly challenging. As a result, students are less likely to demonstrate outcomes faculty hope to see. Yet expanding the capstone beyond a single term would likely require the buy-in from and coordination with stakeholders within and beyond the individual academic department (e.g., faculty senate if course approvals/changes are necessary, the registrar, advising staff).

Support

McGill (2012) found that the "most important contributor to student satisfaction or dissatisfaction in capstone appears to be capstone faculty" (p. 500). Students want the capstone supervisor to mentor and advise them. The

Strada-Gallup College Student Survey (see Crabtree, 2019) offers insight into what this might look like: Students value faculty who care about them as individuals, encourage them to pursue their goals, and get them excited about learning. Yet there is room for improvement. In a recent study of HIPs quality (Kinzie et al., 2020), roughly half of students participating in a capstone reported opportunities for substantive interaction with faculty and peers—the kinds of interactions that lead to perceptions of faculty support. Quality of mentoring or faculty contact may also vary by major. For example, students in the arts and humanities were more likely to report supportive relationships with faculty mentors than students in business, the social sciences, or STEM fields (Crabtree, 2019). Faculty in these fields may need additional training to develop supportive learning environments within and outside classrooms. Institutions may also need to revisit course loads and reward structures to ensure that faculty have the time, flexibility, and incentives to mentor students involved in capstones.

Centers for teaching and learning are ideal partners to develop training for faculty leading capstone experiences. For example, the University of South Carolina's Center for Teaching Excellence offers a certificate on applying the principles of integrative and experiential learning (IEL) in various educational environments. The workshops emphasize setting the stage for reflection in service-learning, study abroad, internships, and other HIPs so students can make connections across curricular and cocurricular learning experiences, engage diverse perspectives, and synthesize and transfer knowledge to new contexts. Faculty who complete the certificate are eligible for grant funding to create new experiential learning opportunities, incorporate them into an existing course, or develop team-taught interdisciplinary courses. The IEL certificate model could be adapted at other institutions to help faculty prepare to facilitate a range of culminating experiences in the senior year.

Students may also need access to resources (e.g., work or lab space) and financial support (for equipment and supplies, printing, travel, or other expenses) to complete a capstone. Students who work part time or full time may find internship, fieldwork, or practical training requirements particularly trying. Grants, stipends, and community partnerships are possible strategies for alleviating financial barriers. For example, at the University of South Carolina, corporate partners host student teams addressing a funder-identified problem in the College of Engineering's two-semester design capstone (Horn, 2018). Institutions need to ensure that financing a capstone experience is not a barrier to participation among low-income students—many of whom may be first-generation students or members of racially or ethnically minoritized groups.

Conclusion

As institutions initiate, develop, and implement capstone experiences, administrators and faculty must contend with the tension between flexibility in design and delivery and creating an experience that consistently achieves broad institutional goals for seniors. Critics may contend that inconsistencies across the forms of capstone experiences signal a lack of rigor or value across these experiences. However, high-level, campus-wide goals help bring clarity to the purposes of individual experiences. Additionally, transparent assessment of outcomes related to capstone participation for graduating seniors and alumni, disaggregated by type, program, and student characteristics, will go a long way to pointing out areas of effectiveness and opportunities for improvement. Moreover, assessment helps institutions understand how well they deliver on the promises made to students.

We would be remiss not to acknowledge the time in which we are writing this chapter. Because of the COVID-19 pandemic, many culminating experiences were interrupted. Experiential capstones, such as internships and student teaching, were canceled or moved online. Test-based capstones were rescheduled or delivered in different formats. The world shifted for many students during a critical point in their education. Surely these changes have taken a mental and emotional toll on students who have questions about their preparation and ability to enter the workforce in a world where unemployment has suddenly spiked. Interruptions to experiences preliminary to the capstone (e.g., first-year experiences, transfer, study abroad, internships) will create ripples for culminating experiences beyond the time frame of the pandemic.

Moreover, the social unrest resulting from police violence and brutality toward Black and other racially minoritized citizens has emphasized how these interruptions disproportionately affect students who have been historically disadvantaged in higher education. Where we have not started asking and acting on questions of access and opportunity, we must increase our attention to ensuring equitable access to the benefits of capstones for all students and not just those who have enough affluence or cultural capital to participate.

References

Boyer Commission on Educating Undergraduates in the Research University. (1998). *Reinventing undergraduate education: A blueprint for America's research universities.* (ED424840). ERIC. https://files.eric.ed.gov/fulltext/ED424840.pdf

Brownell, J. E., & Swaner, L. E. (2010). *Five high-impact practices: Research on learning outcomes, completion, and quality.* Association of American Colleges and Universities.

Crabtree, S. (2019, January 24). *Student support from faculty mentors varies by major.* Gallup. https://news.gallup.com/poll/246017/student-support-faculty-mentors-varies-major.aspx

Finley, A., & McNair, T. (2013). *Assessing underserved students' engagement in high-impact practices.* Association of American Colleges and Universities.

Gardner, J. N., Van der Veer, G., & Associates. (1998). *The senior year experience: Facilitating integration, reflection, closure, and transition.* Jossey-Bass.

Henscheid, J. M. (2000). *Professing the disciplines: An analysis of senior seminars and capstone courses* (Monograph No. 30). University of South Carolina, National Resource Center for the First-Year Experience and Students in Transition.

Henscheid, J. M., Skipper, T. L., & Young, D. G. (2019). Reflection, integration, application: Intentional design strategies for senior capstone experiences. In T. Trolian & E. A. Jach (Eds.), *Applied Learning in Higher Education: Curricular and Co-Curricular Experiences That Improve Student Learning* (New Directions for Higher Education, no. 188, pp. 91–100). Wiley. https://doi.org/10.1002/he.20349

Horn, C. (2018, May 8). *Designing their futures: Senior capstone course gives an entrée into the professional world.* University of South Carolina. https://sc.edu/uofsc/posts/2018/05/designing_their_futures.php#.Y49D_HbMJPY

Kinzie, J. (2013). Taking stock of capstones and integrative learning. *Peer Review, 15*(4), 27–30.

Kinzie, J., McCormick, A. C., Gonyea, R. M., Dugan, B., & Silberstein, S. (2020, November 6). *Assessing quality and equity in high-impact practices: Comprehensive report.* Indiana University Center for Postsecondary Research. https://nsse.indiana.edu/research/special-projects/hip-quality/index.html

Kuh, G. D. (2008). *High-impact educational practices: What they are, who has access to them, and why they matter.* Association of American Colleges and Universities.

McGill, P. T. (2012). Understanding the capstone experience through the voices of students. *The Journal of General Education, 61*(4), 488–504. https://doi.org/10.1353/jge.2012.0029

Mills, T., & Beliveau, Y. (1999). Vertically integrating a capstone experience: A case study for a new strategy. *Journal of Construction Education, 4*(3), 278–288.

National Survey of Student Engagement. (2013). *Promoting high-impact practices: Maximizing educational gains* (NSSE Research Brief No. 1). Center for Postsecondary Research, Indiana University Bloomington.

National Survey of Student Engagement. (2016a). *HIP participation by transfer status by Carnegie classification* [Data table]. Center for Postsecondary Research, Indiana University Bloomington.

National Survey of Student Engagement. (2016b). *NSSE 2016 high-impact practices: U.S. summary percentages by student characteristics* [Data table]. Center for Postsecondary Research, Indiana University Bloomington.

Padgett, R. D., & Kilgo, C. A. (2012). *2011 National Survey of Senior Capstone Experiences: Institutional-level data on the culminating experience* (Research Reports on

College Transitions No. 3). University of South Carolina, National Resource Center for the First-Year Experience and Students in Transition.

Rhodes, T. L., & Agre-Kippenhan, S. (2004). A multiplicity of learning: Capstones at Portland State University. *Assessment Update, 16*(1), 4–5. https://doi.org/10.1002/au.161

Rowles, C. J., Koch, D. C., Hundley, S. P., & Hamilton, S. J. (2004). Toward a model for capstone experiences: Mountaintops, magnets, and mandates. *Assessment Update, 16*(1), 1–2, 13–15. https://doi.org/10.1002/au.161

Wawrzynski, M., & Baldwin, R. (2014). Promoting high-impact student learning: Connecting key components of the student experience. In P. L. Eddy (Ed.), *Connecting Learning Across the Institution* (New Directions for Higher Education, no. 156, pp. 51–62). Wiley. https://doi.org/10.1002/he.20083

Young, D. G., Chung, J. K., Hoffman, D. E., & Bronkema, R. (2017). *2016 National Survey of Senior Capstone Experiences: Expanding our understanding of culminating experiences* (Research Report No. 8). University of South Carolina, National Resource Center for the First-Year Experience and Students in Transition.

PART 2
Exploring Capstone Experience Models

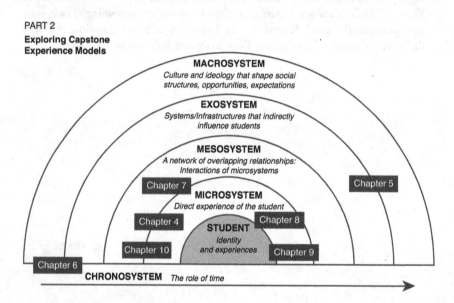

PART TWO

EXPLORING CAPSTONE
EXPERIENCE MODELS

Caroline J. Ketcham, Anthony G. Weaver, and Jessie L. Moore

C hapters in this section examine models of culminating experiences (e.g., seminar courses, independent research projects, capstone ePortfolios, etc.), with examples from multiple institutions and strategies for adapting them for readers' own campus contexts. These chapters span across the socioecological framework and give readers tangible ideas and resources to support implementation in their context. Focusing on the levers and mission salient to your institution makes the models in this section applicable to all readers. Each chapter highlights the challenges and opportunities that the different layers of the socioecological framework play in decisions made about their specific context.

We begin with chapter 4, "Where There's a Will, There's a Way: Implementing a Capstone Experience for General Education," by looking at a large institution that has designed and implemented a capstone experience for all. The authors discuss how the micro- and mesosystems specifically related to the programs, with limited room to add courses, impacted the decisions made in capstone design. This should give all institutions a model to think about when the barrier to implementation is scale. This general education model is followed by an example from the biosciences field in chapter 5, "Preparing Students for the Fourth Industrial Revolution." This field classically culminates with research experiences and a systems approach to hearing the drivers of the exo- and chronosystems demanding graduates with a broader range of professional experiences. This chapter's takeaways benefit readers in the sciences broadly and also other fields where the capstone is often deeply rooted in the traditions of the field. Having a broad array of fresh examples with very handy resources is a great starting point.

These examples are followed by chapter 6, "How Two Australian Universities Achieved "Capstones for All": A Change Management Perspective," which provides a comparison of how a required capstone emerged at two Australian universities with vastly different contexts. The voice of the founding leaders for these experiences is useful to readers as they balance the drivers at the macro- and exolevel within their socioecological context with a sharp focus on the student experience. Chapter 7, "Adapting a Capstone: Projects and Portfolios Across Four Courses and Three Institutions," shares a capstone example that has morphed across disciplines, universities, and faculty, keeping the heart and art of the course true while considering the impacts of the micro- and mesosystems of their context. It is a refined example of how staying true to the goals and adapting to the values of a campus can lead to really impactful capstone experiences for student and faculty development.

In chapter 8, "Just a Few Minutes of Your Time: Using Qualitative Survey Data to Evaluate and Revise a Capstone Project at an Early College Network," readers are given a model set right at the intersection between the student experience and microlevel impacts implementing student experiences systematically to improve the capstone experience. Additionally, the faculty from Bard Early College remind readers that our students experience these integrated and impactful curricula along their academic journey. As professors in higher education, we often assume knowing what students come prepared to do, but our colleagues in high school and early college contexts are scaffolding integrative and complex experiences for the students entering our walls. How can we ask about or assess those skills and use them to advance the experiences in our institutions?

The last two chapters put students intentionally as integral to the experiences created. Chapter 9, "Students-as-Partners and Engaged Scholarship: Complementary Frameworks," highlights the importance of student perspective to the goals and assessments of the experiences we implement, emphasizing that the microsystem is dependent on the experiences and identities of the students. Let's challenge higher education to implement this resource into our vision of the future of higher education. Finally, chapter 10, "Designing Democratic Spaces: Public-Facing Civic Capstone Courses," levels this idea up and emphasizes that if we ignore the skills, expertise, values, and experiences of our students, we miss the mark of what is possible. It challenges educators to put democratic pedagogy and civic service as the central outcome to a college education. This transition isn't easy, but it is necessary as we consider the layers of the socioecological framework as more fluid and dynamic than our structures have ever considered. If we want to keep up a societal context that expects our workforce to have knowledge, skills, expertise, and experiences that translate and transform, we must be prepared to do things differently.

We are confident these examples will give readers models to consider. What should be noted is how the mission and goals of their specific programs and institutions drove decisions and choices even as the changing landscape and demands of higher education were the same across all contexts. We are confident readers will find useful nuggets in each example and hope these ignite ideas for implementation and change agents at their institutions; our society needs this.

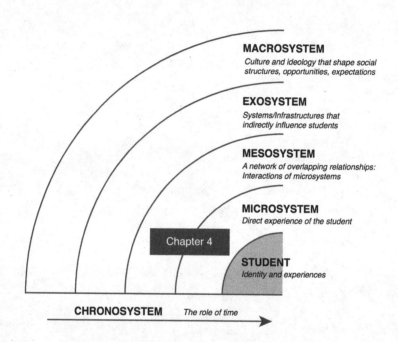

MACROSYSTEM
Culture and ideology that shape social structures, opportunities, expectations

EXOSYSTEM
Systems/Infrastructures that indirectly influence students

MESOSYSTEM
A network of overlapping relationships: Interactions of microsystems

MICROSYSTEM
Direct experience of the student

Chapter 4

STUDENT
Identity and experiences

CHRONOSYSTEM   *The role of time*

WHERE THERE'S A WILL, THERE'S A WAY

Implementing a Capstone Experience for General Education

Carol Van Zile-Tamsen, Janet Bean, Christina Beaudoin, David I. Lewis, and Tania von der Heidt

As institutions of higher education consider ways to incorporate high-impact practices into the undergraduate curriculum, the general education capstone is an underutilized option that deserves more attention. This case study analysis examines a general education capstone at the University at Buffalo (UB), State University of New York (SUNY). This capstone is of particular interest not only because it is the culminating requirement of general education rather than of a degree program, but also because the institution is a large, research-intensive institution where universally required general education capstones are less common (see chapter 1). Furthermore, the UB capstone uses an ePortfolio as its signature assignment, a high-impact practice (HIP) in its own right (Watson et al., 2016). How did UB overcome the obstacles that are inevitable with large-scale curricular change? This institution's experience can provide insights about the challenges and opportunities of implementing a general education capstone. This chapter describes the UB capstone experience and demonstrates how its design elements map to Bronfenbrenner's (1974) socioecological framework, as suggested in the introduction.

Institutional Context

UB is the largest and most comprehensive institution in the SUNY system, awarding over 8,000 degrees each year and enrolling nearly 22,000 undergraduates in over 125 degree programs. UB is a member of the American Association of Universities, a consortium of top research institutions in the United States. Demographic characteristics of the undergraduate population are reported from the most current *Common Data Set* (University at Buffalo, 2019). These students are primarily full-time, degree-seeking students. Just over half identify as White (55%) and male (56%).

Among non-White domestic students, 7% identify as Hispanic, 8% as Black or African American, 0.4% as Native American or Alaskan Native, 16% as Asian, 0.1% as Native Hawaiian or Pacific Islander, and 2% as two or more races. Just under 20% of undergraduates are first-generation college students (M. Whitford, personal communication, July 31, 2020), and 30% fall within the lowest income group. Approximately 29% of entering fall undergraduates are transfer students, and approximately 14% of all undergraduates are international students.

With regard to organizational structure, UB comprises 12 academic units that deliver the university's educational programs. The Division of Academic Affairs, headed by the vice provost for academic affairs (VPAA), is a central support unit providing oversight and support for academic programs, central advising for undecided undergraduate students, class scheduling, professional development for instructors, support for assessment work, and oversight and governance for the undergraduate general education program. The deans of the academic units and the VPAA report to the university provost, the chief academic officer.

The UB Curriculum Office reports to the dean of undergraduate education and coordinates the delivery of general education across the 12 academic units with guidance from a committee governance structure. The assistant vice provost for undergraduate education directly supervises the UB curriculum director. The day-to-day oversight of the capstone experience is provided by the capstone coordinator, with assistance from a full-time instructor.

The UB Capstone: UBC 399

The UB Capstone, a one-credit mentored course (UBC 399), was launched in 2016 as part of a revised general education program called the UB Curriculum. The revised general education program was based on design principles promoted by the Liberal Education and America's Progress (LEAP) Campus Action Network of the Association of American Colleges and Universities (AAC&U; Budwig & Jessen-Marshall, 2018), as well as evidence-based high-impact educational practices, including a first-year seminar, an ePortfolio, and the capstone (Kuh, 2008; Van Zile-Tamsen et al., 2018). With the design of the UB Curriculum and the culminating capstone course, the student is placed firmly at the center of the ecosystem. The program's focus is on providing a meaningful general education experience that allows students to follow personal interests, while building an integrated knowledge base.

The goal of UBC 399 is creation of an integrative ePortfolio that allows students to demonstrate their learning and achievement through the first 2 years of their undergraduate course work. *All* undergraduates, regardless of major, including those transferring from other institutions, must complete UBC 399 prior to graduation. For most students, UBC 399 is taken at the end of general education coursework, typically in the junior year, and they are encouraged to enroll as soon as they have completed their UB Curriculum requirements.

With instructor guidance, students reflect on and work to integrate completed coursework into a more holistic and interconnected knowledge base. Chapter 1 identified common drivers of capstone experiences. At UB, the primary rationale for the required general education capstone comes from the planful design of the UB Curriculum to foster the thinking skills of integration and reflection (Kohler & Van Zile-Tamsen, 2020; Van Zile-Tamsen et al., 2018), explicitly addressed in the course description:

> The Capstone is not a seated class, but rather a digital space set aside for thinking, reflecting, and integrating elements of the program through the creation of a Capstone ePortfolio: a multi-media, web-based platform where students will gather and integrate their learning experiences at UB into a meaningful whole, demonstrating their growth and development as learners. Students will be able to keep (and modify) this ePortfolio as they transition into the job market, graduate study, or other endeavors. (UB Curriculum, 2019, p. 1)

Additional desired outcomes include career/future goals (addressed in the course description), as well as application, core competencies, and self-directed learning (UB, 2013; 2014).

Governance of the Capstone

The faculty committee charged with designing the capstone experience proposed the one-credit mentored learning experience, UBC 399. At the committee's recommendation, delivery and oversight of UBC 399 was placed in the UB Curriculum Office within the Division of Academic Affairs rather than within one of the 12 academic units. This approach is in direct contrast to the typical approach to instructional delivery at UB, where courses and academic programs are designed, developed, and delivered by faculty members in academic units. This organizational structure was seen as essential for establishing and maintaining the integrity of the capstone as a common experience for students in all majors and ensures that there is a supportive exosystem (Bronfenbrenner, 1974) for delivery of the general education program and the capstone. This central management of UBC 399 is viewed as one of the key factors for its successful implementation. As described by the vice provost for academic affairs,

> The campus had to say we're doing this, and the capstone had to be delivered centrally . . . this capstone actually is for all students, and if you embedded it in any one unit . . . you may lose the importance of the capstone to assess [learning in] general education.
> [Further,] we were relying on the capstone as the point of . . . integrative learning. And that was such a key piece of the program that it seemed like that needed to be protected and brought in more central.

As of a result, the UB Curriculum Office is responsible for all aspects of the capstone experience, including hiring and supporting instructors, scheduling sections, delivering instruction, and supporting students. This office reports to the dean of undergraduate education, who convenes the faculty oversight committees for general education, the UB Curriculum Steering Committee, and the Diversity and Integrative Learning Subcommittee responsible for periodic review and assessment of UBC 399.

In addition to ensuring that UBC 399 was delivered centrally, the faculty committee had to address the number of credit hours and how this new course would fit into curricular plans. It soon became apparent that a typical three credit hour course was problematic for high-credit programs like engineering. As a compromise, the capstone became a one-credit mentored learning experience. With student learning being at the very center of program and course design, the implementation committee established the mentored model at scale, and this serves as the mesosystem (Bronfenbrenner, 1974), providing support for scaffolded integration and knowledge construction throughout the capstone experience.

Once implementation began, it became evident that a communication plan was needed to address confusion about the purpose of the capstone experience among all campus audiences. Many faculty members believed that it was going to be disciplinary specific for majors, while many advisors were under the impression that it was centered on career exploration. Students were hearing conflicting messages from both groups. As described by the dean of undergraduate education:

> One of the challenges has always been ensuring that the leadership, the administrative leadership really understands exactly what the capstone is, how and why it was designed in the way that it was . . . so that people's expectations are appropriately aligned [with] the outcomes of the class.

The UB Curriculum Office developed and distributed fliers and short videos to communicate the purpose of the capstone experience. In addition, UB Curriculum staff presented to advisors and to instructors who taught other components of the general education program. Through these communications, they emphasized the need for students to have general education artifacts for the capstone ePortfolio. A Capstone Excellence event was designed as a way for students to showcase high-quality capstone ePortfolios for the campus community. This disciplined communication plan has been effective in eliminating misconceptions about the purpose of the capstone.

UBC 399 Structure and Delivery

The foundation of the capstone experience largely rests on the shoulders of two full-time clinical instructors who teach, coordinate, and administer UBC 399, including supervising the instructional team of graduate teaching assistants (TAs) and adjunct instructors. With just over 2,000 students needing to complete UBC 399 each term, these clinical instructors manage a complex balancing act to ensure the integrity of the capstone is maintained. This balancing act includes offering a sufficient number of sections while ensuring that instructional costs are within budget. The initial plan was to supplement the two clinical instructors with only TAs, but because of tuition reimbursement, this is the most expensive instructional model. The UB Curriculum Office instead took advantage of the fact that UB employs a large number of staff with terminal degrees who hold professional positions and are actively seeking more interaction with students. Hiring the most qualified as adjuncts is a creative way to extend instructional resources at low cost.

With 70 students per section, one of the most important aspects of the delivery of the capstone, according to all of the interviewees, is the emphasis on continuous improvement efforts to ensure that the capstone not only runs like a well-oiled machine, but also remains a stress-free experience for instructors and provides a positive and meaningful learning experience for students. The primary mechanism through which these objectives are achieved is through standardization across course sections, achieved with instructor training, a common course syllabus with common assignment guidelines and ePortfolio template, and regular meetings during the semester. However, balancing section consistency with unique contributions of instructors is important. Instructors primarily express their individuality in the mentoring relationship through conversation and feedback within the ePortfolio. In actuality, the standardization of course materials, the availability of instructional resources, and the support provided through regular meetings allow more time for instructors to engage in the mentoring process. This process of standardization also limited instructors to common reflective and integrative assignments essential to the creation of the ePortfolio, which more closely aligns with expectations of a one-credit class. This approach to course design and instructional delivery provides a supportive microsystem (Bronfenbrenner, 1974) for the student experience, taking the form of a collaborative relationship with the capstone instructor who provides a scaffolded experience to promote student cognitive development.

This close relationship between instructors and students also benefits the endeavor in a more holistic way, allowing instructors to gain much useful qualitative information about the effectiveness of the capstone. The instructors are then able to share this information with UB Curriculum staff and modify the surrounding ecosystem as needed to ensure a quality experience delivered at scale. This feedback loop allows for continuous course improvements that range from such minor changes as language used in course assignment descriptions to selecting a new platform for the ePortfolio system.

The Capstone ePortfolio

ePortfolio was identified as the eleventh HIP (Watson et al., 2016) and, because of the promise of ePortfolios for promoting scaffolded instruction of higher order thinking skills (Eynon & Gambino, 2017; Reynolds & Patton, 2014), the general education redesign committee incorporated an ePortfolio project to promote reflection and integrative learning (Van Zile-Tamsen et al., 2018). Embedding ePortfolio creation in UBC 399 provides the mechanism through which scaffolded mentoring is used to promote reflection and integration of the undergraduate learning experience, the primary learning outcomes of the capstone, and the UB Curriculum as a whole. In its essence, the ePortfolio is the mechanism through which the student experiences the individualized supports from the micro- and mesosystem

(Bronfenbrenner, 1974). Components of the UBC 399 ePortfolio are described in detail in Kohler and Van Zile-Tamsen (2020).

Integration occurs as students reflect on their learning experiences and select and connect artifacts that best exemplify their achievement of UB Curriculum learning outcomes. Since this is the first time that most of these students have been asked to engage in explicit reflection and to create meaningful connections among past courses, the instructor's role as mentor is essential for success. All of the interviewees note the visible window that the ePortfolio provides into student achievement of these learning outcomes. For example, as the dean of undergraduate education describes,

> It's amazing to me how they've been able to have a pretty sophisticated understanding of the role that general education is playing in their overall education and . . . the different components of a relatively complicated general education structure . . . and how students are able to understand why they engaged in that structure, and what all the different components have to do with one another.

In addition to the support provided by the individual instructor, the UB Curriculum Office has devoted resources to support students as they work to complete the ePortfolio and achieve the key learning outcomes of reflection and integration. An ePortfolio help site was created, along with video tutorials on using the ePortfolio platform. The UBPortfolio Walk-In Lab, supervised by the clinical instructors, is staffed with undergraduate eMentors who provide ePortfolio assistance. Instructors conduct in-person office hours in the lab to provide assistance with specific assignments.

> Students have their instructor, obviously, who's their first point of contact, but they do have the lab. And even if their particular instructor isn't here at a particular time, there are almost always, if not always, one, if not two, clinical instructors, as well as TAs. We have close to fifteen eMentors.

Assessment findings suggest that UBC 399 is achieving its stated objectives of the development of reflection and integrative learning skills (Kohler & Van Zile-Tamsen, 2020; UB Curriculum Diversity and Integrative Learning Committee, 2020). Review of final ePortfolios provides direct evidence of integration, reflection, and application of skills, with over 70% of students in the assessment sample categorized as highly proficient or exemplary by the assessment team. In addition, over 80% recognize that completion of the capstone experience provides valuable benefits, including increased metacognitive and reflective skills and an increased ability to identify meaningful connections across disparate courses and disciplinary areas (Kohler & Van Zile-Tamsen, 2020). Further, instructors report that being a part of the student's learning process and seeing this learning reflected in the ePortfolio is very rewarding.

Continuing Challenges

In spite of the success of UBC 399, there are challenges as the institution tries to ensure a high-quality experience at scale. First, the perceived importance of UBC 399 among some students continues to present challenges. As with many courses that are labeled general education courses, there can be difficulties getting students to take them seriously and put forth their best effort. Next, because UBC 399 is required for all incoming transfer students, and many have completed most, if not all, of their general education requirements at other institutions, they begin the capstone with little preparation or extended orientation to the UB Curriculum requirements or to the process of integration. Finally, for the majority of undergraduate degree programs, UBC 399 has been placed into the third year curricular plan. However, more students wait until their senior year than expected. Seats are limited, and there is a potential that students who wait until the last minute might have difficulty enrolling.

Conclusions and Implications

The careful cultivation of UB's general education capstone experience, UBC 399, has resulted in visible benefits to student learning, as evidenced by the experiences of key capstone personnel, student reflections on the value of the experience (Kohler & Van Zile-Tamsen, 2020), and direct evidence of integration, reflection, and application of skills in student ePortfolios (UB Curriculum Diversity and Integrative Learning Committee, 2020). UB Curriculum staff and capstone instructors are guided by the original goals the faculty committee members had for the capstone, and they have stayed true to these goals in spite of barriers that have emerged. In addition, they engage in sustained continuous improvement efforts to ensure that the integrity of the capstone is maintained.

While UBC 399 has experienced growing pains and continues to face some challenges, it has been extremely successful in meeting the objectives laid out by the general education redesign committee. Brofenbrenner's (1974) socioecological framework can help explain why such a large and potentially unwieldy experience has been successful. At the center of the model is the student, where the focus of higher education should be, and where the focus of the UB capstone experience firmly rests. Instructors (microsystem) meet students where they are to provide an individualized mentored experience (mesosystem) at scale to promote reflection and integration.

The governance and oversight of the capstone experience (exosystem) has been shaped in such a way that the focus is allowed to remain on the student. Policies, procedures, and supports are designed in such a way to promote student achievement of desired learning outcomes. Further, the planful design of the exosystem and the microsystem has been influenced by the macrosystem of evidence-based higher education. Easily described in a short chapter, the effort needed to design and implement this effective capstone experience actually spanned more than 5 years and required the institution to stay committed to student learning in spite of challenges, not the least of which relates to financial constraints.

Implications for Faculty Who Teach or Direct Capstones

The story of UB's general education capstone has implications for those who teach or direct capstones at other institutions. With its use of the ePortfolio, UB's capstone provides the space and support for all students to reflect on their learning. To maintain the focus on the student, those who teach or direct capstones must be fully aware of the desired student learning outcomes and commit to helping students achieve them through high-quality instruction and mentoring activities. Further, it is important that instructors are transparent in their communications to students about the "why" of the capstone experience so that students' learning is explicit and that requirements are equitable across sections so that all students have a common experience. Finally, including faculty, capstone directors, and campus champions in systematic, periodic, and "candid" assessment will promote continuous improvements and enhance the likelihood of success.

Implications for Administrators and Institutions

The UB capstone provides a powerful mechanism for the assessment of student learning. However, the same feature that makes this learning experience so effective—its emphasis on student reflection and integration in a multidisciplinary space—also creates structural and budgetary challenges. Maintaining a student focus and the integrity of the experience through an adequate budget model that provides for high-quality instruction is absolutely essential for any successful capstone experience. Because the capstone is not housed within an academic unit, placing the capstone within the appropriate organization is essential to maintain the integrity of the capstone. In addition, campus-wide conversations about the capstone should occur early and often and should address the timing and sequencing of the capstone experience for students in all majors, especially those with high credit hour requirements.

In the end, a universally required capstone delivered at scale can be daunting to think about. However, if a commitment to the student-centered focus is maintained, it can be done. As the newest member of the UB Curriculum/Capstone team advises, "Know that where there's a will, there's a way . . . . The message that I would send to folks is that it can be done. . . . It's impressive that it's come together the way it has."

References

Bronfenbrenner, U. (1974). Developmental research, public policy, and the ecology of childhood. *Child Development, 45*(1), 1–5. https://doi.org/10.2307/1127743

Budwig, N., & Jessen-Marshall, A. (2018). Making the case for capstones and signature work. *Peer Review, 20*(2), 4–7.

Eynon, B., & Gambino, L. M. (2017). *High-impact eportfolio practice: A catalyst for student, faculty, and institutional learning.* Stylus.

Kohler, J., & Van Zile-Tamsen, C. (2020). Metacognitive matters: Assessing the high-impact practice of a general education capstone ePortfolio. *International Journal of e-Portfolio, 10*(1), 33–43. https://www.theijep.com/past_10_1.cfm

Kuh, G. D. (2008). *High impact educational practices: What they are, who has access to them, and why they matter.* American Association of Colleges & Universities. https://www.aacu.org/publication/high-impact-educational-practices-what-they-are-who-has-access-to-them-and-why-they-matter

Reynolds, C., & Patton, J. (2014). *Leveraging the eportfolio for integrative learning: A faculty guide to classroom practices for transforming learning.* Stylus.

UB Curriculum. (2019). *UBC 399 course syllabus.*

UB Curriculum Diversity and Integrative Learning Committee. (2020). *Capstone assessment report 2019–20.*

University at Buffalo. (2013). *Provost's Committee on General Education: Preliminary report to the Curriculum and Assessment Task Force.*

University at Buffalo. (2014). *Progress report of the General Education Committee.*

University at Buffalo. (2019). *Common data set 2019.*

Van Zile-Tamsen, C., Hanypsiak, K., Hallman, L., Cusker, E., & Stott A. M. (2018). The capstone ePortfolio: High impact practice for general education. *AePR: The AAEBL ePortfolio Review, 1,* 24–35.

Watson, C. E., Kuh, G. D., Rhodes, T., Light, T. P., & Chen, H. L. (2016). ePortfolios—The eleventh high impact practice [Editorial]. *International Journal of ePortfolio, 6,* 65–69. https://www.theijep.com/past_6_2.cfm

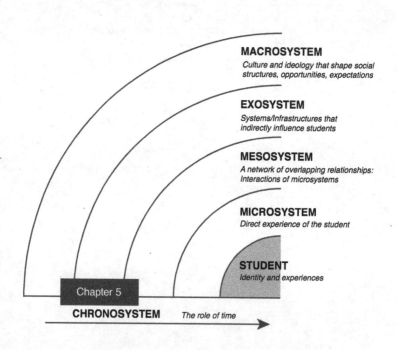

MACROSYSTEM
*Culture and ideology that shape social
structures, opportunities, expectations*

EXOSYSTEM
*Systems/Infrastructures that
indirectly influence students*

MESOSYSTEM
*A network of overlapping relationships:
Interactions of microsystems*

MICROSYSTEM
Direct experience of the student

STUDENT
Identity and experiences

Chapter 5

CHRONOSYSTEM   *The role of time*

PREPARING STUDENTS FOR THE FOURTH INDUSTRIAL REVOLUTION

David I. Lewis, Janet Bean, Christina Beaudoin, Carol Van Zile-Tamsen, and Tania von der Heidt

We are currently in the fourth industrial revolution (4IR), a world and workplace governed by robotics, artificial intelligence, digitization, and automation (Schwab, 2016). There is a need for employees who can create new tasks for robots or do the things robots cannot currently do. Recruiters require graduates with different skill sets, the so-called 4IR skills (Gray, 2016). Appropriately designed capstones provide a unique opportunity for students to develop and apply these 4IR skills, but also to showcase their acquisition to educators, graduate recruiters, and most importantly, to themselves.

The majority of undergraduate students in bioscience programs in the United Kingdom undertake a research-based assignment in their final year, a requirement of Accrediting and Regulatory Bodies (Institute of Biomedical Sciences, 2017; Quality Assurance Agency, 2019; Royal Society of Biology, 2020). For the vast majority, this comprises a laboratory-based, fieldwork, or literature project (Cowie, 2005). Despite the emphasis on a culminating research experience in UK bioscience programs, less than 10% of students go on to careers in research, the majority leaving science altogether (Lewis, 2020d). Therefore, while these traditional research projects, with their focus on research experience, may have been relevant 50 years ago, they do not enable the majority of current bioscience graduates to be "workplace ready" (Deloitte, 2018). Radical change was required, involving a total rethink of the purposes, practices, and outcomes of undergraduate research projects, in order to better prepare students for an increasingly challenging 21st-century workplace.

This chapter describes the principal author's (David Lewis) 19-year journey in taking a discipline-specific final year undergraduate research project course, and evolving it into an innovative, interdisciplinary course comprising a sector-leading portfolio of 16 project opportunities for students—a combination of traditional research projects, scientific and industry-relevant capstones, and capstones with a civic or societal focus in the same course.

The process and lessons learned are applicable to all disciplines, not just the biosciences or wider STEM, or to the United Kingdom, but to educators and institutions across the world seeking to develop global graduates who have the potential to lead initiatives to resolve the major challenges facing mankind.

Historical Background and Drivers

The biosciences research project course was first offered at the University of Leeds (UK) in 2001 as a core for all final-year students (~200 p.a.) on four programs (physiology, medical sciences, pharmacology, neuroscience) offered by the School of Biomedical Sciences. In keeping with Leeds being a large, public, research-intensive university, all projects were research-focused, with students undertaking either a laboratory-based project or critical literature review. To give critical review students experience of experimental design, they had to write a grant proposal for a pilot study to take research in the area of their review forward. The module learning outcomes encapsulated this focus on research experience by ensuring students

- acquired an in-depth knowledge and understanding of a research topic in the biomedical sciences;
- practiced basic laboratory skills, acquired new laboratory skills, and further developed experimental design skills; and
- improved their written and oral communication skills.

In 2014 the university, with its core mission of research-based learning, introduced the "Leeds Curriculum," with the requirement that all undergraduate students, irrespective of discipline, undertake a significant research project in their final year of study, one of only five UK universities to have this mandatory requirement (University of Leeds, 2014; see also chapter 1).

Evolution Into a Sector-Leading, Interdisciplinary, Multiopportunity Capstone Experience

Lewis increasingly recognized that his course, with its research focus, was not serving his students' needs. Few were going into careers in research, and it didn't provide the work experience or develop the broader skills required for careers outside of research (Lewis, 2017). A radical rethink of its purpose, practices, and outcomes was required.

In the United Kingdom, universities are free to set their own curricula, guided by the Quality Assurance Agency for Higher Education discipline-specific benchmark statements. The Biosciences Benchmark Statement (QAA, 2019, para 3.3) requires students to "plan and perform a research project" (the term *capstone project* is largely unknown in the United Kingdom). Across the sector, students were undertaking laboratory-based, fieldwork, or literature reviews (Cowie, 2005). However, the statement permits students to "work outside of the laboratory or field environment, for example, in education or in the public understanding of science," (paragraph 7.5) providing the authority to totally reshape the purpose and ethos of the course, to create many different project opportunities and experiences for students. At that time, there was no UK biosciences accrediting body.

As a highly experienced science communicator, Lewis regularly facilitated ethical debates in local high schools. Recognizing this would make an ideal alternative project, he collaborated with one student to codeliver an ethics-focused workshop at the 2005 Leeds Festival of Science (Lewis, 2011). The event was a huge success, so the next year, the scheme was expanded and delivered directly in local schools.

These projects were not hypothesis-driven research projects. Instead, they provided engaging educational activities. They also inspired students who facilitated the events, and massively contributed to their personal and professional development, providing both a service-learning (Salam et al., 2019) and capstone experience (Kuh, 2008). The narrow research-focused course had been transformed into a capstone course.

Other faculty, recognizing the substantial benefits to students, progressively joined the team, bringing with them new ideas, expertise, and skill sets. Their contacts expanded the team's network of external partners (e.g., primary care physicians, small and medium enterprises). Together, they cocreated new capstone formats (see Figure 5.1).

Figure 5.1. Progressive development of research and capstone projects.

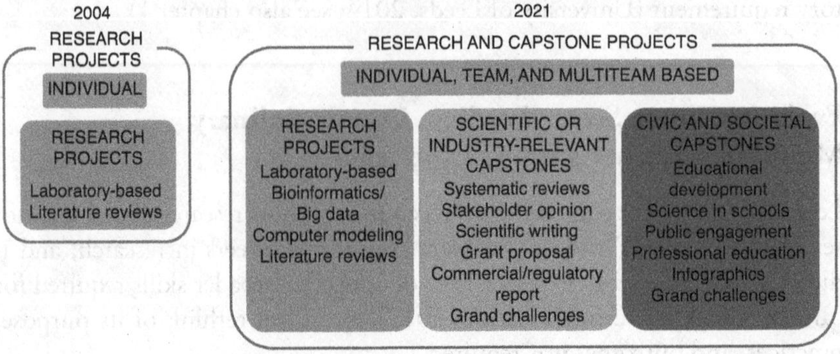

New Ethos, New Learning Outcomes

With the broadening portfolio of non-research focused capstones, the old learning outcomes no longer fit and therefore a new set were created:

- apply knowledge, understanding, and skills gained in earlier years of their program to a problem relevant to the biomedical sciences
- gather or generate information, critically analyzing this information to address this problem
- gain new knowledge, understanding, and skills in creating a solution to, or output for, this problem
- develop and apply skills required in employment, including 4IR skills
- effectively communicate the outcomes and outputs of this enquiry-based learning experience

Capstones for the 21st-Century Workplace: Developing and Showcasing Fourth Industrial Revolution Skills

The team has progressively created a sector-leading portfolio of capstone opportunities, a combination of both scientific or industry-relevant capstones, and those with a civic or societal focus (Figure 5.1). These are offered alongside an expanded range of traditional research projects.

The principal purpose of the course, and of capstones themselves, is personal and professional development, and preparation for the workplace. Each format of capstone preferentially develops specific skills and attributes and provides work experiences most relevant to particular career pathways. Table 5.1 offers examples.

More detail on individual research or capstone projects, what each entails, the skills developed, and career pathways can be found in the accompanying

TABLE 5.1

Capstone Brief, Skills Developed, and Potential Career Pathways for Examples of Industry-Relevant and Civic/Societal Capstones

Capstone	Brief	Skills Developed	Career Pathways
Commercial or technical reports (industry-relevant)	Create a commercial or technical report for a client (e.g., SME, external organization). Could be related to any area of their business or activities (e.g., market analysis, industry standards, policy). Includes the discovery, collation, and critical analysis of information, conclusions, and recommendations. May include an evaluation of the outcomes or impact of their activity.	Research skills, ICT skills, communication skills, numerical and analytical skills, critical thinking, independent working, use of initiative, planning and organization skills, self-management	Careers that require commercial or technical reports, or other defined styles of writing (e.g., scientific writing, regulatory affairs, policy). Careers where you collate, analyze and report, or storyboard, or graphically display information in areas you may not have significant expertise in (e.g., business, marketing, regulation)
Science in schools (civic and societal)	Create and deliver interactive teaching sessions in elementary, middle, or high schools. Topic must be in relevant state or national curricula. Ideally something that the school cannot deliver themselves (lack of expertise/resources). Includes *some* evaluation of the effectiveness of the activity.	Creativity, problem-solving, communication to diverse audiences, storyboarding, planning and organization, independent working, resilience	Careers that require excellent verbal communication skills, including education, resource development, medicine, sales and marketing, or leadership roles

guides for students and educators, respectively (Lewis, 2020a, 2020c; see also the supplementary materials at www.centerforengagedlearning.org/books/cultivating-capstones). The created capstones are not specific to the biosciences. With their focus on personal and professional development rather than research experiences, they can be adopted and implemented by educators from any discipline, institutional type, or country. These approaches are also scalable; each year, this course has 320 students enrolled and 52 faculty contributing.

Offering a broad portfolio of both research and capstone projects enables students to decide exactly what they want to get out of their project (e.g., personal and professional development, research/work experience, safe space to "try out" career options) and choose accordingly. The portfolio should therefore be advertised to students, not based on topic or approach, but on skills and attributes developed, and career pathways these may lead to.

In the workplace, teamwork predominates over individual endeavor, and is often critical to success. The 4IR skill set includes many that can only be developed through teamwork (e.g., service orientation, people management; see Deloitte, 2018). To fully realize the developmental benefits of teamwork, all research and capstone projects (except critical reviews) are offered principally as team-based rather than individual opportunities. We have taken it further, embedding "team within teams," inclusive collaborative partnerships, and high-impact educational practices throughout including:

- Mentors (educators) guide and support their mentees (students) as they undertake their capstone. Mentors give mentees ownership, allow them to make mistakes, reflect on these and learn from them (*reflective learning*, Helyer, 2015).
  Mentees allocated to the same capstone work collaboratively, as a team, to achieve its outcomes. They develop as a *learning community* (Healey et al., 2014), mentoring and supporting each other. "Instead of becoming stressed and demoralized, we worked through the problem optimistically as a team; using our initiative, defining what the problem was, what our options to move forward were and seeking help where appropriate" (BSc Physiology).
- Mentees collaborate with their mentor to cocreate new formats of capstone. The first 2 years of a new format are developmental, partners working collaboratively not only to achieve the capstone outcomes but also to develop the format and guidance (*students-as-partners*, Healey et al., 2014).

- Developing *partnerships* with *external organizations* (e.g., SMEs, civic organizations), identifying their organizations' needs for specific outputs that they don't have the resources to deliver (e.g., patient information leaflets for primary care physicians), creating capstones that deliver these outputs.

There is no standard way a team functions. Mentees (students) are given ownership of their team, allowed to decide how the team will function, assigning roles/responsibilities based on their expertise and skills, and reassigning, if required, as the capstone progresses. It is critical that all buy into the team-based approach and ethos, that the outcomes and outputs are cocreated and collectively owned by the team as a whole.

Increasing Equality and Inclusion

Increasing inclusion and reducing educational inequality have been at the forefront of the team's mind from the start. Inclusive learning partnerships, where everybody can contribute their individual ideas, expertise, and skills, and all are equally valued and respected, are the bedrock of this course. By offering a broad portfolio of opportunities, each utilizing and developing different skills and attributes, there is something for every student, an opportunity to excel, irrespective of background. Diverse backgrounds within the team enrich the experience for all. Students seize this opportunity, visibly growing in confidence as their capstone progresses. We encourage them to regularly reflect on their experiences, to demonstrate to themselves the transformative impact of their capstone. They become role-models, in turn inspiring others from disadvantaged backgrounds.

We have reimagined relationships. Instead of students and supervisors, it's mentees and mentors. Mentors give mentees ownership of their capstone, allow them to make mistakes and to learn from them (Helyer, 2015). This learning is less achievable in a student/supervisor relationship. Mentees work to a client brief, enabling them to undertake their capstone at a time and place of their choosing, unless constrained by the requirements of the brief. They have the option to decide when, within the academic year, they want to undertake it.

We give them the freedom to choose the primary assessment tool (e.g., academic paper, commercial report, reflective ePortfolio), the one that is most authentic/appropriate for their capstone but also best showcases their knowledge, skills, and understanding to us as educators, to potential employers, and most importantly, to themselves—a realization of what they personally can achieve given the opportunity.

Achieving Student and Faculty Buy-In

Faculty were initially concerned about the academic equivalence of capstones to traditional research projects, that they were an "easy" option. To overcome these fears, the principal assessment was the same for both, a dissertation. The difference being what was required for each section; for example, for a "science in schools" capstone; the introduction would be from the educational rather than science literature. Dissertations were also blind second-marked by faculty who didn't supervise capstones. This achieved two things: faculty acceptance of academic equivalence but also recognition of the potential and benefits of capstones. They increasingly joined the team, mentoring capstones and cocreating new formats.

Once capstones had been "de-risked" (see next section) and the purpose and benefits of these shared, students, particularly those not intending to go onto careers in research, needed no further prompting. They welcomed the opportunity. However, it is critical to "sell" different capstones based on the skills they develop and work experience they provide given that students view projects historically offered in their discipline as the "gold standard." To overcome this, a Capstone Choices lecture and *Choosing Your Capstone* guide (Lewis 2020a; see also the supplementary materials) outline what each capstone involves, the skills developed, and the careers it can lead to. Students then chose their capstone or research project based on their developmental needs and/or future career intentions.

Support for Students and Faculty

Capstones are not without their challenges, for both students and faculty. However, with appropriate scaffolding and support, these can be overcome. Capstone courses, with their high credit tariffs, are a high-risk educational experience. To get student buy-in, there is a need to "de-risk" them, to provide opportunities for students to gain experience of the different educational tools/methodologies and assessments in earlier years of their program.

Initially, we introduced workshops, for example, on public engagement, to support students. Subsequently we created a comprehensive program of core activities threaded throughout earlier years of our degrees where students gain experience of the different approaches and skills used in capstones (Lewis, 2020e), culminating in a core Advanced Skills course that runs in parallel with the capstone course. Students opt to attend the units within this

Figure 5.2. Progressive development of skills and attributes through an Advanced Skills course.

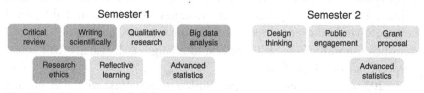

Note. Core = dark grey, optional = light grey.

course that develop the skills required for their individual capstone and/or future career intentions (Figure 5.2).

It is equally important to support your faculty, for most of whom capstone activities will be outside of their comfort zones or previous experience. Faculty new to mentoring capstones are assigned a mentor who shares hints and tips, and often comentors mentees with them in their first year on the team. They have full access to all student support resources and can attend the previously described skills units if they wish. We have also created a how-to-do-it guide, one page for each capstone format, specifically for faculty (Lewis, 2020c; see also the supplementary materials).

Student and Faculty Reflections

We have given our students a voice, the opportunity to decide what they want to get out of their capstone, and to choose accordingly. They love them. Capstones inspire them and promote personal and professional development: "Cannot stress enough how much this project has helped me develop as a young professional" (BSc Physiology).

They open students' eyes to new career opportunities: "Always loved working with children. This capstone has allowed me to realize it may be my 'calling'" (BSc Neuroscience).

They help develop key skills and enhance employability for careers outside of research: "Excellent opportunity to demonstrate your aptitude in a scientific, non-laboratory working environment" (BSc Medical Sciences).

Students have grasped capstones wholeheartedly, excelling academically. Their course marks are significantly higher than those of students undertaking traditional research projects (2020–2021 Academic year: mean ± SD = 71.4±4.4% vs 68.4±5.8%, $p<0.05$).

Students are voting with their feet. In 2020/21, 26% selected capstones as their first choice of project—a massive cultural shift given laboratory projects have traditionally been viewed as the gold standard in the biosciences.

Faculty, in a very research-focused discipline and institution, increasingly (a) recognized the academic rigor, parity of experience compared to research projects, and exceptional benefits of capstones to students and (b) joined the team. "Modern science involves a lot more facets than just bench work—scientific communication, KTP, policy, lobbying etc. It widens their career prospects" (associate professor).

In 2021/22, 95% of faculty contributing to the course will be mentoring a capstone, a phenomenal "cultural" shift given we are a research-intensive institution, with the expectation students will gain a research experience through their project.

Future Directions

The University of Leeds has a new student education strategic objective, to broaden its portfolio of undergraduate research projects such that every student, irrespective of discipline, has the opportunity to undertake a capstone project—an institutional realization of the transformative potential of capstones. Within the biosciences, we are continuing to broaden our capstone portfolio, focusing on developing opportunities that address civic or societal responsibilities. We have introduced team-based Grand Challenges capstones, with the intention that, in the future, these become interdisciplinary and multidisciplinary transnational educational opportunities where students work in partnership with peers in other countries on global grand challenges or UN Sustainable Development Goals.

Impact Across the Biosciences

Increasing numbers of bioscience students, despite enrolling on a science program, do not like laboratory work and are opting for careers outside of research or even science. Recognizing this, bioscience faculty globally are broadening their portfolios of project opportunities to include capstones. COVID-19, with the subsequent closure of campuses and laboratories, has massively increased the rate of adoption of capstones globally, using our resources (see the supplementary materials) as guides. We have inspired faculty to rethink the purpose of final-year research projects and opened their eyes to the potential of capstones:

"You have been an inspiration to me personally to rethink the objectives of final-year projects, and for that I am truly grateful." Professor, Eire.

"Becoming a cornerstone on which a full curriculum review is being built." Professor, Canada.

We have inspired sector-wide change. Instead of returning to their old ways as the world emerges from the COVID pandemic, bioscience faculty globally plan to further increase capstone opportunities in their programs going forward. Our work has resulted in both the two UK bioscience Accrediting Bodies incorporating our capstone concept into their project criteria (Institute of Biomedical Sciences, 2020; Royal Society of Biology, 2020).

Implications for Faculty Who Teach or Direct Capstone Experiences

Capstones are a high-impact educational practice; however, educators globally have yet to fully realize their transformative (significantly increase knowledge, understanding, and skills) and translational (prepare students for the world of work) potential. The activities and approaches described in this chapter are applicable and achievable in any discipline, institution, or country.

Faculty, in any discipline, who teach or direct capstone experiences need to think beyond established practices, discipline, and other silos, to think laterally, and take good practice from around the world and adapt it to their own programs or discipline.

We all need to broaden the portfolio of capstone opportunities within our individual programs so there is something for every student, moving from seminars and taught courses to team project-based active-learning opportunities in order to maximize student personal and professional development, and better prepare them for the diversity of careers they go onto. An increased focus on global civic and societal responsibilities will help develop truly global graduates, equipped with the skills and attributes to be able to lead significant change in the world.

Implications for Administrators and Institutions

Higher education is going to be a challenging marketplace globally for the foreseeable future. Those institutions that survive and prosper are those that stand out above the crowd, that develop graduates with the skills and attributes to be leaders in whatever career they go into, truly global graduates (Lewis, 2020b, 2020e). Capstones can provide this unique selling point. However, it will require institutions to fully commit to capstones, to provide a broad portfolio of capstone opportunities, make them mandatory, and sufficiently resource their delivery (see chapter 1).

Implications for Society

The benefits of a capstone experience for all are phenomenal. Graduates will be equipped with the skills and attributes to make a difference in the world. Employers will have graduates who can fully develop and evolve their businesses in an increasingly challenging global marketplace. Institutions, through student capstones, will better address society's needs, and their own civic and societal responsibilities and missions. Society will be better equipped to tackle the substantial challenges facing the world.

References

Cowie, R. J. (2005). *A snapshot of final year practice in UK bioscience departments.* www.bioscience.heacademy.ac.uk/ftp/SIG/projectsurvey.pdf

Deloitte. (2018). *Preparing tomorrow's workforce for the Fourth Industrial Revolution: For business—A framework for action.* https://www2.deloitte.com/content/dam/Deloitte/global/Documents/About-Deloitte/gx-preparing-tomorrow-workforce-for-4IR.pdf

Gray, A. (2016). *The 10 skills you need to thrive in the Fourth Industrial Revolution.* World Economic Forum. https://www.weforum.org/agenda/2016/01/the-10-skills-you-need-to-thrive-in-the-fourth-industrial-revolution/

Healey, M., Flint, A., & Harrington, K. (2014). *Engagement through partnership: Students as partners in learning and teaching in higher education.* York Higher Education Academy. https://www.heacademy.ac.uk/node/23784

Helyer, R. (2015). Learning through reflection: The critical role of reflection in work-based learning (WBL). *Journal of Work-Applied Management, 7*(1), 15–27. https://www.emerald.com/insight/content/doi/10.1108/JWAM-10-2015-003/full/html

Institute of Biomedical Sciences. (2017). *Criteria and requirements for the accreditation and re-accreditation of BSc (Hons) in biomedical science.* https://www.ibms.org/resources/documents/criteria-and-requirements-for-the-accreditation-and-re/

Institute of Biomedical Sciences. (2020). *Final year research or capstone projects.* https://82b1248a-8d51-4814-ab1c-ba8f72828534.filesusr.com/ugd/4b6beb_402a92c0f60344cc92c1c20e91ecbae3.pdf

Kuh, G. (2008). *High-impact educational practices: What they are, who has access to them, and why they matter.* Association of American Colleges and Universities.

Lewis, D. I. (2011). Enhancing student employability through ethics-based outreach activities and open educational resources. *Bioscience Education, 18*, 1–3. https://doi.org/10.3108/beej.18.7SE

Lewis, D. I. (2017). Extra-curricular partnerships as a tool for enhancing graduate employability. *International Journal of Students and Partners, 1*(1). https://doi.org/10.15173/ijsap.v1i1.3052

Lewis, D. I. (2020a). *Choosing the right Final Year research, Honours or Capstone project for you. Skills, career pathways and what's involved.* https://bit.ly/Choosing-BioCapstone

Lewis, D. I. (2020b). Final year or Honours projects: Time for a total re-think? *Physiology News, 119*, 10–11. https://www.physoc.org/magazine-articles/final-year-or-honours-research-projects/

Lewis, D. I. (2020c). *Final year research, Honours or Capstone projects in the biosciences: How to do it guides.* https://bit.ly/BiosciCapstones

Lewis, D. I. (2020d). Final year undergraduate research project or a "Capstone Experience"? Time for a re-think. *British Journal of Clinical Pharmacology, 86*(6), 1227–1228. https://bpspubs.onlinelibrary.wiley.com/doi/epdf/10.1111/bcp.14266

Lewis, D. I. (2020e, August 5). Post-COVID education: eLearning and the new world of education. *Pharmacology Matters.* https://www.bps.ac.uk/publishing/pharmacology-matters/august-2020/post-covid-education-elearning-and-the-new-world

Quality Assurance Agency. (2019). *Biosciences Benchmark Statement.* https://www.qaa.ac.uk/docs/qaa/subject-benchmark-statements/subject-benchmark-statement-biosciences.pdf

Royal Society of Biology. (2020). *The accreditation handbook.* https://www.rsb.org.uk/images/accreditation_home/RSB_Overall_Handbook_Sept_2019_September_2020_Implementation.pdf

Salam, M., Iskandar, D. N. A., Ibrahim, D. H. A., & Farooq, M. S. (2019). Service learning in higher education: A systematic literature review. *Asia Pacific Education Review, 20,* 573–593. https://doi.org/10.1007/s12564-019-09580-6

Schwab, K. (2016). *The Fourth Industrial Revolution: What it means, how to respond.* World Economic Forum. https://www.weforum.org/agenda/2016/01/the-fourth-industrial-revolution-what-it-means-and-how-to-respond/

University of Leeds. (2014). *The Leeds Curriculum.* https://ses.leeds.ac.uk/leedscurriculum

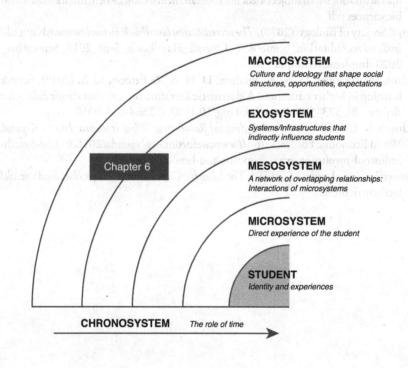

6

HOW TWO AUSTRALIAN UNIVERSITIES ACHIEVED "CAPSTONES FOR ALL"

A Change Management Perspective

Tania von der Heidt, Carol Van Zile-Tamsen,
David I. Lewis, Janet Bean, and Christina Beaudoin

The significance of capstones in undergraduate higher education is well established (i.e., Budwig & Jessen-Marshall, 2018; Kinzie, 2018). Capstones provide culminating learning experiences, opportunities for students to synthesize learning, as well as closure and transition to post-graduation life. The Boyer Commission's seminal report (1998) recommended a universal capstone for all undergraduate degrees offered at research universities "to ensure that the educational experience is drawn together . . . at the end of the curriculum that corresponds to the capstone of a building or the keystone of an arch" (p. 36).

While faculty and administrators at the time recognized the value of a capstone experience, few followed the recommendation and implemented or even discussed a universal capstone requirement (Katkin, 2003). A recent systematic analysis of 600 colleges and universities in the United States, United Kingdom, and Australia found only a limited number of institutions in the United States (15%), Australia (5%), and United Kingdom (4%) required capstones in all baccalaureate degrees (see chapter 1). Research into the universal capstone requirement is emerging and focuses on the United States. Notably, in 2015 the Association of American Colleges and Universities launched the Liberal Education and America's Progress (LEAP) challenge, "Engaging in Capstones and Signature Work," which involved a consortium of eight U.S. colleges and universities—all committed to curricular change that incorporates capstones—with findings presented in a special edition of *Peer Review* (e.g., Hayden-Roy et al., 2018). In the Australian university context limited research is available on the universal capstone requirement. Lee and Loton (2017) have studied style, scope, and purposes of capstones at Australian universities extensively, but not the institution-wide requirement for undergraduate capstones.

This chapter helps close this gap by highlighting how the universal capstone requirement evolved—from conception, through implementation, to present practice—at relevant Australian universities. First, literature on institutional change is reviewed, and the scope of inquiry is outlined. Next the Australian higher education context and the two institutions are introduced. The method is summarized and results are presented in terms of key themes, and conclusions are drawn. This research has implications for any institution seeking to implement capstones.

Institutional Change for Universal Capstones

Introducing an institution-wide capstone involves some degree of planned organizational change. Three frameworks are often used to describe such change. Each of these is briefly reviewed in the following before considering them in the context of institution-wide capstones, specifically in two Australian universities.

Types of Strategic Institutional Change

Strategic change can be described in terms of scope and time (Balogun & Hope-Hailey, 2008). The extent or scope of change refers to the breadth of change across an organization, or depth of culture change required. Change of limited scope is considered a realignment of strategy; more extensive change, going beyond the existing business model or culture, is transformational. Srikanthan and Dalrymple (2004) also pointed to these two general options for a higher education institution to transform itself for teaching (before considering how to transform its students)—to redesign the processes and structures or to muddle through the present system.

Similarly, these two main change approaches align with evidence from the LEAP Consortium regarding faculty development as it pertains to introducing an institution-wide capstone requirement. One change approach is more incremental and decentralized, and situates capstones within the context of existing offerings; another makes capstones part of a significant curricular reform with more deliberate, centralized, and comprehensive approaches

TABLE 6.1
Types of Strategic Change/Scope of Change (End Result)

		Transformation	*Realignment*
Speed of change (time)	**Incremental**	Evolution	Adaptation
	Rapid	Revolution	Reconstruction

Note. Adapted from Whittington et al., 2020.

to faculty programming (Budwig & Low, 2018). Hayden-Roy et al. (2018) recommended a wider scope of change in which the process for providing universal capstones is from the grassroots and involves the larger campus community, including students. Egan et al. (2018), too, advocated a "collective effort in defining signature work on our campuses [in order to] share a more nuanced vision of how . . . it might play out in practice" (p. 11).

Reflecting on the processes of change at the eight LEAP institutions, Hayden-Roy et al. (2018) observed that none of the institutions mandated capstones; rather, they "emerged from preexisting institutional priorities and faculty engagement, and in most cases, they were driven by institutional research or the systematic use of research on effective teaching and learning" (p. 12). The authors acknowledged the tolerance within each institution for "messiness" in making the necessary curricular revisions. These comments suggest that, in addition to the extent of institutional change, the temporal factor of change needs to be accounted for. The speed of change in an organization may be incremental to allow time for learning to occur, or it may be rapid (a big bang) to ensure a fast response to a crisis. Based on scope and time dimensions of change, Balogun et al. (2016) distinguished four generic types of strategic change, as shown in bold in Table 6.1.

Process of Change and Force Field Analysis

Lewin's conceptualization of planned change provides two further useful tools for analyzing change for institution-wide capstones. First, Lewin (1952) viewed planned change efforts as an iterative three-step process:

- unfreezing—preparing a system for change to ensure people are ready for it
- changing—making actual changes after having properly diagnosed the problem and examined alternatives
- refreezing—stabilizing the system after change through providing appropriate resources, reinforcement, and rewards

In reflecting on the implementation of capstones within the consortium, Hayden-Roy et al. (2018) reiterated the importance of budgeting necessary incentives and rewards for faculty who need to undertake the necessary changes, as well as monitoring carefully the success of the new or fortified curriculum and undertaking adjustments.

Secondly, Lewin's (1951) force field analysis helps in thinking about the dynamic nature of various forces in a situational field. Notably, in the unfreezing stage of the change process, the forces to direct behavior away from the status quo need to be increased, and the restraining forces that hinder change need to be decreased (Swanson & Creed, 2014). Scholars recognize that an institution's brand promise around distinctive attributes provides a strong driving force for change, which has relevance for effectively introducing and maintaining institution-wide capstones. Kuh (2013) argued that, together with a mission that informs and sustains the institutional brand, coherence can be brought to the student experience such that what was promised to students is actually fulfilled. Driskill et al. (2019) suggested that the mission statement needs to be "coconstructed" to "create positive contagion within the [higher education] organization" (p. 80). With reference to the LEAP Consortium, Hayden-Roy et al. (2018) reflected that "the changes were shaped by each school's identity and what they wished to provide for their students" (p. 12).

The Research Approach

The scope of the exploratory study reported here is to gain an initial understanding of the change relating to the introduction of the institution-wide capstone requirement at two Australian universities in 2019. Guided by the preceding literature, Table 6.2 shows how the five main themes relating to each of the three change phases were studied.

TABLE 6.2
Themes Explored in the Study

	Change-Related Theme Studied				
Three Change Phases	*Drivers*	*Barriers*	*Scope*	*Time*	*Continuity and Impact*
Unfreezing	✓				
Changing			✓	✓	
Refreezing					✓

Context

Australia has 42 universities, of which 37 are public institutions, and all are research-active. There is no requirement for capstones within bachelor degrees, as per the Australian Qualifications Framework. Therefore, universities adopt different positions in relation to capstones—from being silent to providing guidelines regarding capstone unit design to mandating capstones in all bachelor's degrees.

A search was undertaken by the lead author of publicly available documents on capstone and capstone experiences at university level for all 42 Australian universities. The search yielded only two universities with an institutional capstone requirement. Both universities are based in Melbourne, Victoria. The University of Melbourne (UM) is one of Australia's leading research-intensive universities, as well as being one of its oldest and largest (45,000 full-time equivalent students in 2019). La Trobe University (LTU) is younger, has about half the number of students, and is recognized for its commitment to excellence in teaching, learning, and research. UM is ranked 32nd worldwide, while LTU is ranked in the 301–350 band (Times Higher Education, 2019).

UM's capstone policy statement, which can be found in its Courses, Subjects, Awards and Programs Policy document, states:

> Capstone in bachelor degrees 4.21. Bachelor degrees must contain a capstone experience which is intended to: (a) offer both disciplinary and cohort coherence; (b) function as a bridge between the undergraduate experience and the next stage of study or work; (c) consolidate the content and skills acquisition components of the major area of study; and (d) apply those skills and experience in the capstone. (Melbourne Policy Library, 2009, para. 1)

LTU's capstone institutional requirement in 2019 is contained in Section 3— Policy Statement Graduate Capabilities for Undergraduate Students Policy:

> The University will define a set of La Trobe University Graduate Capabilities for each college to: Describe in appropriate discipline-specific terms; Develop agreed GC standards of student performance of these capabilities at three points in each course—Cornerstone (first year), Mid-point, and Capstone (final year); and, At each of those three points, the standard for expected student achievement for each graduate capability will be defined at three quality levels. (LaTrobe University, n.d., para. 7)

Methodology

To gain insights into the evolution of the institutional capstone requirement, a qualitative style of research was called for. The interview research followed Kvale and Brinkmann's (2009) recommended systematic, seven-step progression to ensure that it lived up to scientific criteria—namely, thematizing, designing questions, interviewing, transcribing, analyzing, verifying, and reporting.

Findings

The coded and condensed views of both participants are reported jointly for both institutions in terms of the main a priori themes and the emerging subthemes.

Phase 1: Unfreezing

Both participants indicated that internal factors were driving the change for institution-wide capstones at their respective institution. In the case of UM, there were two main internal drivers: a new incoming vice chancellor (in 2005) and "a proliferation of UG [undergraduate] programs—an unravelling, loss of coherence, process of accretion [e.g., adding exemptions/exceptions] and frustration around a lack of attention being paid to the structure of those programs" (P1).

Two different internal drivers were in play at LTU: a major restructuring in 2013–2014 and a desire by academic leaders to develop graduate attributes/capabilities/essential skills. "They were looking for place in the first, second, and third year where these would be most literally delivered. Capstones were part of that picture" (P2). Further, P2 reported that two external drivers motivated change at LTU: growing pressure around employability of graduates, as well as a national senior teaching fellowship funded by the Office for Learning and Teaching in 2013 and 2015, which led to the report *Capstone Curriculum Across Disciplines: A Snapshot of Current Practice in Australia and Beyond* (Lee & Loton, 2015) and to the capstone curriculum network (Lee & Loton, 2020).

Phase 2: Changing

The participants offered different views on the breadth of change and depth of cultural change across their respective universities.

Scope of Change

P1 described how the introduction of capstones in every major involved everybody in every degree program: "On a university-wide basis, there was a huge amount of goodwill of openness to the idea of certain core principles."

In terms of depth, academics in charge of the six programs were asked "to rethink, to go back to first principles, wipe the slate clean, and come up with what the program (and the capstone) should look like, rather than adding things on all the time."

At LTU the scope of change appears to have been distinctly narrower. P2 indicated that "a top-down approach was adopted. They put it in policy and told everyone to do it. So people effectively just picked a subject and called it a capstone." P2 wished for a wider scope of involvement:

> The ideal process always you do as a part of curriculum renewal piece of work, so you look at it holistically. You co-design around the principles. Give people opportunities to come to talk together about what a capstone might look like.

In fact, P2 envisaged a preferred scenario in which "running course design workshops with students involved in the design process with capacity building is the first step."

Speed of Change

The time taken to introduce the change at both institutions varied. P1 from UM reflected on "a very significant transition period for a couple of years, where we had many members who were both teaching out the old programs and teaching in the new one." P1 outlined a 3-year timeline from conception (discussion and approval by University Council in 2006), curriculum design in 2007 (a new capstone within every major within each of the programs), and implementation in 2008.

By contrast, according to P2, LTU adopted the institution-wide capstone at the end of the same year (2014) in which they were first workshopped.

Barriers to Implementation

In terms of the barriers to institution-wide capstone implementation in their university, the participants' offered divergent views across five subthemes. P1 noted that UM was challenged by intrafaculty negotiations: "Within each department there was plenty of fighting about what's a capstone going to look like." According to P1, the second problem at UM was budgetary in nature: "A large sum of money was required to fund the introduction of the Melbourne Model, as staff were doing double loads teaching out the old programs and teaching in the new one."

P2 identified three barriers to implementation faced by LTU. First, the lack of genuine leadership: "As far as I can tell, there was no real engagement by vice chancellor and pro vice chancellor in that process and what it might mean. So filtering down was a challenge."

A second barrier at LTU related to the convergence of implementing capstones with a major organizational restructure from five faculties to two colleges with 11 schools. P2 cautions that "trying to do it [introduce capstones] during a [restructuring] change process points to the difficulty of the exercise."

The third problem reported by P2 was the lack of involvement of academics in the process: "The capstone requirement simply appeared; there was not much working through with people involved; this meant that there was a lack of knowledge. There was very limited support material and activity apart from wheeling me in."

Phase 3: Refreezing

Participants were asked to share their thoughts on how the change had stabilized in the refreezing phase, on conditions for continuity, and the impact of the change.

Standard Practice

When asked how the institution-wide capstone requirement was currently practiced across the institution, the participants' responses varied somewhat. P1 indicated that capstones are a normal part of the UG curriculum with the only variation being

> the balance between "do you have a capstone with a focus on developing an academic coherence at the need of a UG program" or "do you have a focus instead that's more forward-looking, more towards the bridge, as to where the degree is taking you," or whether you have both.

However, P2 mentioned that capstones at LTU are run in a variety of ways:

> Some are single subjects, some are double-weighted; some are interdisciplinary, some are very discipline focused. For the professionally accredited ones, we've just done a whole set of changes around these courses, particular for health sciences, and those will be largely placements. That gives us this very disparate group—some of which may or may not actually be capstones.

Resourcing

In terms of resourcing the delivery of capstones through workload, neither institution seems to cater especially for capstones. P1 noted that UM "did not have a model that said we're going to find some money for people to design capstones." P2 explained that because the academic workload system at LTU does not allow for variations, "at local level we add things into the service component to compensate for additional workload where it exists."

Monitoring

Both participants indicated an absence of monitoring the design and performance of capstones across their institution postimplementation. P1 elaborated that at UM capstones might be reviewed as part of the 5-year course review and acknowledged the future need to "formally build in a process of review."

Similarly, P2 indicated that LTU is about to go through a curriculum renewal architectural program "where all will surface. I think that we will get much clearer about the types of capstones that we offer and more consistent about the way they are delivered. We will also be using them much more consistently as a benchmarking tool."

Impact

Participants were asked about whether the impact of capstones was being measured (e.g., in terms of student success, gaining employment, or entering graduate school). Neither participant was aware of such evaluation initiatives within their institution. However, both participants firmly believed that the institution-wide capstone requirement provided their respective universities with a competitive advantage. P1 elaborated how capstones may be viewed as an essential part of UM's brand identity and promise: "It's implicit in the Melbourne Model. The capstone sways students to UM. It's one of the most powerful arguments we have internally—the idea of greater academic coherence."

Discussion and Conclusions

This chapter explores the stories of capstone conception and implementation through executive academic interviews at the only two Australian universities with universal undergraduate capstones. The study provides initial insights into the complex forces driving capstone change, implementation, and perceived success.

Each institution adopted a considerably different approach to their capstone requirements. At UM the institutional take-up of capstones was part of a much larger change initiative. At the heart of the radical new strategic plan, "Growing Esteem," articulated in 2005, was the "Melbourne Model," with the objective of creating an outstanding and distinctive "Melbourne experience" for all its undergraduate students. A key element of the model is that all majors should culminate in a capstone experience in the third year. P1 recounted how in 2007 all academics were involved in redesigning their curriculum. UM showed a commitment, not just to capstones, but also to a democratic process or rational persuasion (Schermerhorn et al., 2011). In terms of the four strategic change types shown in Table 6.1, UM's change for universal capstones may be thought of as evolutionary (transformative in scope and incremental in speed).

By contrast, at LTU a more autocratic, almost forced coercion approach appears to have been followed. The participant recalled that the university initiated its capstone in the final year requirement recently (in 2015) to help demonstrate to students the value of their degree. However, P2 perceived the capstone implementation process as top-down with limited buy-in from staff. This suggests that the initial change was of a reconstructive nature (realignment of scope; rapid change). P2 feared that some of the capstones may be in name only. Hence, further transformation of curriculum across the institution is currently underway.

The findings of this exploratory study tend to confirm those of the 2015–2018 LEAP Engaging in Capstones and Signature Consortium. Generally speaking, an evolutionary (gradual, inclusive) approach to conceiving and implementing capstones, such as at UM, is preferable to a reconstructive (rapid, restricted) approach, such as at LTU. In any case, given the significance of capstones for institutional strategy, as well as for teaching and learning, it appears that a deliberate/planned approach is preferable to one that is emergent/laissez-faire, especially in the absence of a systematic use of scholarly learning and teaching research in an institution.

For faculty who teach or direct capstone experiences one implication of this study is to consider the particular role of their capstone within the faculty or the institution's capstone framework. Reflecting on the rationale for the capstone may identify room for improvement with the capstone course or its fit with the aims of a program, the faculty, and even the institution. Through the interviewing and research process, the lead author certainly gained valuable insights into how capstone development and implementation may occur more effectively at her home institution.

The findings also indicate that sound leadership and coordination by administrators is vital to facilitating and promoting genuine, institution-wide, active participation in the conception, implementation, and/or review processes. As demonstrated by UM's Melbourne Model, capstones may be an essential part of a bigger program, which might need to be more effectively accounted for.

To further our understanding of how institutions adopt and implement capstones wholesale, future research could contrast these Australia examples with those of universities in other countries. Future research may also concentrate on exploring and measuring the varied impacts of institution-wide capstones, such as on student satisfaction, employability, and higher degrees research. Regardless of the research focus of these future efforts, campuses internationally would benefit from considering how understanding the scope and speed of their planned adoption of capstones can guide strategic institutional change.

References

Balogun, J., & Hope-Hailey, V. (2008). *Exploring strategic change* (3rd ed.). Pearson.

Balogun, J., Hope-Hailey, V., & Gustafsson, S. (2016). *Exploring strategic change* (4th ed.). Pearson.

Boyer Commission. (1998). *Reinventing undergraduate education: A blueprint for America's research universities* (ED424840). ERIC. https://files.eric.ed.gov/fulltext/ED424840.pdf

Budwig, N., & Jessen-Marshall, A. (2018). Making the case for capstones and signature work. *Peer Review, 20*(2). https://www.aacu.org/peerreview/2018/Spring

Budwig, N., & Low, K. (2018). Institutional readiness for signature work. *Peer Review, 20*(2), 20–23. https://www.aacu.org/peerreview/2018/Spring

Driskill, G., Chatham-Carpenter, A., & McIntyre, K. (2019). The power of a mission: Transformations of a department culture through social constructivist principles. *Innovative Higher Education, 44*, 69–83. https://doi.org/10.1007/s10755-018-9449-8

Egan, M., Kneas, K., & Reder, M. (2018). Defining and framing signature work on your campus. *Peer Review, 20*(2), 8–11. https://www.aacu.org/peerreview/2018/Spring

Hayden-Roy, P., Elgren, T., Kneas, K., Malsky, M., & Reder, M. (2018). Processes of curricular change and strategies for organizing signature work. *Peer Review, 20*(2), 12–14. https://www.aacu.org/peerreview/2018/Spring

Katkin, W. (2003). The Boyer Commission report and its impact on undergraduate research. In J. Kinkead (Ed.), *Valuing and Supporting Undergraduate Research* (New Directions for Teaching and Learning, no. 93, pp. 19–38). Wiley.

Kinzie, J. (2018). Assessing quality and equity: Observations about the state of signature work. *Peer Review, 20*(2). https://www.aacu.org/peerreview/2018/Spring

Kuh, G. (2013). Promise in action: Examples of institutional success. In D. H. Kalsbeek (Ed.), *Reframing Retention Strategy for Institutional Improvement* (New Directions for Higher Education, no. 161, pp. 81–90). Wiley.

Kvale, S., & Brinkman, S. (2009). *Interviews: Learning the craft of qualitative research interviewing* (2nd ed.). SAGE.

La Trobe University. (n.d.). *Graduate capabilities for undergraduate students policy.* https://policies.latrobe.edu.au/document/view.php?id=218&version=1

Lee, N., & Loton, D. (2015). *Capstone curriculum across disciplines: A snapshot of current practice in Australia and beyond—Survey report.* Victoria University. http://vuir.vu.edu.au/36310/

Lee, N., & Loton, D. (2017). Capstone purposes across disciplines. *Studies in Higher Education*, *44*(1), 134–150. https://doi.org/10.1080/03075079.2017.1347155

Lee, N., & Loton, D. (2020). *Capstone curriculum*. Australian Government Office of Learning and Teaching. https://www.capstonecurriculum.com.au/

Lewin, K. (1951). *Field theory in social science: Selected theoretical papers*. Harper & Row.

Lewin, K. (1952). Group decision and social change. In G. Swanson, T. Newcomb, & E. Hartley (Eds.), *Readings in social psychology* (pp. 459–473). Holt, Rinehart.

Melbourne Policy Library. (2009). *Courses, subjects, awards and programs policy (MPF1327)*. University of Melbourne. https://policy.unimelb.edu.au/MPF1327

Schermerhorn, J. R., Davidson, P., Poole, D., Simon, A., Woods, P., & Ling Chau, S. (2011). *Management: Asia-Pacific edition* (4th ed.). John Wiley & Sons.

Srikanthan, G., & Dalrymple, J. (2004). A synthesis of a quality management model for education in universities. *International Journal of Educational Management*, *18*(4), 266–279. https://doi.org/10.1108/09513540410538859

Swanson, D., & Creed, A. (2014). Sharpening the focus of force field analysis. *Journal of Change Management*, *14*(1), 28–47.

Times Higher Education. (2019). *World university rankings 2019*. https://www.timeshighereducation.com/world-university-rankings/2019/world-ranking#!/page/0/length/25/sort_by/rank/sort_order/asc/cols/stats

Whittington, R., Regner, P., Angwin, D., Johnson, G., & Scholes, K. (2020). *Exploring strategy* (12th ed.). Pearson.

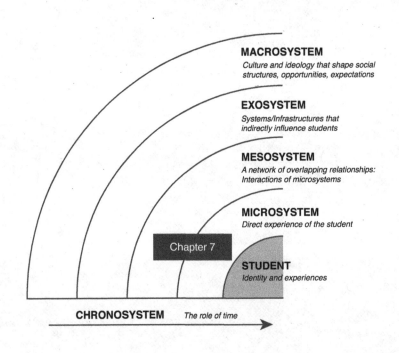

MACROSYSTEM
Culture and ideology that shape social structures, opportunities, expectations

EXOSYSTEM
Systems/Infrastructures that indirectly influence students

MESOSYSTEM
A network of overlapping relationships: Interactions of microsystems

MICROSYSTEM
Direct experience of the student

Chapter 7

STUDENT
Identity and experiences

CHRONOSYSTEM   *The role of time*

7

ADAPTING A CAPSTONE

Projects and Portfolios Across Four Courses and Three Institutions

Sandra Bell, Frederick T. Evers, Shannon Murray, and Margaret Anne Smith

This chapter examines the adaptation of a capstone course across four institutions and the development of a core ePortfolio project that highlights student skills and accomplishments. We focus on the ways a capstone course can adapt to different institutional contexts, to a variety of disciplinary subject matter, as well as to changing technology, and how it can connect students to broader alumni and work communities. Our goal in developing these courses was to address gaps in students' knowledge and in instructors' goals; we wanted to celebrate our various disciplines but also to make our students and our institutions aware of the transferability and flexibility of the many skills learned throughout the degree.

Central to each of our courses is a portfolio showcasing the skills and accomplishments students gained through their degrees. Evidence for ePortfolios as a "high-impact practice" is persuasive (Moore, 2016; Mueller & Bair, 2018). As our own practices evolved from one context and institution to the next, we were aware of the importance of three principles in particular: framing the portfolios as "portable, expandable, updatable" (Kuh et al., 2017, p. 10); insisting on an authentic audience and purpose that goes beyond the classroom (Moore, 2016); and devoting significant class time to scaffolding the work of collecting, selecting, reflecting, and connecting (Parkes et al., 2013).

Our four capstone examples, each one building and adapting from an earlier iteration, suggest varying pathways for other instructors eager to implement a transitional experience for senior arts students. Varying though our experiences have been, we recognize a number of common issues at the student, faculty, and institutional levels. Without a program requirement for such a course, senior-level students might struggle to find space among other demands of the major, and they may simply not understand the value of either the capstone or the ePortfolio if these are new concepts. For faculty, we recognize the enriching experience of interdisciplinary team teaching for these courses but run into workload issues and the teaching demands of our own departments; both can make mounting these courses unsustainable without institutional support. And finally, for institutions, we identified the strongest impacts when the courses involve a team of instructors, career counselors, and alumni officers, as well as a network of speakers, career mentors, and community leaders. Our biggest takeaway: At a time when support for a liberal arts education appears to be waning, a course that opens a space for reflection on the uses of such an education and on the accomplishments of graduates is appreciated by students and institutions alike. This chapter will move through four narratives grounded in our specific institutions and contexts and will highlight how such ideas and practices can be adapted for different circumstances.

Improving Opportunities and Addressing Gaps in a Discipline (Frederick T. Evers)

I designed the capstone course Transition From School to Work in 1997 and offered it each year through the Department of Sociology and Anthropology at the University of Guelph in Ontario; other instructors took it over in 2001. There are 37 students in the course in a typical year. The course is based on the research project "Making the Match Between University Graduates and Corporate Employers" (Evers et al., 1998). In this study, 1,610 university students and university graduates rated themselves on 17 skills grouped within four "Bases of Competence." This course fulfills fourth-year requirements for students in sociology and anthropology and is an applied "capstone" that examines the issues, research, and models in the transition from university to employment.

There are two overall objectives to the course: academic and experiential. The academic objective considers the first-year studies and senior-year studies literature in sociology, sociology of education, sociology and anthropology of work, human resources, and career development (Gardner et al., 1999). A number of critical concepts related to the workplace are investigated (e.g., organizational culture; global webs; work structures and processes; differences among private, public, and not-for-profit organizations; contract vs. permanent work arrangements). The academic opportunities afforded by this course are numerous and address gaps in the literature that students study in their programs.

The experiential objective of the course is addressed through a "Skills Portfolio" and an "Action Sociology and Anthropology Project." Each student prepares a skills portfolio—a three-ring binder when I taught the course, now an ePortfolio—containing a personal mission statement, résumés in alternate formats, example cover letters for a job, record of job interviewing experience, and a presentation (with support material) of the development of skills in each of the four bases of competence: managing self, communication, managing people and tasks, and mobilizing innovation and change (Evers et al., 1998).

Students also work on an action project, which involves creative applications of sociology and anthropology to issues in each student's transition to the workplace. The action project can be on any topic that is consistent with what the students intend to do with their degrees. The action project becomes part of the skills portfolio, demonstrating the students' ability to apply their knowledge of sociology or anthropology. Each student will be involved in a class presentation (individually or in a team) to report the results of the action project.

The students receive a grounding in skill areas that we know from the bases of competence are important in the workforce for university graduates. We found four bases and within each base four or five specific workplace skills (for a total of 17 skills).

> 1) Managing Self: Learning, Personal Organization, Personal Strengths, and Problem Solving and Analytic; 2) Communicating: Interpersonal, Listening, Oral Communication, and Written Communication; 3) Managing People and Tasks: Coordinating, Decision-Making, Leadership and Influence, Managing Conflict, and Planning and Organizing; 4) Mobilizing Innovation and Change: Ability to Conceptualize, Creativity, Innovation and Change, Risk-Taking, and Visioning. (Evers et al., 1998, pp. 40–41)

The students comment on their abilities in each of these specific skills in the skills portfolio and provide support material. Some skills are more difficult to evaluate than others; for example, *visioning* is "the ability to conceptualize the future of the company and provide innovative paths for the company to follow" (Evers et al., 1998, p. 40), whereas *oral communication* is more straightforward: "the ability to present information verbally to others, either one-on-one or in groups" (p. 41).

Although no longer offered by me (I'm a professor emeritus), the course is still being offered to fourth-year students. The students respond well to the course. It allows them to think about and plan what they will do when they finish their degrees.

Adapting to New Disciplines in a New Context (Shannon Murray)

The University of Prince Edward Island is a small institution—about 4,000 students—in Atlantic Canada and the only university in the province. After teaching in UPEI's English Department for about a decade, my colleague Jane Magrath and I became increasingly concerned about the frightening transition English and other arts majors faced as they left university. We all had the general sense that, even as they were doing research on Shakespeare's sonnets or giving presentations on Joyce's *Ulysses,* they were practicing, at a very high level, transferable skills that would be valued in a variety of different workplaces. But how could we make that general sense clearer and more intentional, and as a result guide our students to greater confidence as they planned their next steps?

When I met Fred Evers in 2001, his innovative and highly successful capstone course for anthropology and sociology students seemed a promising model for the English Department version that eventually became the faculty-wide course Capstone in Arts. Our disciplinary focus shifted—from the history, value, and purpose of a literary education to the history, value, and purpose of an arts degree generally—but the core of the course remained the same: a discussion of readings designed to integrate what they learned, guests who talked about their own career paths and a career-focused assignment, and workshops that led to a career portfolio.

We sought to incorporate all four of the principles outlined in *The Senior Year Experience:* integration, reflection, closure, and transition (Gardner et al., 1997). For the students, however, it was the transition and especially the career portfolio that engaged them most. We designed the portfolio to have a few requirements and many options. Students could choose their own virtual platforms (we started with paper portfolios but now are completely digital), highlight and organize in a way to make sense for them, and add as many elements as they liked, but all portfolios had to include

- work goals
- a statement of work
- an annotated list of their important skills, linked to evidence and the artifacts to support their claims

- at least three letters of reference
- a résumé and a CV
- as many artifacts (research essays, slideshows, videos, reference letters, reports, photographs, and so on) as they needed to support any claims they made in their work philosophy or skills list

We emphasized two principles. First, they should think in terms of both an archive portfolio and a purpose-built portfolio. The archive is the one that holds all possible examples of their work, while the purpose-built portfolio could be selected and aimed at a specific employer or occasion. The archive needed to be in a form that they could easily access but also could be backed up. (They didn't want to lose all their work if one platform shut down or got prohibitively expensive.) And second, they should think of this as a living document, one that could be added to, changed, and revised with each new experience or opportunity.

Typically, a 3-hour class begins with a discussion of readings about the value, history, and purpose of a liberal arts education; the second hour is a conversation with guests from the community, alumni who share their stories, or workshops from our campus career counselors or work-integrated learning specialists; and our final hour focuses on workshopping some aspect of the portfolio. For each portfolio requirement, we work in an overlapping 3-week workshop pattern: In the first week, students are introduced to a requirement; the next week they bring a draft for peer editing; and in the third week they submit it to me for feedback. A typical week's workshop might look like this: introducing how to request strong letters of reference, peer editing of the statement of "work philosophy," and handing in the final draft of "work goals."

In the almost 20 years of the capstone, we've seen changes not only because of the shift from English majors to all arts majors but also because of the changes in our institutional context. A reduction in our campus teaching load as well as in full-time teaching staff has made it more difficult to justify team teaching the course, and my original collaborator left the university. An elective in most departments, the course is now a requirement for a new interdisciplinary major, which has increased enrollment. And we now have career counselors and an entire office devoted to experiential and work-integrated learning to draw on, which has been a great support. Most importantly for me, there are now two other instructors who have offered the course in rotation with me. My greatest worry was that, when I retire, the course might be retired with me. I now have much greater hope that the work of easing the transition to work for liberal arts students will continue at UPEI.

Expanding Disciplines and Broadening Access (Sandra Bell)

I heard Shannon Murray talk about her capstone course at a teaching confer-ence in 2015 and was thoroughly impressed by her student presenter taking us through the ePortfolio he had developed. I immediately knew that this type of course would be useful for my students in English. The University of New Brunswick on the East Coast is a large, comprehensive university with approximately 11,000 students across two main campuses; my campus in Saint John is relatively small, with approximately 2,000 students, 70% of whom are from the region. Saint John, on the Bay of Fundy, has a history of fishing, forestry, and oil industries, and while some of the workforce is shift-ing into more varied information technology and tourism sectors, these tra-ditional industries still form a strong base. I knew that a course that reflected on and celebrated the potential of the arts in society and work would be very welcome to students who were still answering the old "What are you going to do with an arts degree?" question. What it also provided was guidance and support for instructors and the institution when explaining the importance of our disciplines in the wider context of employment.

At a small campus, with approximately 600 students enrolled in the Faculty of Arts each year, it would be difficult to find the numbers to fill a regularly taught capstone course of this type if the intake were limited to one discipline. Our arts faculty thus agreed that the course would count as an elective toward the bachelor of arts degree for students from any discipline. With a multidisciplinary student base, we would shape our course around explorations of three main areas: the benefits of a liberal arts degree for the individual and society, the skills developed, and the possible avenues for employment; it would be called Liberal Arts: Essential Skills. The culminat-ing project would be the ePortfolio—a document celebrating the student's skills, experiences, and future potential.

After preliminary discussions with students, we recognized that what we had imagined to be a capstone course—a final term course providing an opportunity to reflect on a whole degree—could be equally advantageous to students in their second and third years; in fact, it might provide students in earlier years the opportunity to discover gaps in their knowledge and experi-ence that they could then work on filling with specific courses, volunteer work, and employment before they completed their degree. While a larger campus might be able to scaffold the steps of the course across different years—for example, discussing skills in the second year, introducing alumni and careers in the third, and researching careers and developing the portfolio in the final year—our small campus could afford the commitment to one course taught every other year, so opening the course to students at varying stages of their degree ensured healthy numbers. Students in their fourth year could reflect on their degree and get more of a capstone experience, while those in their second and third years could apply what they learned in our course to their future education and development.

To get a better understanding of how the liberal arts could be discussed, we started with Martha Nussbaum's (2010) *Not for Profit: Why Democracy Needs the Humanities*, as well as a variety of recent articles, both scholarly and popular, from online newspapers, journals, and magazines. Students expanded their understanding of the many ways arts was both defended and attacked, and how arts knowledge and skills were useful in employment as well as in personal growth and community development.

Assignments were developed so that students practiced the skills we discussed (critical reading, writing, listening; research; presentation skills) and students reflected on their own practices and goals. They researched potential career options and interviewed someone in a field of interest; presenting this information to their peers opened everyone's eyes to the broad employment possibilities. As a final project, we used the ePortfolio as established by Shannon Murray at UPEI, using the student example provided in the online supplemental resources for this book. Rather than a discipline-specific product, the ePortfolios were student-specific. The ePortfolio was a creative means by which students could practice their technology skills and show off their successes in their undergraduate career along with their employment and volunteer history; the ePortfolio was also designed to be a useful tool in applying for future employment. An example from a UNB Saint John student is also found in the online supplemental resources.

In discussing employment options with our arts students, we provided broad possibilities but local examples, relying heavily on our alumni office; there were many UNB Saint John alumni working locally in a variety of interesting careers who were very willing to come into our class and discuss their career paths. Students met alumni of different ages who had diverse educational backgrounds and often unusual stories about their routes to successful employment; this element of the course was so popular that we increased the number of visits in the second iteration of the course to 12 alumni guests.

UNB Saint John plans on continuing to offer Liberal Arts: Essential Skills in alternate years. The Canadian news magazine *Macleans* included the course in its article on the employability of arts graduates entitled "Yes You Will Get a Job With That Arts Degree" (Lewington, 2022). At the Atlantic Association of Universities teaching conference in October 2018,

Margaret Anne and I presented a paper titled "When the Student Becomes the Content: Developing a Cross-Disciplinary Arts Course With a Focus on Essential Skills." And student response has been overwhelmingly positive.

Planning for a New Institutional Context (Margaret Anne Smith)

I have recently left UNB Saint John to take on the leadership role at St Stephen's University, a tiny liberal arts university in New Brunswick. As I transition from faculty member to administrator and from one institution to another, I will bring our capstone course with me. The course's strengths and emphases on interdisciplinarity, community networking, skills development, and the ePortfolio (which integrates all these strengths) can make it a program highlight and enhance our current course offerings.

As a new course, the capstone will suit my new institution's current strengths as I assess them: an interdisciplinary focus, small seminar-style classes, creative arts students (who have been told they will never find meaningful work), and a strong alumni network. The feedback from our students at UNB Saint John indicates that this approach to a course (empowering students, asking them to determine some of the content, encouraging them to practice skills on the spot in the classroom, inspiring them to seek out new challenges) works. Students wholeheartedly participated in speaking and listening exercises; talked about creativity and empathy as cultivated in arts classes, and how these values are needed in the world; researched interesting careers and interviewed strangers; formed a tight cohort of supportive and enthusiastic peers; gained new self-awareness and insights; and made key connections between learning and doing. They finished the course with more curiosity and greater confidence—two of the objectives of any learning experience. After facilitating (rather than "teaching") this course twice, I am a better educator and better listener. This experience has clear implications for what active learning looks like in the classroom.

There are practical outcomes from our experience for instructors and institutions: We need to articulate why we are teaching and learning certain subjects. We need to be realistic about the financial costs of learning and the necessity of meaningful work for our students that pays their bills. Administrators need to hear from our frontline professors and our students about what resonates with students about work postgraduation. Students do not simply want school, then job; they want a meaningful education that inspires them and leads to significant work. A liberal arts program is not job training but should help them make the connection between learning and doing and give them essential skills. The final project, the ePortfolio, helps do this; it becomes a shareable artifact on an easily accessible tech platform that both celebrates and integrates who students are, what they have accomplished so far, and where they hope to go.

Finally, there is a huge and generally untapped resource in our alumni. Alumni visits were a highlight for the students at UNB Saint John, and guests spoke with humor, passion, and candor about the challenges of finding real careers in our economically challenged region. Each one presented highly relevant information and experience—and demonstrated their wide variety of paths and vast array of careers. I am an academic who graduated with a BA more than 3 decades ago; students need to hear from younger, more recent graduates who know what life is like right now outside the walls of the university. Some of our students found mentors in these alumni guests and were given access to invaluable resource networks that are well beyond the reach of many undergraduates. As postsecondary institutions develop a focus on experiential learning and skills development, it makes sense to tap into preexisting alumni networks of loyal graduates with workplace expertise who are willing to devote time to mentoring current students. A recent survey of St. Stephen's alumni reveals that an overwhelming majority would love to connect with students and share what they have learned since graduation.

I have found a new collaborating colleague and we will offer this capstone at St. Stephen's University in winter 2021. Our goal? More student comments like this one: "I have more confidence in myself and my degree."

Conclusion

The adaptation of this capstone over time and across institutions highlights some key components for the establishment of similar courses, especially in the contexts of students, faculty workload, and institutions.

While students benefit from a discussion of the skills learned alongside the disciplinary content in their degrees and from a consideration of possible avenues of employment, unless the course is accepted as a requirement or elective for their majors, students may simply not have space in their final year timetables to take the courses. Encouraging departments to build the capstone into majors will enable students in a cramped final year to include this valuable course. Conversely, shaping such a course more broadly along interdisciplinary lines and opening it to students in earlier years can work for smaller campuses, and help students become more aware of what and why they are learning.

Our various experiences suggest that team teaching—especially for faculty across disciplines—is enriching both for the student and the faculty experience, but issues of workload and other departmental teaching duties can deter faculty from working with others. A recognition by administrators of the importance of team teaching and of recognizing it as a full course rather than a portion of one is essential to the sustainability of the model.

For the institution, all our experiences demonstrate that the courses work best when they involve a team, both on campus and off. Ideally, staff from career offices and alumni affairs should be included early in planning for these courses, to extend the network of speakers, mentors, and career contacts.

The main lesson we have learned is that both our students and our institutions appreciate a course that provides the opportunity for reflection on the usefulness of the degrees in the arts and for celebration of the accomplishments of our senior students.

References

Bell, S., & Smith M. A. (2018). *When the student becomes the content: Developing a cross-disciplinary arts course with a focus on essential skills.* Atlantic Association of Universities Teaching Showcase, Halifax, Nova Scotia, Canada.

Evers, F. T., Rush, J., & Berdrow, I. (1998). *The bases of competence: Skills for lifelong learning and employability.* Jossey-Bass.

Gardner, J. N., Van der Veer, G., & Associates. (1997). *The senior year experience: Facilitating integration, reflection, closure, and transition.* Jossey-Bass.

Kuh, G., O'Donnell, K., & Schneider, C. G. (2017, September/October). HIPs at ten. *Change, 49*(5), 8–16.

Lewington, J. (2022, November 15). Yes you will get a job with that arts degree. *Macleans.* https://education.macleans.ca/getting-a-job/yes-you-will-get-a-job-with-that-arts-degree/

Moore, J. L. (2016, July 27). *ePortfolio as high-impact practice* [Blog post]. Center for Engaged Learning. https://www.centerforengagedlearning.org/eportfolio-as-high-impact-practice/

Mueller, R. A., & Bair, H. (2018). Deconstructing the notion of ePortfolio as a "high impact practice": A self-study and comparative analysis. *The Canadian Journal for the Scholarship of Teaching and Learning, 9*(3), Article 6.

Nussbaum, M. (2010). *Not for profit: Why democracy needs the humanities.* Princeton University Press.

Parkes, K. A., Dredger, K. S., & Hicks, D. (2013). ePortfolio as a measure of reflective practice. *International Journal of ePortfolio, 3*(2), 99–115.

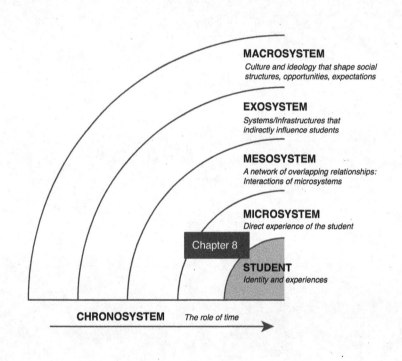

8

JUST A FEW MINUTES
OF YOUR TIME

Using Qualitative Survey Data to Evaluate and Revise a Capstone Project at an Early College Network

Matthew Park, Paul Hansen, Guy Risko, and Joshua Walker

Although the size and shape of capstone projects differ between institutions, their purposes are generally similar from high school to graduate school, and across disciplines. In order to evaluate and revise a capstone project at any type of institution, qualitative survey data drawn from both instructors and students are invaluable, not only because the information highlights strengths and weaknesses for possible revision, but also because it leads students to critically reflect upon the purpose of their own capstone experience.

In their third and fourth year at a Bard Early College, students enroll in the Bard Seminar, a sequence of interdisciplinary humanities courses culminating in an independent research project. The capstone experience (which we call the "Inquiry Project") is a graduation requirement for students earning an associate degree concurrently with a high school diploma. This chapter illustrates how qualitative data collection is a crucial tool for improving capstone experiences and the student learning outcomes associated with them, especially in a multi-institutional context. Data collection, evaluation, and revision require administrative support and a coherent structure to be effective, presenting unique challenges with faculty spread across six states.

The Bard Early Colleges are a network of 10 schools that offer a rigorous liberal arts curriculum embedded within a public high school. Students have the opportunity to graduate in 4 years while earning both a high school diploma as well as an associate degree, tuition-free. The majority of the Bard Early College faculty hold terminal degrees in their field, which means that the same faculty members teach both high school and college courses in one building.

Since 2001, when Bard College partnered with the New York City Department of Education to create the first Bard High School Early College (BHSEC) campus, the network has expanded and currently includes 10 campuses from Baltimore to Cleveland, located primarily in cities with historically underrepresented populations. The network was founded on the belief that many students are ready for college-level work earlier than age 18 and that by providing students an opportunity to earn college credits while still enrolled in a public high school, the Bard Early Colleges can increase the rate at which students continue their education. Although every campus teaches a similar curriculum, structural differences arise from the individual partnerships between Bard and each of the partner districts. With 10 campuses in two time zones, the network's institutional variety presents curriculum development and program evaluation challenges. To address these challenges, administrators appoint program chairs to oversee courses taught at multiple campuses, including the 2-year Bard Seminar.

The Bard Seminar asks students to read texts ranging from Descartes to Toni Morrison as they consider questions such as "What does it mean to be human?" and "What is freedom?" Across all four semesters, close reading and small discussions support a significant amount of informal and scholarly writing. Far from being an isolated exercise in textual study, students are required, through Socratic methodologies, to engage in a discursive and collaborative process of reading, writing, discussion, and debate that deepens their inquiry, develops community, and requires acknowledgment of and engagement with other perspectives (Fisher & Frey, 2015; Gillies, 2014; Walsh-Moorman, 2016). As Dewey (1910/1991) has argued, inquiry is a part of active learning that is "transactional, open-ended, and social" in nature (Walsh-Moorman, 2016, p. 72).

The seminar focus shifts toward writing in the final semester, when each student is engaged in an independent capstone research project. Although there are variations between campuses, the capstone project typically culminates in a research essay of approximately 10 pages. Each student chooses a topic based on both their interests and reading from previous semesters, and then submits a formal proposal to their instructor. The Bard Early Colleges student population is incredibly diverse, so the topics chosen for the capstone project run the gamut from the (mis)representation of minority populations in film to the incorporation of neuroscience-driven meditation practices in elementary schools. A wide range of approved topics creates particular challenges for the faculty, but the benefits gained through self-directed research outweigh the challenges. Although both faculty and students find the cap-stone project challenging, both agree that its importance extends beyond the purely academic accomplishment of producing a research paper. The cap-stone project is the culmination of a challenging associate degree, provides valuable preparation for earning a bachelor's degree, and encourages lifelong independent learning.

The Bard Seminar is the signature component of our network's peda-gogical model. The seminar program chair and the faculty regularly reexam-ine and assess how we coach students through the capstone process. With administrative support, we survey faculty and alumni to revise our teach-ing practices continually. As Duncheon and Muñoz (2019) have argued, a network-based approach, grounded in collaboration and analysis, might be more successful at preparing students not only for capstone projects but also for the world beyond isolated schools. We hope that our findings will ben-efit faculty and administrators at other multicampus institutions, as well as instructors of transfer students who might have completed a capstone project as part of an associate degree.

This chapter is divided into three sections. The first section is written by Matthew Park, the program chair of Second Year Seminar and an assistant professor of history at BHSEC in Newark, New Jersey. Following Park's over-view of the program evaluation process, Joshua Walker, an assistant professor of history at BHSEC in Cleveland, describes his experience as an instructor of Second Year Seminar. The chapter concludes with some forward-looking remarks from Guy Risko, who teaches the seminar courses and serves as the dean of collegiate studies in Cleveland.

A Network Approach to the Capstone Experience

This section makes three related claims: that the creation of a program chair with travel funding kickstarted essential processes of dialogue and revision across the Bard Early College network, that surveying faculty and graduates was vital in discovering the best ways to implement a useful capstone project, and that collaboration across a network, facilitated by a program chair, leads to a more effective capstone project.

When I became the program chair of Second Year Seminar in the Bard Early College network, I knew very little about the course outside of my campus at BHSEC Newark. Indeed, I quickly discovered that few people in the network knew what was happening at other campuses, including the capstone project. During a network-wide meetup of Second Year Seminar teachers in 2019, one campus had never heard of the capstone project while other campuses wondered about the efficacy of assigning a 10-page, student-directed research paper. Given the expansion of the BHSEC network, which opened new campuses in three major cities in 5 years and turned another campus from part time to full time, it was clear that the need for connection had become greater than ever. Creating a program chair position that bridged the divide between different campuses made it possible to achieve meaningful connections across the network. As Duncheon and Muñoz (2019) have argued, a network approach to evaluating and revising capstone experiences can significantly improve students' coherence across the network.

I began by using my budget as program chair to visit five of the six BHSEC campuses teaching Second Year Seminar and speak with faculty about their experiences and vision for the program's future. Campus visits were beneficial because they allowed me to make personal connections and identify professors at each campus who were excited to forge new relationships across the network. These campus visits, and the travel budget that supported them, were the necessary building blocks that created buy-in across the network for a systematic review of our Second Year Seminar program. The experience also validated what Jonathan Becker (2019) has found: Bard successfully created an "ecosystem of engagement" (p. 38) although it is underfunded compared to peer institutions.

The next step was to create a comprehensive survey that would deepen my understanding of the capstone project and its importance across the network. This was especially important given the huge gaps in the study of capstone projects in high schools despite their implementation since the 1990s (Kannapel, 2012). The National Survey of Student Engagement, for example, tracks capstone experiences at bachelor's-granting institutions, but not high schools or early colleges that grant associate degrees, leaving large lacunae to fill.

I opted for an open-ended survey that would produce qualitative data so that professors and graduates could elaborate on and clarify their thoughts. I asked one professor at each campus to be my representative in charge of speaking to their peers about the importance of the surveys, distributing, and collecting them. I was able to collect surveys from the majority of professors who have taught Second Year Seminar across the network and from many graduates who had moved on from the Bard Early Colleges to earn bachelor's degrees at other institutions. Perhaps the most surprising result of the survey was that every respondent affirmed the capstone project as central to the Second Year Seminar experience.

Every BHSEC graduate who responded to the survey indicated that their capstone experience had prepared them to succeed in their next adventure beyond the network, which validates Kuh's (2008) claim that students who have completed capstone projects report deep learning. One student from BHSEC Newark cited their experience with the seminar program as "extremely beneficial to my growth as a thinker, reader, and writer" and specifically praised the opportunity for "forming my own thoughts and experiences and developing into meaningful analyses." Another student from New Orleans agreed: "I am glad I was able to prepare myself for reading them (difficult texts) in Bard before I was almost left to bear it on my own in college." A student from Newark opined: "I think Seminar has helped my writing improve in many ways, from the first essay to the last 10-page (Inquiry Project) paper." Some identified the capstone project as the most meaningful experience of their BHSEC career, including one student from BHSEC Cleveland who wrote:

> My most successful writing experience in Seminar was my Senior Capstone Project. I think the open-endedness of the project itself was liberating. . . . I was able to produce a piece of work that I could identify with and do my own research and make arguments in the same ways that the authors we read did.

As Candace Thompson and Kennedy Ongaga (2011) have argued, our model for the capstone project has clearly created "high expectations" that "support a college-bound culture for historically underrepresented students" (p. 50). This is all the more important because, as Kuh (2008) has pointed out, historically underserved students are also the least likely to have access to the very high-impact educational practices that we offer in the Bard Early College network, including seminar, a writing-intensive curriculum, undergraduate research, and capstone projects.

Faculty similarly expressed support for Second Year Seminar's scope, including the capstone project, across the network. When asked whether college-level inquiry and capstone projects worked at their campus, faculty universally responded that it is working. At New Orleans, a professor stated, "It really works on our campus because it does! I've seen it! We're in our third year! . . . Our alumni often tell us that they arrive on their next institution's campus ready to do 10-page research papers and for that they are so grateful!" At the oldest BHSEC, in Manhattan, another professor claimed that they had seen "20 years of success. . . . I am confident it can and will continue to work here." A professor at BHSEC Queens echoed these sentiments, exclaiming, "I have no doubts at all, having done it several times over." This feedback establishes that faculty across the network see their students producing impressive, college-level work. It counters misleading narratives that the work being done in early colleges is watered down or not sufficiently rigorous (Mangan, 2016). Studies have shown that students at early colleges graduate high school at higher rates, are more likely to be prepared for college than peers at traditional secondary education institutions, and are similarly prepared compared with peers attending postsecondary colleges and universities (Edmunds et al., 2017).

Utilizing these results, faculty can now target specific points of weakness in the capstone experience, find new ways to reach and support their students, and share best practices across the network. For example, I have been designing modules that will help students who fear the capstone project and don't see how it relates to them (Park, 2021). Across the network, other professors, including the authors of this paper, are working on similar initiatives.

Teaching a 10-Page Research Essay at an Early College

A specter is haunting my classroom—the specter of 10 pages.

I teach the Second Year Seminar course at BHSEC Cleveland. In seminar, students get to choose their capstone research topic (in consultation with the instructor), and many feel genuinely thrilled with the opportunity to explore an issue that matters to them. They also appreciate the steps we take to scaffold the project. Instructors help students practice writing research questions, proposals, and annotated bibliographies. At the Cleveland campus, students learn to experiment with electronic research databases and visit Cleveland's exceptional public library to find sources. They make notecards and outlines, formulate theses, and type sloppy rough drafts (Foss & Waters, 2007; Lamott, 1995). They visit our school's writing center and edit each other's papers. At the end of the term, students present their work at a research showcase open to our school community.

However positive these experiences turn out to be, many students are terrified to begin. They express high levels of anxiety about the length of the essay, especially when the number "10" appears in the assignment description. In the past, I have modified the page length requirement on my syllabus, turning it from a "10-page essay" to a "seven-to-10-page essay." I instructed students who were nervous about page length to focus on the "seven" instead of the "10." In my grading rubric for the paper's final copy, I deemphasized page count in favor of the number of sources analyzed. Students got full credit for the "evidence" section of the rubric if they analyzed at least six scholarly sources, regardless of how many pages it took them to do this.

These interventions provided a differentiated experience in which each student's abilities and personal interests determined how long their project needed to be. They also played to my suspicion of the pedagogical value of length requirements. I further suspect that they helped students overcome the fears they express at the beginning of each semester. But I worry that these accommodations also allowed my students and me to dodge a question that lies at the heart of the 10-page terror: What is the purpose of long and challenging writing assignments?

I plan to use Park's qualitative survey responses, described previously, to help students answer this question for themselves. Park's questions for graduates, including the following, asked them to process their experience in seminar and, for those who pursued additional higher education, to relate it to other institutions' expectations:

- If you were to describe the purpose/goals of seminar to someone outside of the BHSEC community, what would you say?
- Did Second Year Seminar prepare you for your ongoing education? In what ways? Did you find that the texts you read were useful or the skills you developed came in handy?
- Keeping in mind that Second Year Seminar should be equivalent to a sophomore-level college course, do you feel like the workload was appropriate in terms of how much you were asked to read and write?
- Looking back, do you see Second Year Seminar in the same or a different light based on your new experiences? What has changed or not?

Before we begin working on the research project, I plan to have students write informally about goals they wish to accomplish with their projects. We will then read alumni responses to Park's questions. Students will follow this with more informal writing in which they assess whether former students seem to have accomplished the goals that the current students described. For example, if my current students said their objective was to be "more ready for their next college," they would evaluate whether Park's correspondents felt that seminar made them more ready. If their course objective was to "learn something, but not have too much homework," we'll evaluate whether respondents felt satisfied with the learning process in seminar and whether they felt that the workload was too burdensome.

Follow-up activities could include assignment reviews and interviews with alumni. For the assignment reviews, students read assignment prompts and syllabi from research and writing courses submitted by alumni attending other colleges and universities. Students annotate the prompts and label features similar to or different from our course requirements in seminar. Alfred E. Guy Jr. (2009) used a similar process at the end of his courses to get students to connect skills they learned in his class to other classes on campus. I will also invite alumni to guest lecture in my course. They will talk about expectations at their new institutions and compare them to what they experienced in seminar.

My students will write reflection paragraphs to process what they have learned from these activities. They will describe whether the surveys, the syllabi, and the guest lecture changed their ideas and feelings about my course. Does it seem like the course will help them to prepare for what's next? Does a 10-page paper still seem unreasonable?

I am committed to allowing students to answer these questions openly and honestly. For students who know that they have no intention of continuing on to a 4-year college or university, the ideas expressed by alumni might seem irrelevant to them. I am open to negotiating a lower page length requirement for these students in exchange for a specified grade. However, I hope that the students who plan to complete a bachelor's degree will find in Park's surveys the answers I would have given them at the start. What is the point of long and challenging writing assignments? To help us to explore the world and to prepare us to succeed wherever we go next. With this in mind, I hope many will choose on their own to finally confront the 10-page demon. Although numerous studies, personal experiences, and our network survey have shown that capstone experiences are highly demanding of faculty, they have also confirmed that they are highly rewarding and meaningful for all involved (Hauhart & Grahe, 2015; Laye et al., 2020).

Internal and External Applications of the Bard Early Colleges' Network-Wide Qualitative Survey Data

The data collection and analysis led by Park grounded our faculty and administrators in a shared vision of the capstone project. As educators and scholars engaged in a radical reimagining of the K–16 system, we saw in the survey data that a shared expectation of semester-long research projects supports student preparation for their move to a 4-year college or university. It helps students transition from our relatively small, supportive environment to a more extensive, independent system by demonstrating their capacity for developing research questions, diving into library stacks and databases, and producing polished academic writing. Such an overwhelmingly clear shared belief has also begun to serve as a guidepost about using data collected from multiple sources in the future.

One readily available option is using alumni networks and survey results to produce a cycle of self-reflection related to student experience as many move on to 4-year institutions. Although a lagging indicator of our capstone project's relationship with contemporary norms of university pedagogy, graduate surveys help us know the relationship between our seminar sequence and the academic expectations of students at 4-year institutions. As a result of our multistate network, our alumni base enrolls at institutions across the country and internationally. By nurturing a culture of participation in these kinds of surveys, we believe we can adapt and change our capstone project quickly and with fidelity to the expectations placed on our graduates. These surveys, however, are our hardest to get completed. Our campuses graduate nearly 700 students per year, and it is difficult to reach many of them afterward. A more robust secondary to postsecondary communication pipeline must engage the students socially.

We are also planning to use surveys to support a series of scaled assessments of the seminar course focused on equity and transferability of skills. Completing a capstone project demonstrates the ability to produce independent, academic work successfully; however, it does not necessarily help us identify students' strengths and weaknesses vis-à-vis social-emotional learning or a student's willingness to request support from faculty or other services. Moving forward, we are looking to produce an instrument that will measure these skills and help faculty identify gaps in students' knowledge about working independently. Collaborating on assessing student independence and ingenuity should help us ensure that not only can our students produce high-quality academic work but that they can do so in the context of either a larger university or future career.

The network of early colleges spans two time zones, five major metropolitan areas, and graduates hundreds of students with both a high school diploma and an associate degree. While our mission and model might be particular, organizations and institutions of various sizes and types can take a few key points from our experience. First, the cross-campus collaboration worked best when the stakeholders were diverse. Administrators, faculty, students, and alumni all had different experiences, and those differences appeared across multiple campuses. Mere faculty collaboration may have changed our perspective on the capstone project and highlighted differences in experiences that were less impactful on our students than we may have thought. The vibrancy of our shared vision of seminar also speaks to the survey data's ability to assess the strengths and weaknesses of a set of expectations. Institutions that share curricular designs or pedagogical models might see similarities in smooth or rough communication or adherence to a set of beliefs about culture. In the Bard Early College network, we saw how our differences paled in comparison to the agreed-upon importance of the capstone project. By highlighting what stakeholders thought was working, we can build upon what is shared rather than what is assumed to be shared.

References

Becker, J. (2019). Bard College: An ecosystem of engagement. *Journal of Community Engagement & Higher Education, 11*(1), 38–52. https://discovery.indstate.edu/jcehe/index.php/joce/article/view/519

Dewey, J. (1991). *How we think.* Prometheus. (Original work published 1910)

Duncheon, J. C., & Muñoz, J. (2019). Examining teacher perspectives on college readiness in an early college high school context. *American Journal of Education, 125*(3), 453–478. https://doi.org/10.1086/702731

Edmunds, J. A., Arshavsky, N., Lewis, K., Thrift, B., Unlu, F., & Furey, J. (2017). Preparing students for college: Lessons learned from the early college. *NASSP Bulletin, 101*(2), 117–141. https://doi.org/10.1177%2F0192636517713848

Fisher, D., & Frey, N. (2015). *Text dependent questions, grades 6–12: Pathways to close and critical reading.* SAGE.

Foss, S. K., & Waters, W. (2007). *Destination dissertation: A traveler's guide to a done dissertation.* Rowman and Littlefield.

Gillies, R. M. (2014). Developments in classroom-based talk. *International Journal of Educational Research, 63*, 63–68. https://doi.org/10.1016/j.ijer.2013.05.002

Guy, A. E. (2009). Process writing: Reflection and the arts of writing and teaching. In T. Vilardi & M. Chang (Eds.), *Writing-based teaching: Essential practices and enduring questions* (pp. 53–70). State University of New York Press.

Hauhart, R. C., & Grahe, J. E. (2015). *Designing and teaching undergraduate capstone courses.* Wiley.

Kannapel, P. J. (2012). *High school capstone courses: A review of the literature.* Appalachian Regional Comprehensive Center at Edvantia. https://files.eric.ed.gov/fulltext/ED539346.pdf

Kuh, G. (2008). *High-impact educational practices: What they are, who has access to them, and why they matter.* American Association of Colleges and Universities.

Lamott, A. (1995). *Bird by bird: Some instructions on writing and life.* Penguin Random House.

Laye, M. J., Boswell, C., Gresham, M., Smith-Sherwood, D., & Anderson, O. (2020). Multi-institutional survey of faculty experiences teaching capstones. *College Teaching, 68*(4), 201–213. https://doi.org/10.1080/87567555.2020.1786663

Mangan, K. (2016, July 22). As dual enrollments swell, so do worries about academic rigor. *Chronicle of Higher Education.* http://www.chronicle.com/article/As-Dual-Enrollments-Swell-So/237220

Park, M. (2021). Scaffolding independence applied: Research focus. *Early College Folio, 1*(1).

Thompson, C., & Ongaga, K. (2011). Flying the plane while we build it: A case study of an early college high school. *The High School Journal, 94*(2), 43–57. https://doi.org/10.1353/hsj.2011.0000

Walsh-Moorman, B. (2016). The socratic seminar in the age of the Common Core: A search for text-dependent discourse. *The English Journal, 105*(6), 72–77.

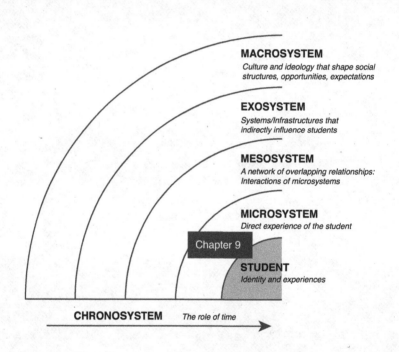

9

STUDENTS-AS-PARTNERS AND ENGAGED SCHOLARSHIP

Complementary Frameworks

Andrew J. Pearl, Joanna C. Rankin, Moriah McSharry McGrath,
Sarah Dyer, and Trina Jorre de St Jorre

Since 2018, we have worked under the auspices of the Center for Engaged Learning to participate in a Research Seminar on Capstone Experiences. In broad terms, our research group was tasked with better understanding student diversity and identity in capstone experiences in higher education. This challenged us to examine diversity within our own institutions, how that diversity is represented, and how students are influenced by or understand the ways in which institutions represent diversity. Given the centrality of student perspectives to our research focus, we employed a students-as-partners (SaP) approach to examine the public messaging of colleges and universities related to equity, diversity, and inclusion (EDI). Specifically, we asked how institutions referenced capstone experiences on public-facing websites, and if there were any explicit connections made between EDI and capstone experiences (Rankin et al., 2022). In this chapter, we reflect on the process of doing this analysis in collaboration with students at the University of Calgary, why a SaP approach was well suited to our goals, and the parallels between the principles that undergird both SaP work and engaged scholarship.

The Capstone Course

This chapter reflects on studying capstones as a capstone project. The University of Calgary's undergraduate community rehabilitation and disability studies (CRDS) program, where author Rankin is on the faculty, requires a practicum experience as its capstone. The learning outcomes for this practicum include developing leadership skills, enhancing inclusion, reflecting on past service delivery to inform future decision-making, building a collaborative network for action, and strengthening research skills (Rankin, 2020). We presented our collaboration as an option for students seeking to fulfill their practicum requirement, providing them with a pathway to dive deeply into our research questions and develop the requisite research abilities, growing as potential agents of change.

One of our fundamental research goals is to better understand the structural barriers to student success, particularly for students from minoritized and marginalized backgrounds, and ultimately to dismantle those barriers to enable the success of underrepresented students. We focused on the inherent barriers encompassed by student–instructor dynamics and ways to engage in the process of teaching and learning as a "dynamic endeavor" that "keeps the flame of scholarship alive" (Boyer, 1990, pp. 23–24). Therefore, for us, a research project about students and their experiences would have been inauthentic without students playing an integral role. Without centering and listening to students, we would not have been able to fully address our research questions, or to know if we were asking the right questions in the first place. In this chapter, we use two parallel conceptual frameworks to demonstrate how a capstone experience might be more participatory for students.

Two cohorts of student coresearchers were initially involved in the project. The faculty disciplinary expertise and research experience was complemented by the student coresearchers' insight into the student learning experience, which established the importance of the student coresearchers not simply as subjects of the research or data points but as necessary at every level of the research process, including the identification of the questions being asked, the data collection and analysis, and the reporting and interpretation of the findings. Because the students were all enrolled in a capstone practicum course themselves, they had a vested interest in learning more about how a student's intersecting identities might impact their experience in a capstone course.

Students-as-Partners

To enable integrative learning for our student researchers, we employed a SaP approach, which can be defined as a "reciprocal process through which all participants have the opportunity to contribute equally, although not necessarily in the same ways, to curricular or pedagogical conceptualization, decision-making, implementation, investigation, or analysis" (Cook-Sather et al., 2014, pp. 6–7). Had students been given the traditional research assistant role in our project, they might have achieved their stated learning goals, but would have done so in a way that reinforced traditional hierarchies and power dynamics between faculty and students. Treating students as coresearchers as part of the capstone experience gave them more space to create and affect meaningful change, reflecting Healey et al.'s (2014) description of SaP as "a relationship in which all involved—students, academics, professional services staff, senior managers, students' unions, and so on—are actively engaged in and stand to gain from the process of learning and working together" (p. 12).

We first understood the impact of this approach on our research when we began coding website data on diversity (Rankin et al., 2022), with one aspect in particular underscoring the importance of a SaP approach in our case. Initially, the first cohort of student researchers reviewed institutional websites and recorded their interpretations of emerging thematic elements. Next, two of the faculty researchers analyzed the same websites using the themes identified by the students as a priori codes. Then, a second cohort of students followed the same procedure, to strengthen the validity of the analysis and subsequent findings. While not surprising in retrospect, we were initially surprised that the students' interpretation and coding of the responses from the first cohort of student coresearchers differed between the faculty researchers and the second cohort of student coresearchers. Relying solely on the academic insight and expertise of the faculty researchers alone would have left our analyses incomplete.

As the research process unfolded, we noticed how a SaP approach can serve to advance the principles discussed in the *Full Participation* catalyst paper (Strum et al., 2011). This paper brings together multiple initiatives in higher education that are often treated separately: diversity, public engagement, and student success. The authors argued that integrating these ideas as interconnected and mutually beneficial can serve "as a nexus for the transformation of communities on and off campus" (p. 3).

Full participation first means building pathways to social and economic citizenship, particularly for students from communities that have not been afforded access or enabled to succeed. Second, it involves connecting the knowledge resources of the academy with the pressing and complex problems facing multiple communities. Finally, full participation also involves building the capacity and commitment of diverse leadership equipped to tackle these social problems. We link this to our research process in terms of the importance of relationships, as "students' experiences of full participation and engagement, in their capstone experience, are influenced by how and with whom they interact on the faculty, and these interactions are in turn shaped by the values affecting faculty members' choices and priorities" (Strum et al., 2011, p. 5). We hoped that by demonstrating our values, to share power in the research process, our student coresearchers would in turn understand the knowledge production process to be "rooted in and accountable to multiple communities" (p. 4). Further, these principles are consistent with the American Association of Colleges and Universities essential learning outcomes, which "define the knowledge and skills gained from a liberal education, providing a framework to guide students' cumulative progress" (AAC&U, n.d.). Through AAC&U's LEAP initiative, the essential learning outcomes are closely associated with high-impact practices, like capstone experiences.

The Norms of Engaged Scholarship

One of the critical elements of the *Full Participation* catalyst paper is community engagement, and the remainder of this chapter explores ways to democratize knowledge by overlaying the fundamental norms of community-engaged scholarship (CES) onto how we work with SaP. We will discuss the parallels between these two bodies of literature and how these CES and SaP principles manifested in the collaboration with our student coresearchers through their capstone practicum experiences. Finally, we will present our thinking on how these parallels might play out moving forward.

Campus Compact, a national coalition of colleges and universities dedicated to the public purposes of higher education, has articulated six norms of engaged scholarship that are intended to guide the "generation of new knowledge through the combining of academic knowledge and community-based knowledge, eliminating a hierarchy of knowledge and a one-way flow of knowledge outward from the college or university" (Campus Compact, n.d., para. 3). The first norm of engaged scholarship is a *participatory epistemology* that "shifts the position of students from knowledge consumers to knowledge producers and shifts community groups from being subjects or spectators of the research process to collaborators in knowledge generation and problem solving" (Campus Compact, n.d., para. 4). A participatory approach to engaged scholarship holds the promise for the "freedom . . . to imagine new possibilities, transform old ways of knowing, and pursue original ideas" in a way that "sustains the entire operation" and serves to "uphold the integrity of a community" (Peralta, 2017, p. 52). The flow of knowledge production and consumption becomes more cyclical and purposefully repositions the roles of those involved in scholarly endeavors.

Next, engaged scholarship should be *collaborative research*, where disciplinary expertise is "combined with community-based knowledge, eliminating a hierarchy of knowledge and a one-way flow of knowledge outward from the college or university" (Campus Compact, n.d., para. 4). The SOFAR (students, organizations in the community, faculty, administrators on campus, and residents in the community) model (Bringle et al., 2012) provides a useful framework for understanding the types and complexity of relationships that exist in CES, often part of capstone experiences. All are represented in this model and each is involved in "reaching out, up, and across institutional and social structures to engage members with greater or complementary influence, power, and resources" (p. 15).

The third norm of CES involves *knowledge experts from outside the academy*.

> Along with a valuing of the knowledge and experience that both academics and nonacademics bring to the processes of education and knowledge production comes the reframing of who is a peer in the peer review process and the recognition that in certain circumstances the expert will be a noncredentialed, nonacademic collaborator. (Campus Compact, n.d., para. 4)

This principle redefines who is considered a peer in the knowledge production enterprise; we recognize the importance of "the local knowledge of community stakeholders in defining the problem to be addressed, a shared understanding of the problem, and designing, implementing, and evaluating the actions to be taken to address the problem" (Saltmarsh et al., 2009, p. 9). The democratization of knowledge is not fully possible until we begin "dismantling traditional conceptions of who qualifies as a peer in peer review" (Ellison & Eatman, 2008, p. x).

This links to the fourth norm of engaged scholarship: rethinking *scholarly artifacts as publications*, including "expanding the understanding and valuing of scholarly products beyond publication in highly specialized disciplinary journals" (Campus Compact, n.d., para. 4). One manifestation of these alternative "products" of scholarship is CES4Health.info (Jordan et al., 2012), which was developed and is coordinated by Community-Campus Partnerships for Health. The site includes a wide range of policy briefs, tool kits, documentaries, evaluation tools, and so on—all peer-reviewed.

Fifth, engaged scholarship also should have *impact*, leading to "actionable and useful knowledge" (Campus Compact, n.d., para. 4), such as policy change or social action. An alternative conceptualization of the quantitative "impact factors" computed by academic journals, this idea of impact connects to Boyer's (1990) "scholarship of application," which asks "How can knowledge be responsibly applied to consequential problems? . . . Can social problems themselves define an agenda for scholarly investigation?" (p. 21).

Finally, engaged scholarship is inherently *transdisciplinary*: It moves beyond the bounds of academic disciplines and "combines multiple disciplinary knowledge within the college or university with knowledge that exists and is generated outside the college or university" (Campus Compact, n.d., para. 4). This process of "making connections across the disciplines, placing the specialties in larger context, illuminating data in a revealing way" (Boyer, 1990, p. 18) allows for addressing "pressing social, civic, economic, and moral problems" (Boyer, 1996, p. 11).

Applying the Norms to Students-as-Partners

The remainder of this chapter explores in more depth how CES can be overlaid onto SaP by applying these two bodies of literature as they manifested in the collaboration with our student coresearchers. We identify connections between the CES norms and the literature on SaP, discussing how our work mirrored a CES project despite the lack of designated community partner organizations. We suggest how these parallel approaches may be woven together in capstone programs. For brevity's sake, we have sorted the norms of engaged scholarship into three larger domains:

- power dynamics of knowledge (participatory epistemology, collaborative research, and knowledge experts from outside the academy)
- outputs (scholarly artifact as publications and impact)
- transdisciplinarity

Power Dynamics of Knowledge

Reconceptualizing who has agency in the research production process is at the core of both engaged scholarship and a SaP approach. Just as the positions of both community and campus partners in engaged scholarship are shifted away from traditional hierarchies of knowledge, a SaP approach "subverts the traditional power hierarchy between learners and teachers by repositioning partners as learners and teachers" (Mercer-Mapstone et al., 2017, p. 14). Implicit in this redefinition of power dynamics and hierarchies is the acknowledgment that different types of knowledge, perspective, and experiences are equally valuable to the partnership (Cook-Sather et al., 2014), which requires giving space to be authentic in their contributions. This reciprocity demands "openness to new ways of working and learning together" (Healey et al., 2016, p. 9) and goes against the "customs and culture of higher education" (Mercer-Mapstone et al., 2017, p. 2).

We also observed new power relations in terms of the previously noted capstone researchers' learning outcome of "building a collaborative network for action," which occurred through participating in knowledge production. By seeing how their findings could be used to improve capstone programs, student researchers came to understand the process of cocreation that they would be able to use in future endeavors. Here we see an opportunity for SaP projects to move beyond the principle of reciprocity and embrace cocreation. We link this directly to a parallel evolution in CES. Iowa Campus Compact (Trebil-Smith, 2019) investigated the perceptions of community-based organizations partnering with universities and found that "a partnership focusing on reciprocity typically begins with one or both partners bringing their preestablished goals and ideas to the table," whereas "cocreation means developing goals together that serve each partner's mission and needs" (p. 31). Long-term planning is necessary to develop this type of project, and incorporating students creates time limitations in terms of the academic calendar and student tenure.

Outputs

Evaluating the products of SaP projects and their impact requires considering the intended audience for those products and who in the partnership is benefiting from their dissemination. While peer-reviewed publications remain the primary currency in higher education—particularly for those faculty members on the tenure track—these publications rarely carry the same weight for students. Even though some students (e.g., those who are interested in graduate school) may value peer-reviewed publications, this is not the case for all students. Hence, Mercer-Mapstone's (2017) call for new genres of writing and reporting in SaP projects. Cook-Sather et al. (2019) mentioned opportunities to plan, host, and moderate events, and Dunne and Zandstra (2011) provided examples of three dissemination models, including a student-run project blog, a campus-based student conference, and a series of case studies. Each of these offers ways for students to move beyond being consumers of higher education and engage in the process of "knowledge creation and thought leadership" (National Union of Students, 2012, p. 12), as they begin to have a stronger voice in the dissemination and application of findings to new contexts.

In our project, the student coresearchers have been included as coauthors on the projects to which they contributed. Through our conversations with them, the students felt that this further legitimized their roles as true partners in the research process. In addition, for the students whose futures include continued study in graduate school, a peer-reviewed publication was especially meaningful. Students also gained access to new leadership opportunities based on this scholarly work, such as being invited to attend the International Institute for Students as Partners on the basis of their capstone work.

Building from both the CEP and SaP bodies of literature, instructors should work collaboratively with students to establish shared definitions of output and impact. Lubicz-Nawrocka (2019) specifically advocated for the possibility of how cocreation in the curriculum holds promise for impacting communities beyond the university, a recommendation reflective of Strum et al. (2011). If we accept that full participation can be achieved at the nexus of an intentional commitment to diversity, equity, and inclusion; community engagement; and student academic success and engagement, then a SaP approach can fulfill its promise as the future of student engagement in higher education (Matthews, 2016).

Transdisciplinarity

Going beyond interdisciplinarity, transdisciplinarity work not only brings together different professional/disciplinary perspectives but also purposefully integrates academic disciplines with nonacademic partners, highlighting the importance of knowledge and theory development for the scientific community as well as the broader society (Tress et al., 2005). Dimon et al. (2019) suggested that SaP projects are ripe for transdisciplinarity, and Healey et al. (2014) pointed to the potential for creating learning communities and/or communities of practice that are "structured around a common theme and can span multiple subjects or disciplines" (p. 26).

Although all of our student coresearchers currently come from a single discipline (disability studies), our project spans multiple disciplines due to the interdisciplinary nature of our research and the diverse training of the faculty team (biology, disability studies, education, geography, public health, and urban planning). We are also adding student researchers from the University of Alabama who are pursuing a variety of academic programs, making the student cohort interdisciplinary as well. By creating space for these peer researchers to interact with each other in the context of a capstone project, we aimed to foster what Fitzgerald et al. (2017) called "T-shaped" students, who have depth of knowledge and a breadth of collaborative skills in order to solve "global problems that transcend disciplinary parameters . . . with entrepreneurial and innovative solutions" (p. 40). We believe this capstone experience has provided the student partners with a platform to see beyond the boundaries of traditional disciplinary silos, and to get past the barriers that traditionally define who is a knowledge expert, and who is not.

Conclusion

Because they are recognized as high-impact educational practices, capstone experiences have the potential to provide students with the opportunity to integrate theory with practice and to synthesize their learning (Kinzie, 2013; Kuh, 2008; Padgett & Kilgo, 2012). Based on our experience, we see the SaP approach as a useful framework for instructors to adopt in supporting students to achieve the full promise of capstone experiences. Faculty members involved in designing and implementing capstone experiences should consider how purposeful partnerships with students can foster students' academic learning and development, but also students' abilities to see beyond traditional academic power relationships as they begin the process of "unlearning hierarchies" (Guitman et al., 2020, p. 61). This applies not just to their academic experience but also the larger enterprise of engaged scholarship, with its imperative to reconsider who are the producers and consumers of knowledge.

The value of a SaP approach, however, goes beyond student learning. In our experience, working with student coresearchers has made our work stronger, in line with Cook-Sather et al.'s (2019) assertion that students provide insight and perspective that would have otherwise been unavailable to faculty researchers. Instructors who are thinking about integrating a SaP approach into a capstone experience should consider how adding in new perspectives and ways of knowing from their student partners can strengthen how they ask and seek to answer their research questions. Because our research is primarily concerned with the student experience, we found viewing our partnership with the students as a form of CES to be particularly useful. As faculty and administrators continue to develop capstone programs, we encourage them to continue exploring the parallels between CES and SaP to rethink and expand who is involved in the knowledge production and application process.

Acknowledgments

Our research would not be possible without the contributions of several student coresearchers: Roberta Armitage, Daania Chaudhary, Anoushka Jere, Kerstin Ruediger, Shalaine Sedres, Samiah Sheriff, and Saania Zafar.

References

Association of American Colleges and Universities. (n.d.). *Essential learning outcomes*. https://www.aacu.org/essential-learning-outcomes

Boyer, E. L. (1990). *Scholarship reconsidered: Priorities of the professoriate*. Carnegie Foundation for the Advancement of Teaching.

Boyer, E. L. (1996). The scholarship of engagement. *Journal of Higher Education Outreach and Engagement, 1*(1), 11–20. https://openjournals.libs.uga.edu/jheoe/article/view/666

Bringle, R. C., Clayton, P., & Price, M. (2012). Partnerships in service learning and civic engagement. *Partnerships: A Journal of Service-Learning and Civic Engagement, 1*(1), 1–20. http://libjournal.uncg.edu/prt/article/view/415

Campus Compact. (n.d.). *Ernest A. Lynton Award for the Scholarship of Engagement*. https://compact.org/impact-awards/ernest-a-lynton-award/

Cook-Sather, A., Bahti, M., & Ntem, A. (2019). *Pedagogical partnerships: A how-to guide for faculty, students, and academic developers in higher education*. Elon University Center for Engaged Learning. https://www.centerforengagedlearning.org/books/pedagogical-partnerships/

Cook-Sather, A., Bovill, C., & Felten, P. (2014). *Engaging students as partners in learning and teaching: A guide for faculty*. John Wiley & Sons.

Dimon, R., Pettit, L., Cheung, C., & Quinnell, R. (2019). Promoting botanical literacy with a mobile application—CampusFlora—using an interdisciplinary, student-as-partners approach. *International Journal for Students as Partners, 3*(2), 118–128. https://doi.org/10.15173/ijsap.v3i2.3671

Dunne, E., & Zandstra, R. (2011). *Students as change agents: New ways of engaging with learning and teaching in higher education*. University of Exeter/ESCalate/Higher Education Academy. http://escalate.ac.uk/downloads/8244.pdf

Ellison, J., & Eatman, T. K. (2008). *Scholarship in public: Knowledge creation and tenure policy in the engaged university*. Imagining America. https://imaginingamerica.org/wp-content/uploads/TTI_FINAL.pdf

Fitzgerald, H. E., Van Egeren, L. A., Bargerstock, B. A., & Zientek, R. (2017). Community engagement scholarship, research universities, and the scholarship of integration. In J. Sachs & L. Clark (Eds.), *Learning through community engagement: Vision and practice in higher education* (pp. 31–51). Springer.

Guitman, R., Acai, A., Mercer-Mapstone, L., Mercer-Mapstone, L., & Abbot, S. (2020). Unlearning hierarchies and striving for relational diversity. In L. Mercer-Mapstone & S. Abbot (Eds.), *The power of partnership* (pp. 61–72). Center for Engaged Learning. https://www.centerforengagedlearning.org/books/power-of-partnership/

Healey, M., Flint, A., & Harrington, K. (2014). *Engagement through partnership: Students as partners in learning and teaching in higher education*. The Higher Education Academy. http://www.tandfonline.com/doi/full/10.1080/1360144X.2016.1124966

Healey, M., Flint, A., & Harrington, K. (2016). Students as partners: Reflections on a conceptual model. *Teaching & Learning Inquiry: The ISSOTL Journal, 4*(2). https://doi.org/10.20343/teachlearninqu.4.2.3

Jordan, C., Gelmon, S., Ryan, K., & Seifer, S. D. (2012). CES4Health.info: A web-based mechanism for disseminating peer-reviewed products of community-engaged scholarship: Reflections on year one. *Journal of Higher Education*

Outreach and Engagement, 16(1), 47–64. https://openjournals.libs.uga.edu/jheoe/article/view/922

Kinzie, J. (2013). Taking stock of capstones and integrative learning. *Peer Review, 15*(4), 27–30.

Kuh, G. D. (2008). *High-impact educational practices: What are they, who has access to them, and why they matter.* Association of American Colleges and Universities. http://hdl.voced.edu.au/10707/232146

Lubicz-Nawrocka, T. M. (2019). "More than just a student": How co-creation of the curriculum fosters third spaces in ways of working, identity, and impact. *International Journal for Students as Partners, 3*(1), 34–49. https://doi.org/10.15173/ijsap.v3i1.3727

Matthews, K. E. (2016, September 5). Students as partners as the future of student engagement. *Student Engagement in Higher Education Journal, 1*(1), 1–5. https://sehej.raise-network.com/raise/article/view/380

Mercer-Mapstone, L., Dvorakova, S. L., Matthews, K. E., Abbot, S., Cheng, B., Felten, P., Knorr, K., Marquis, E., Shammas, R., & Swaim, K. (2017). A systematic literature review of students as partners in higher education. *International Journal for Students as Partners, 1*(1). https://doi.org/10.15173/ijsap.v1i1.3119

National Union of Students. (2012). *A manifesto for partnership.* https://www.nusconnect.org.uk/resources/a-manifesto-for-partnership-2013

Padgett, R. D., & Kilgo, C. A. (2012). *2011 national survey of senior capstone experiences: Institutional-level data on the culminating experience.* National Resource Center for the First-Year Experience and Students in Transition.

Peralta, K. J. (2017). Toward a deeper appreciation of participatory epistemology in community-based participatory research. *PRISM: A Journal of Regional Engagement, 6*(1), 45–56. https://encompass.eku.edu/prism/vol6/iss1/4

Rankin, J. C. (2020). *Practicum I & II* [Disability studies syllabus]. University of Calgary.

Rankin, J. C., Pearl, A. J., Jorre de St Jorre, T., McGrath, M. M., Dyer, S., Sheriff, S., Armitage, R., Ruediger, K., Jere, A., Zafar, S., Sedres, S., & Chaudhary, D. (2022). Delving into institutional diversity messaging: A cross-institutional analysis of student and faculty interpretations of undergraduate experiences of equity, diversity, and inclusion in university websites. *Teaching & Learning Inquiry, 10.* https://doi.org/10.20343/teachlearninqu.10.10

Saltmarsh, J., Hartley, M., & Clayton, P. H. (2009). *Democratic engagement white paper.* New England Resource Center for Higher Education. https://repository.upenn.edu/gse_pubs/274/

Strum, S., Eatman, T. K., Saltmarsh, J., & Bush, A. (2011). *Full participation: Building the architecture for diversity and community engagement in higher education.* Imagining America. https://surface.syr.edu/cgi/viewcontent.cgi?article=1001&context=ia

Trebil-Smith, K. (2019). *Perceptions of partnership: A study on nonprofit and higher education collaboration.* Iowa Campus Compact. https://iacampuscompact.org/perceptions-of-partnership/

Tress, G., Tress, B., & Fry, G. (2005). Clarifying integrative research concepts in landscape ecology. *Landscape Ecology, 20*(4), 479–493. https://doi.org/10.1007/s10980-004-3290-4

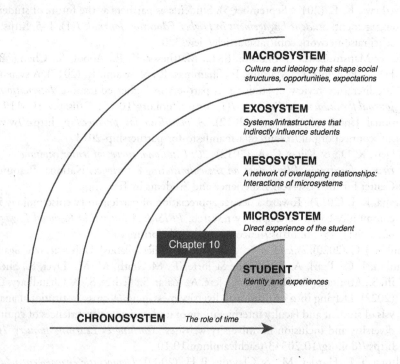

DESIGNING DEMOCRATIC SPACES

Public-Facing Civic Capstone Courses

Cindy Koenig Richards, Nicholas V. Longo, and Caryn McTighe Musil

Clarion calls in the United States to heed the democratic, public purposes of colleges and universities have come at moments of great crisis: establishing a new nation after the Revolutionary War or responding to the vacuum after the swift collapse of most European democracies during World War II. We are again at such a moment. A cascade of catastrophes (e.g., deteriorating democratic structures, systemic racism, catastrophic climate change) demands higher education invest their intellectual, social, and economic resources to educate equity-minded, socially responsible graduates capable of collective problem-solving. When colleges and universities educate for democracy, they not only expand economic opportunities, but also heighten graduates' obligations to improve the quality of life for others through their public actions.

A Crucible Moment: College Learning and Democracy's Future (National Task Force, 2012), released at the White House and the product of multiple stakeholders, laid out an ambitious agenda for higher education to better prepare graduates as constructive civic actors in a diverse, divided, and unequal democracy. Some spaces for deeply informed democratic habits are well represented in institutional policies and practices, student life, the curriculum and pedagogy, and the fertile soil of campus–community partnerships where pressing societal problems can be tackled cooperatively. *A Crucible Moment* revealed, however, that most students' majors were largely a civic-free zone.

A key recommendation from the national report was to attend to this untilled disciplinary land so majors could be sites for educating for a just and equitable democracy. Faculty should consider, the report suggested, "the public purposes of their respective fields, the civic inquiries most urgent to explore, and the best way to infuse civic learning outcomes progressively across the major" (p. 32). Disciplinary learning culminates for many majors in capstone courses, space that beckons for more expansive democratic reinvention and intellectual investment. This chapter introduces overarching conceptual frameworks for these civic-rich capstones and two in-depth institutional case studies to illustrate how public-facing, justice-oriented capstone courses can serve as touchstones for educating for democracy, even as they hone disciplinary skills that serve graduates well in the workplace.

Cultivating Civic Professionals

Our chapter describes how capstone courses in a student's major can be leveraged to promote the civic mission of colleges and universities. As Kevin Kecskes (2015) argued, "An engaged department agenda invites faculty to envision intentional, *collective* action focused more squarely and publicly on the public purposes of the discipline" (p. 62). Capstones offer the opportunity for sustained attention to grappling collaboratively about big ideas and wicked problems. Hoy and Wolfe (2016) added that civic pathways ending with capstone experiences such as those in many Bonner colleges are an essential part of education for engaged citizens. Hoy and Wolfe argued that such robust approaches lead to "collaborative and even collective impact models" with a "deeper focus on systemic solutions" (p. 8).

Civic capstones most effectively meet current crises if they are justice-oriented, making questions of diversity, equity, and agency central to learning and community-based experience. Students can deepen their knowledge about democracy and its gaps, expand their skills in civic practice, develop stronger values that are oxygen for democratic culture, and acquire necessary experience enacting public problem-solving. In short, they become effective civic professionals.

As Figure 10.1 expresses, in addition to conceptual frameworks for capstones that include diversity, equity, and agency, faculty construct such courses suffused by distinctive disciplinary knowledge, methods, and pedagogies. Students' experiences in public-facing capstones also will be collaborative, reflective, and public.

The findings of Civic Prompts in the Major: Designs in Social Responsibility and the Public Good, a multiyear project launched in 2015 and directed by Caryn McTighe Musil, were simultaneously sobering and

Figure 10.1. Diagramming public-facing capstones.

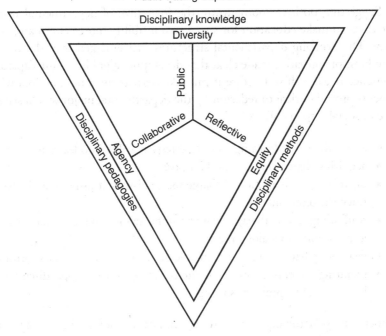

uplifting. Civic Prompts involved departments from 270 institutions that participated in a range of projects from national calls for examples and minigrants to participation in institutes and webinars to the production of online case studies and publications. The sobering discovery was how much work there is to do in the major and how civic initiatives within departments too often depend on a handful of professors rotating through select designated courses as opposed to department-wide commitments that reach every major. Impressively, many were strengthening departmental civic learning goals, adding courses, and inserting more hands-on assignments. And yet only a handful of departments had public-facing, problem-solving capstones.

Compounding issues, many majors largely exclude social issues as relevant to their discipline. While 61% of seniors responding to a National Survey of Student Engagement shared that they "often" or "very often" connected learning to societal problems or issues in their major, the ranges spanned from as high as 78% in social sciences to as low as 38% in physical sciences, math, and computer science (Swol & Musil, 2017). Convincing all disciplines that knowledge for which they are stewards can be linked to social, economic, political, or cultural contexts and issues is essential before public-facing capstone courses can become the norm.

Suggesting positive momentum, the first wave of departmental teams were eager to make education for social responsibility more central and pervasive. The evolving departmental structures that emerged over the 6-year Civic Prompts initiative made clear that developing a public-facing capstone experience needs rich soil before it can take permanent root. The following elements proved critical to redesigning the departmental major with a strong sense of social responsibility:

- embedding civic learning and social responsibility into learning goals
- acquiring shared language and purposes
- organizing the major around large societal issues or using those issues to teach the discipline
- scaffolding civic pathways throughout the major offering distinctive civic learning outcomes along the way
- facilitating hands-on projects in at least one course before the capstone
- requiring students in justice-oriented civic capstones to apply disciplinary lenses to public problem-solving

Deliberately structuring majors to culminate in public-facing capstone experiences is good for teaching disciplinary knowledge, educating for democratic responsibility, and supporting future job prospects. Hart Research Associates (2015) reported that 87% of employers say they would be more likely to consider hiring a candidate who had completed an advanced, comprehensive senior project. Pairing the power of capstones in improving students' job prospects with the power of imbuing such graduates with a civic consciousness can drive both economic prosperity and democratic commitments.

William M. Sullivan (2005) conceptualized such an entwining when he coined the phrase "civic professional" to describe a way to "humanize modern work and improve the equity and quality of contemporary life" (p. 31). Sometimes referred to as "democratic professionalism" (Dzur, 2019) or "citizen professionalism" (Boyte, 2008), this idea explicitly connects professional and civic identities. In their rubric for civic professionalism, Koritz et al. (2016) argued Sullivan's term "attends particularly to the education of civic-minded graduates who understand the civic responsibilities that accompany their decisions and action in the world of work" (p. 7). Public-facing civic capstones serve as strategic locations for the production of future civic professionals able to demonstrate mastery of an area of study and an understanding of how work "demands accountability and responsibility on the part of the professional toward the larger public" (p. 27).

Equity, diversity, and justice need to be integrated even more explicitly as necessary dimensions of a civic professional. Doing so sharpens democratic sensibilities and practices while benefiting the public through the participation of a diverse group of community members. Sylvia Hurtado has long pointed out how environments with diverse people, engagements across differences, and inclusive curriculums are linked to the development of democratic dispositions and capacities. Hurtado et al.'s (2012) research found a correlation between students exposed to an inclusive curriculum and their development of "pluralistic orientation" skills, such as "perspective taking, tolerance of different beliefs, openness to having their views challenged, ability to negotiate controversial issues, and ability to work cooperatively with diverse people" (p. 11). Similarly, a multicampus research study by Patricia Gurin et al. (2011) on intergroup dialogue courses identified an equally positive set of cascading outcomes: "greater increases in their understanding race, gender, and income inequality; their intergroup empathy and motivation to bridge differences; and their commitment to post-college social and political action" (p. 48).

Tania D. Mitchell, a Civic Prompts consultant, also investigated factors that contribute to students' social justice commitments. Mitchell (2008) identified several elements that enhance practicing democratic equity, which should influence the design of civic capstones: providing a social change orientation, projects that work to redistribute power, and opportunities to develop authentic relationships.

Through this process, students begin to develop disciplinary knowledge, but also learn to engage broader publics across multiple differences. Students in civic capstone courses learn to become facilitators, task sharers, and cocreators, as opposed to simply narrow specialists. Albert Dzur (2019) invited us to frame the development of future professionals around the question: "How can professional actors help mobilize rather than immobilize, expand rather than shrink democratic authority?" (p. 3). A student in one of our capstone courses recast the question: "How can we enter a space that has become professionalized and create dialogue with other people (coworkers) about democratizing the space? How do we engage in these conversations as new employees who are new to the working world?"

This process occurs in capstone courses when faculty model equity-minded civic professionalism in teaching and learning. Drawing on our experience developing and implementing civic capstones, we amplify three design principles for educating future leaders in our communities and outline concrete assignments, offering resources that can be used in capstone courses in any discipline.

Case Studies

The following case studies, a global studies capstone at Providence College and a communication and media capstone at Willamette University, were selected as leading models in the Civic Prompts project. In addition to these models at private universities, we recognize that public institutions also have innovative public facing civic capstones models, such as the interdisciplinary, theme-driven seminars in the School of Humanities and Communication at California State University, Monterey Bay. These cases demonstrate a shared commitment to deepening knowledge about our democracy and its limitations, expanding civic skills through practice, strengthening commitments to democratic values, and giving students experience in public problem-solving. To support these democratic aims, the capstones are designed to be public, collaborative, and reflective.

Establishing Civic-Oriented Capstones

Civic capstones offer the opportunity for connecting multiple high-impact practices. But because of the possibility for high reward, it takes extensive planning and buy-in to develop and sustain this focus. These cases also demonstrate the need for feedback loops, which enable the capstone teaching and learning experiences to be revised to stay relevant over time.

In a communication department at Willamette University, civic-oriented capstones emerged from a transformative season followed by years of development and growth. In the context of national calls to action (e.g., *A Crucible Moment*), an external review, and ongoing conversations with students, department faculty redesigned the major program to enact a commitment to civic learning. The department changed its learning objectives, curriculum, structure, and name. Through this process, the Civic Communication and Media Department built a new framework for democratic learning that is deeply rooted in its discipline (Richards, 2017). By design, the new curriculum connects communication education and civic professionalism at every level of the major. Two introductory courses develop understanding of disciplinary history, theory, and methods in relationship to democratic practice. Then, elective courses provide opportunities for students to transform knowledge into action, often through project-based learning, community engagement, and internships.

This scaffolded approach culminates in the capstone, a one-semester course in which every senior completes a signature project on communication in civic life. Initially, these projects took the form of individual research essays. While some students embraced independent research, many advocated to work more closely with each other to address what they saw as critical issues, from climate change to digital disinformation. Responding to students—and civic capacities they developed through the new curriculum—department faculty created a new capstone design to support problem-focused, publicly engaged, collaborative research communities.

The first iteration of this capstone design emerged in 2017, during the first 100 days of the Trump administration. The prior semester, as part of a project-based elective in the major, students led campus events that brought together more than 800 community members to view and discuss the presidential debates between Hillary Rodham Clinton and Donald J. Trump (Richards, 2017). At the conclusion of the course, students wanted to delve into the relationship between digital media and democracy. In response, Cindy Koenig Richards designed a new capstone to support collaborative student research on digital politics, from hashtag activism to presidential campaigning. Assessment of this new capstone emphasized that civic-oriented design can strengthen disciplinary learning and professional skills, and the department determined to continue developing this approach to signature work.

Providence College initiated a new global studies major in 2005 focused on educating the next generation for our global world (Alonso García & Longo, 2013). Like many new interdisciplinary academic programs, the major relied heavily on students selecting from a range of internationally focused courses in a cross-section of disciplines. The program initially offered two separate tracks with unique courses of study—in the humanities or business—with common requirements for all majors to study abroad, become fluent in a foreign language, and write a thesis in a yearlong capstone course. From the beginning, education for global citizenship has been an underlying principle actualized throughout the curriculum, including in the yearlong capstone course.

The capstone has always served as an important point of assessment, where student voice is valued and invited to offer feedback on the major. As such, students in the capstone have been pivotal in making two important changes to the program that help illuminate the power of student voice and how the capstone experience happens in a larger educational ecosystem.

First, given the "cafeteria-style" nature of the entire curriculum—with students in separate tracks, taking very few courses in common—students had very different sets of skills and foundational knowledge when they entered the course as seniors. As a result, the department committed to developing a more developmental curricular experience with a series of courses that connected the intro course to capstone—including a course on globalization and social change, a research methods course, several upper-level electives, a thematic concentration of their choosing, and a one-credit pre–study abroad course. These changes provided students with civic skills to prepare for the capstone experience.

A second shift occurred when a group of students rebelled against the class's single-author thesis requirement. A team of six students in the 2011–2012 capstone course shifted their research project to study the capstone itself and reasoned that the individual research product did not represent the collaborative, interdisciplinary team-based aspects that were hallmarks of the major. As a result, they published a final paper, "Re-Evaluating the Providence College Global Studies Capstone Experience," which helped the department reconceptualize the capstone signature work. The course shifted to a collaborative action research project that includes some initial individualized research (annotated bibliography and literature review) leading to a team-based project partnering with a community-based organization to address a global issue.

Design Principles for Civic Capstones

Our case studies reveal that civic-oriented capstones share aims and design elements, even as they serve different disciplines and institutions. Capstones in a variety of academic contexts can develop civic competencies through three core design principles: public, collaborative, and reflective. In this section, we examine how these design elements support democratic learning and civic agency.

Public

Capstone models at Willamette University and Providence College (a) focus on significant public issues, (b) apply discipline-specific skills to the public issue, and (c) facilitate student dialogue with publics beyond the classroom. In the Civic Communication and Media Department at Willamette University, each capstone focuses on one significant public issue that students engage through research projects of their own design.

Capstone courses in this major focus on different civic issues but share a common objective. All the capstones develop rhetorical agency, "the capacity to act, that is to [communicate] in a way that will be recognized or heeded by others in one's community" (Campbell, 2006, p. 3). Each capstone is conceived to facilitate discourse with communities beyond the classroom, and drawing on their research, students use a variety of media to contribute to public conversations. They produce websites, films, and academic conference papers; broadcast via community radio; and present their work to communication directors, campaign managers, and community organizers.

While Willamette University students focus on a single wicked problem in each capstone, Providence College students work in self-selected teams on the global problem of their choosing. Students spend time sharing their stories and passions, then form into teams of shared interests. The teams conduct literature reviews and stakeholder analyses to develop community partners and culminating project ideas. The course spends time further developing individual and team skills for building reciprocal partnerships, while also exploring issues of power, positionality, and ethical practices for conducting publicly engaged research. Students work in groups on topics such as racial justice, LGBTQ rights, environmental sustainability, immigration, and education. Students then develop publicly engaged products presented to a broader public at the end of the year.

Another aspect of the public-facing dimension of the course at both universities is engagement with alumni. Alumni working at local nonprofits have often been coinstructors in the capstone, and alumni are invited to join the course multiple times each year, as mentors, respondents, and community partners. Alumni share their own vocational stories and career pathways, while offering a real-world perspective on student research projects. Taking advantage of remote learning opportunities, recent capstone courses have organized alumni speakers discussing postgraduate careers, service opportunities, and graduate school experiences, while also supporting opportunities for internships and joint research projects. At both institutions, alumni involvement with capstones became easier to facilitate with remote/hybrid learning technologies adopted during COVID-19.

Collaborative

Justice-oriented civic capstones also share a commitment to collaborative research and learning. For example, civic communication and media capstone courses are designed to foster communities where students engage a complex public problem, together. Through the collaborative work of sharing resources, deliberating actions, and troubleshooting problems, capstone students and faculty develop rhetorical habits of civic friendship (Allen, 2004) and disciplinary knowledge. This pedagogical focus on collaboration makes space for practices essential to civic professionalism, including shared responsibility, openness to having views challenged, the ability to negotiate controversial issues, and the capacity to work cooperatively across differences.

In global studies, the department recognizes that the ability to collaborate is essential for being effective in an interconnected world. Thus, the capstone introduces a set of "habits for civic professionals" that are essential for collaboration, including the ability to cultivate public narratives, listen eloquently, and build reciprocal relationships. Students also are asked to adopt an asset-based approach, analyze stakeholders' interests and power, name and frame problems for public deliberation, and facilitate dialogue as part of the capstone experience. These are developed through a series of assignments and practices throughout the year, including having students share their public narratives and strengths/assets; facilitate various approaches to dialogue and deliberation, including story circles, world cafe, chalk talks, and open space technology; lead workshops and presentations on global issues; and provide critical feedback to peers.

Reflective

Across different disciplinary and institutional contexts, we see reflective practice as a design principle at work in civic-oriented capstones. To support students as they grapple with complex problems that cannot be resolved in one semester, capstones embed reflective practice in class meetings, collaborative work, and culminating assessments. For example, in the capstone on Democracy in the Digital Age, Willamette University students began each class session by discussing what they recently learned, why it matters, and how it will inform next steps. They worked together to do qualitative and computational analyses of more than three million Twitter posts, engaging in reflective thinking as they worked through roadblocks. Incorporating reflective practice throughout a capstone supports civic professionalism, by developing habits of practical wisdom, responsiveness, and persistence. As a pedagogy, reflective practice also supports student agency to create connections between academic knowledge, professional work, and the common good. For example, capstone students write reflections on the relationship between their research and their civic practices, and at the conclusion of the semester they craft résumés that crystallize connections between their signature projects and job opportunities.

In the global studies capstone, students begin the semester by reflecting on their own global studies "cultural autobiographies," offering an opportunity for storytelling and community-building among the majors. Students are often returning from a junior year study away experience which required an intensive community engagement project experience (service-learning course, internship, or action research project), so this activity provides the opportunity to share and reflect on the concentrated intercultural growth fostered through immersion experiences. Further, a final assignment for the capstone course is the same assignment required in each section of GST 101: Introduction to Global Studies—crafting a "philosophy of global citizenship." In capstone, students are asked to revisit—and then rewrite—their current philosophy with a short mission statement and then narrative reflection which asks them to reflect on key courses, readings, and experiences that influenced their updated philosophy. They also reflect on how their own philosophy will guide future choices after graduation. Finally, as a mechanism to curate the diverse experiences in an interdisciplinary major like global studies, students must complete and present their ePortfolio in the capstone, using a Weebly site to implement a "curation of learning" in areas which include civic engagement, along with global awareness, language proficiency, and cultural competency.

Conclusion

Public-facing capstone courses within a major offer democratic spaces where students can work with others to address shared problems. Drawing on the power of disciplinary knowledge, issues, and pedagogies, such courses deepen students' sense of the public purposes of their chosen majors and how to work toward the common good. Thus, the capstone is both a culminating experience and a pivot point.

Ultimately, when students are educated to act publicly, collaboratively, and reflectively through the design of civic capstones, they gain power to hone their skills in the habits of democratic engagement; make questions of diversity, equity, and justice central; and transform knowledge into action. This extends the impact of disciplinary capstones in ways that return to the broader democratic calling of higher education to generate more just, equitable societies where people, the economy, and the planet all flourish.

References

Allen, D. (2004). *Talking to strangers: Anxieties of citizenship since Brown v. Board of Education*. University of Chicago Press.

Alonso García, N., & Longo, N. (2013). Going global: Reframing international service-learning in an interconnected world. *Journal of Higher Education Outreach and Engagement, 17*(2), 31–55.

Boyte, H. (2008). *The citizen solution: How you can make a difference*. Minnesota Historical Society Press.

Campbell, K. C. (2006). Agency: Promiscuous and protean. *Communication and Critical/Cultural Studies, 2*(1), 1–19.

Dzur, A. (2019). *Democracy inside: Participatory innovation in unlikely places*. Oxford University Press.

Gurin, P., Biren (Ratnesh), A. N., & Sorensen, N. (2011). Intergroup dialogue: Education for a broad conception of civic engagement. *Liberal Education, 97*(2), 46–51.

Hart Research Associates. (2015). *Falling short? College learning and career success.* Association of American Colleges and Universities.

Hoy, A., & Wolfe, K. (2016). High-impact learning for self and society: Community-engaged signature work. *Diversity and Democracy, 19*(4), 4–8.

Hurtado, S., Ruiz, A., & Whang, H. (2012). Advancing and assessing civic learning: New result for the diversity learning environments survey. *Diversity and Democracy, 15*(3), 10–12.

Kecskes, K. (2015). Collectivizing our impact: Engaging departments and academic change. *Partnerships: A Journal of Service-Learning and Civic Engagement, 6*(3), 54–72.

Koritz, A., Schadewald, P., & Hubert, H. (2016). *Civic professionalism: A pathway to practical wisdom for the liberal arts* [White paper]. Imagining America: Artists and Scholars in Public Life.

Mitchell, T. D. (2008). Critical service-learning: Engaging the literature to differentiate two models. *Michigan Journal of Community Service Learning, 14*(2), 50–65.

National Task Force on Civic Learning and Democratic Engagement. (2012). *A crucible moment: College learning and democracy's future.* Association of American Colleges and Universities.

Richards, C. K. (2017). A civic-rich framework for liberal education. *Peer Review, 19*(4), 18–21.

Swol, C., & Musil, C. M. (2017). Civic learning in the major by the numbers. *Peer Review, 19*(4), 7.

Sullivan, W. M. (2005). *Work and integrity: The crisis and promise of professionalism.* Jossey-Bass.

PART 3

**Supporting Capstone
Faculty and Staff**

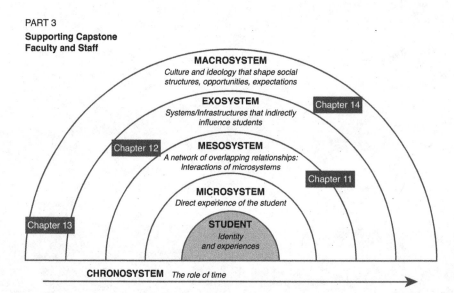

PART THREE

SUPPORTING CAPSTONE FACULTY AND STAFF

Jessie L. Moore, Caroline J. Ketcham, and Anthony G. Weaver

This section explores how institutions can support faculty in designing, implementing, and assessing high-quality capstone experiences. The section's initial chapter, "Understanding Faculty Needs in Capstone Experiences," explores meso- and exosystem components that shape faculty needs when teaching capstones. Drawing from faculty interviews, the authors illustrate faculty perceptions of teaching capstones and offer strategies for reflecting on and discussing issues like accounting for the labor of capstones and aligning expectations for capstones within departments. The chapter's heuristics help faculty, faculty developers, and administrators engage in meaningful conversations about capstones throughout the process of planning, implementing, and assessing them.

The next two chapters then share specific examples of educational advancement initiatives addressing faculty needs when teaching capstones. "The Development of Capstone Assignments Using a Faculty Community of Practice Model" examines how an exosystem-level faculty development initiative enhanced capstone experiences at a community college. While demonstrating how community colleges can be rich sites for capstones, the faculty development process the authors describe could—and should—be implemented across institution types.

"Peer Reviewing to Support Quality Assurance of Capstone Experiences: A View From Australia" takes a wider view, sharing an example of institutions tapping into macrosystem accreditation practices to facilitate a multi-institution peer review of capstone outcomes with the goal of informing future instruction in the participating program's capstone experiences. The authors offer a terrific example of how macrosystem assessment and accreditation could serve as a springboard for capstone design—and redesign. In addition, the process they describe serves as a great model for multi-institutional collaboration in support of academic excellence within state higher education systems, postsecondary athletic associations, or other existing groupings of colleges and universities.

Finally, "Positionality and Identity in Capstones: Renegotiating the Self Through Teaching and Learning" challenges readers to consider how macrosystem cultures and ideologies shape faculty experiences teaching capstones—and in turn, students' experiences; the authors make concrete recommendations for addressing inequities perpetuated by the status quo, and in supplemental materials on the book's website, they share tools for reflection and professional development.

Collectively these chapters illustrate how faculty and administrators can work across a university's socioecological systems to create equitable, high-quality capstones for students. The section's contributors highlight how change at any individual level can positively impact the design and implementation of culminating experiences, but coordination across levels better prepares faculty—both those teaching the capstone and those teaching prerequisite classes—to foster the powerful learning outcomes described in the Introduction and in Part One.

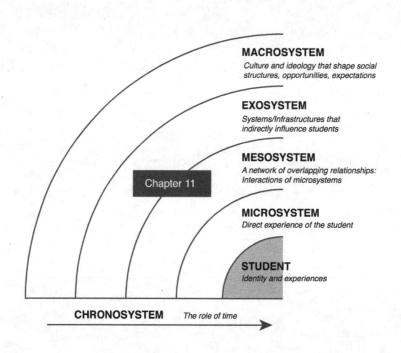

UNDERSTANDING FACULTY NEEDS IN CAPSTONE EXPERIENCES

Morgan Gresham, Caroline Boswell, Olivia S. Anderson,
Matthew J. Laye, and Dawn Smith-Sherwood

How can universities better support faculty who teach capstone experiences (CEs)? We know that CEs have the potential to be meaningful learning experiences for students when capstones are thoughtfully designed and implemented by faculty. Research from our mixed-methods study suggests CE faculty desire more engagement from their colleagues and the institution to ensure the quality of their CE. To illustrate faculty perceptions of teaching CEs, we introduce three faculty composites drawn from our survey and interviews—Megan, Sarah, and Sam—although pseudonyms, their words come from our interviews. As these composites show, there are missed opportunities for conversations around CEs and a perceived lack of conversation that influences how supported faculty feel in teaching them. Additionally, since faculty tend to value these conversations, strategic conversations may shift their perceptions within their specific institutional contexts.

Megan, who frequently teaches her major's capstone, is nearing tenure as a faculty member in the arts. Her specialty is a practical, hands-on discipline, and she is known in her department as a thoughtful, engaged mentor who has encouraged many students into courses in the major. While Megan is excited to work so closely with a diverse group of majors in the capstone course, she's also concerned that her workload in the capstone is increasingly unsustainable. Compared to her senior colleagues, she has more students in her capstone courses, and they require significant guidance as they work to produce both full bodies of work and look toward life after graduation. Conflicted about teaching CEs, Megan is concerned about how she will avoid burnout as she looks to meeting the tenure requirements.

Sarah has been teaching at her institution for 20 years in a relatively small, collegial department that has worked together recently to revise the curriculum for two strands of the major. In the process of that revision, Sarah and her colleagues instituted a required capstone course, which she and two other colleagues take turns teaching. Sarah enjoys teaching the course, and her students love her and the experiences they have taking the course with her. Yet Sarah finds that "the department could be more on board with the course, knowing what's going on and integrating elements of that course [the capstone] into other courses in the majors."

Sam is currently serving as department chair, a position from which they frequently field concerns from students and faculty about the labor required for CEs. Sam also hears from members of the community and alumni how well the capstone prepares students for the workforce. Sam recognizes that they must balance the needs of the students, who are required to have CEs, with the workload and curricular needs of the department and the faculty within.

As part of a multicampus research study, we surveyed 138 faculty teaching CEs and completed 25 follow-up interviews to determine the influences, pressures, and supports faculty face. Drawing from these responses, we created faculty composites of an untenured faculty member, a senior colleague, and a department chair, each of whom has components intertwined from the survey and interviews. Although we did not set out to study faculty conversations per se, our research supports department colleagues as a means of support for the work they do (Roxå & Mårtensson, 2009). In this chapter we explore, with Megan, Sarah, and Sam, some of the important questions they might ask as they make decisions about their CEs. Faculty members' positionality, including gender, plays a role in how they experience tensions around CE development and implementation, and the identities of our faculty composites draw on the positionalities of our respondents.

Specifically, we use heuristics developed from analyzing the results of our survey and interviews; in addition to the heuristics embedded in each story, we share questions for reflection on the book's website. These questions help our faculty identify resources most helpful for them at specific times during the development, implementation, and evaluation of their CEs. Recognizing the importance of institutional context is key to the sustainable success of CEs; our goal here is to help readers identify the multiple roles within and adjacent to their institutions (faculty members, administrators, educational developers, students, alumni, community partners, and governing bodies) and negotiate the conversations that will lead to obtaining the recognition and support needed to successfully maintain CEs.

Megan's Story: "I Think We Need to Do a Better Job of Advocating for the Amount of Diffuse Labor That We Do"

Megan is advancing along the tenure track, her CEs are popular with students, and she enjoys teaching CEs. However, Megan has concerns about her workload and the support she receives from her colleagues for her CEs:

> Sometimes students don't anticipate the workload associated with the course. A lot of people who never teach the course make public claims about what the course should entail.
>
> Students both love and hate integrating; I used community-based pedagogy, which is always challenging, as the real work and academia don't match.

The positive student feedback motivates Megan to do the hard work that CEs require. However, it would be beneficial for Megan to ask herself:

- How much extra time is she willing to continue to devote to teaching CE?
- Is she willing to keep doing this work if it remains uncompensated or unrecognized by the institution?

Similarly, Megan has questions about how her work teaching CE may be reflected in her tenure application: Does publishing on the scholarship of teaching and learning count toward her tenure application?

Megan should ask specific questions about funding, release time, tenure, and promotion criteria, and she should discuss her concerns with a senior colleague mentor. Since many faculty members like Megan may be reluctant to or unsure of how to begin conversations with colleagues or chairs about this aspect of the CE, involving centers for teaching and learning (CTLs) or other academic developers may prove fruitful for initiating and extending these conversations.

Sarah's Story: "I Wish We Even Just Talked About Them More"

Sarah's experience demonstrates a common thread in our research, particularly in the interviews, in which faculty attempted to negotiate for themselves a common definition of the CE in their program or department. In our

composite, Sarah played an integral part in the redevelopment of requirements for the major and the inclusion of the capstone course. Yet she finds
that her department is divided into those who teach the CE and those who
do not:

> I would like my colleagues to be more observant of what happens. And I
> shared a little bit at the end of the semester what we did, but they haven't
> seemed very interested so far. But I hope to keep sharing what we're doing
> and to get their input on it as well.
>
> What happens is that the people who actually teach it, we talk among
> ourselves. . . . People who don't teach those courses are pretty clueless
> about what happens in there. . . . I definitely feel the pressure of some of
> my colleagues not fully knowing what is needed to move students to that
> capstone experience.
>
> I think the other support that I feel is from my colleagues who teach
> them and who have come on to teach them in subsequent years because
> we do recognize the challenges that happen, and we seek each other out
> informally.

From these responses, we see an expressed desire for institutional conversations about the capstone. As we discuss in the following, there are resources
to help faculty implement CEs. However, despite pockets of support, faculty often must initiate these continuing conversations, and given the constraints on their time, although important, these conversations are typically
limited and infrequent. While it may be difficult for Sarah to encourage her
colleagues to continue to have these conversations after the curriculum has
been changed and implemented, she can engage colleagues in conversations
around the following questions that can yield fruitful conversations about
"What is our capstone?" in this departmental context:

- What types of projects do we want our students to do as a part of the CE?
- How can we make sure that our students are prepared to complete the
  work required by the CE?
- What do we want our graduates to be able to do with their projects and
  this degree upon graduation?

As a department, asking questions such as "Where does the CE fit in the
rest of curriculum?," "Who should teach it?," and "How can we make
sure that we are regularly discussing the CE?" fosters community awareness around it (Pifer et al., 2015; Thomson, 2015; Thomson & Trigwell,
2018). Since the chair and departmental colleagues who have taught CE
are the most relied-upon resources used by faculty teaching CE (Laye et al.,
2020), these departmental conversations may lessen the isolation faculty

members expressed when teaching CE while providing a sense of recognition by the department of the labor associated with teaching CE.

Sam's Story: "[D]o I Want to Push at My Colleagues Now That I'm Chair . . . to Do Particular Things in Their Capstone?"

Sam has been a department chair for several years. Prior to becoming chair, Sam taught CE. Again, Sam is a composite, and we drew from both direct statements and implied descriptions from our interviewees. As department chair, Sam oversees the full breadth of the curriculum, and they can help guide conversations to answer questions like where the capstone fits in the curriculum.

> I [am] chair of my department. I think teaching the capstone in some ways helped prepare me to have that kind of view of our curriculum, that I don't know that I would've had otherwise. We have . . . different emphases and even though they overlap, and they all end up in this capstone, I had different levels of knowledge for them.
>
> In introducing [the requirement] to us, they basically said that we as a program already do what would be considered a capstone experience and that production work that students do would be appropriate for fulfilling the capstone and therefore not create additional work. . . . We agreed that we wanted all capstone student proposals to go through the full executive committee.
>
> I was chair. I took 3 years off . . . now I'm chair again. I kept saying for years now, "I want to create some paperwork, a form that students can fill out so that we are tracking who is doing the capstone, so everybody knows what they're doing, and then also some guidelines for students." Because I was answering the same questions over and over. "What can I do for this?" We've written our capstone course in [X] very generally to include really anything. It can be a research project, a travel course, an internship, work on a production. But still, students have questions.

Given Sam's role and their expertise, they walk a difficult boundary between what they would do individually teaching the CE and what the department needs the CE to do. In this leadership role, Sam can guide departmental conversations about the place and the value of the CE.

> And that has been a barrier within my own program, just sharing with people because I have noticed that they don't respond well. And part of it is I'm the chair right now. And so, I have to be thoughtful about how sharing my own experience can come off as, "this is how I think we should do it in our major, do this."

> I think what ended up happening is when we redesigned the program, well, I started to question. . . . I'm not going to lie. It was me. I questioned a lot of stuff. I began to question . . . the quality of work. . . . Because, again, I kept hearing things from external faculty. We have adjuncts here that kept saying that the work being produced was not up to par with other schools, the education they were getting in those two classes was not up to par with other schools, and I agreed.

Sam can steer departmental conversations to discuss the role of academic and design freedom within the confines of meeting the expected curricular goals for the program. Specifically, Sam can address:

- What are the departmental guidelines for the CE?
- What are the student learning outcomes for the CE?
- Are there required components like a test or a paper or a performance?

Academic program chairs face challenges navigating the microcultures of their department and their own position vis-à-vis senior faculty, and academic developers can guide them through this process. As chair, Sam can also reach out to other stakeholders like alumni, students, and academic developers. Chairs can partner with academic developers as fellow developers and intermediaries between program faculty, the department, and larger institutional stakeholders, initiating conversations across these groups. For example, departmental action teams (DAT) work in concert with faculty learning communities to implement institutional change: "DATs are facilitated groups; dedicated facilitators from outside the DAT's department bring expertise in educational research and institutional change, help coordinate logistics, and aim to mitigate the impact of existing departmental power structures within the DAT" (Reinholz et al., 2017, p. 10). Additionally, understanding that capstones should be integrated into a broader consideration of program curriculum, academic developers can facilitate conversations between capstone faculty and program chairs when the instructor or the developer perceives lack of cohesion between CE and programmatic outcomes.

Faculty tasked with implementing the CE often discover that they do not receive recognition for the workload, such as release time, articulated relationship to tenure and promotion, and support and recognition needed for implementation. Scholars have identified 11 high-impact practices (HIPs)—research-based strategies that promote student engagement and deep learning (Kuh, 2008; Kuh et al., 2013). Halonen and Dunn's (2018) aside about faculty frustration with HIPs—that "when these efforts are successful, praise tends to go to the high-impact practice itself" (para. 1) and not the faculty member doing the work—is beginning to be addressed by resources for faculty and administration looking to successfully implement CEs. Chairs like Sam—who have taught CE—are well positioned to guide conversations around faculty workload and the time tax often associated with CE. Sam could share prior courses, assignments, and assessments, and help provide consistent peer review and emotional support during the design, delivery, and assessment stages of the CE.

Listening Is Important: Lessons Learned From Conversations About Faculty Experiences

Before programs or instructors design CEs, our research suggests that all CE stakeholders should engage in a series of conversations about what equitable, high-quality CEs look like within their institutional and programmatic contexts. Given the increasing implementation of CEs, it is important that institutions involve faculty, students, and administrators in the process of their building. Research shows that one of the frequent stumbling blocks to CE success is the lack of institutional support across units of the university. From our survey of 138 CE faculty instructors, less than half of the respondents found the availability of resources "good" or "excellent," with 14% of those surveyed indicating that no resources were available to them. Moreover, the types of resources for which faculty express a desire—a basic agreed-upon definition of what a CE is, colleague-to-colleague professional development, programmatic engagement with design of CE, and examples of CE practices and products—are difficult to locate in existing resource sites. Given that a mere 29% of faculty members feel trained for their faculty roles by their graduate school experience (Hurtado et al., 2012), it is vital that faculty members preparing to develop and teach CEs have access to the resources they need to help them be successful (Lee & Loton, 2019). In the following, we discuss the value of a series of questions that serve as a heuristic for those who wish to promote more structural implementations of CE that are inclusive of the multifaceted faculty needs around HIPs. We focus particularly on questions that may foster conversations across departments and institutions often needed to ensure that structures are in place for the success of individual faculty members who set out to design high-quality CEs.

Questions to Consider: Heuristics for Better Capstones

Citing the growing body of literature that supports how informal conversation can improve faculty teaching, Thomson and Trigwell (2018) described five purposes for midcareer faculty to engage in informal conversations, one of which is improving teaching: "Professional learning is a continuing process, and this study shows that some experienced teachers require and seek support from colleagues to learn more about teaching" (p. 1544). Thomson and Trigwell (2018) examined specifically the role of "mid-career academics' informal, face-to-face, 'corridor,' or 'everyday' conversations in enabling these staff to learn about teaching from colleagues" (p. 1544). Given the influence that these conversations can have, and that many CE faculty members express a desire to have them, we want to provide here some heuristic questions that CE faculty can use to drive those conversations. We suggest that academic developers support the capstone through both formal or semiformal programs that provide participants with resources and structures to have conversations about the role of capstones within curricula and across the institution.

Drawing on Roxå and Mårtensson's (2009) claims about faculty networks—that "university teachers rely on a limited number of individuals to test ideas or solve problems related to teaching and learning" (p. 556)— our research indicates that conversations with colleagues are one of the most valued and engaged resources that support work surrounding capstones. The influence of context on the success of such informal conversations between colleagues within academic units suggests academic developers could use formal development programs—such as interdisciplinary communities of practice—to create opportunities to engage in informal conversations with capstone instructors to provide contextualized guidance for faculty navigating the challenge of engaging colleagues or their program chair in a conversation about the capstone and its place within the curriculum. In an article that our research team has under preparation, we describe significant conversations academic developers may drive as potential resources and support. In this chapter, we have modeled using a heuristic framework to initiate conversations about CEs. Our full list of questions to ask is included in the supplemental resources on the book's website (https://www.centerforengagedlearning.org/ books/cultivating-capstones/).

We recommend that faculty who are tasked with building or implementing a CE, like Megan in our story, review these questions first individually and then with her chair. We suggest chairs like Sam engage faculty about these questions in department meetings and during program assessment. Sarah, as a departmental CE leader, should encourage these conversations with her colleagues, and Sam should use these questions in conversations with the senior administration early in discussions of tenure and promotion. We encourage faculty to share these questions with their colleagues in CTLs as they participate in interdisciplinary faculty learning communities to help develop institutional definitions of CE workload and support.

Our research also indicates that it would be valuable for academic developers and those charged with overseeing CE implementation to study the degree to which preexisting resources supporting capstone design and assessment may also serve as heuristics that provoke the conversations faculty need. For example, does Kezar and Holcombe's (2017) "Tool for Administrators," which provides administrators a series of questions related to the institutionalization of HIPs (Kuh, 2008) such as CE, lend itself to institution-wide conversations about the design and structures of CEs? Quality assurance frameworks such as Hammer et al.'s (2018) "Developing a Generic Review Framework to Assure Capstone Quality" and the Indiana University–Purdue University at Indianapolis (IUPUI) RISE initiative capstone taxonomy could also serve as heuristics to provoke necessary institutional or program conversations about the goals and outcomes of the capstone (Pierce et al., 2019). Freeman et al. (2020) shared their experience designing and implementing the taxonomy and conclude that it offers institutions one possible "tool" to promote "reflection and enhancement for the benefit of faculty, students, and institutions" (p. 13). While we can't know how our composites—Megan, Sarah, and Sam—might respond to CE frameworks such as these, what our research does suggest is that such heuristic devices are essential to ensure the various CE stakeholders engage each other in dialogue before asking faculty to design and offer CEs.

References

Freeman, T. M., Pierce, D., & Zoeller, A. N. (2020). Using the IUPUI Capstone taxonomy to design high-impact-practice capstone experiences for graduating students. *Assessment Update, 32*(4), 6–13. https://doi.org/10.1002/au.30220

Halonen, J. S., & Dunn, D. S. (2018, November 27). Does "high-impact" teaching cause high-impact fatigue? *The Chronicle of Higher Education.* https://www.chronicle.com/article/does-high-impact-teaching-cause-high-impact-fatigue/?bc_nonce=11pr2nkryp9wj51g249dei&cid=reg_wall_signup

Hammer, S., Abawi, L., Gibbings, P., Jones, H., Redmond, P., & Shams, S. (2018). Developing a generic review framework to assure capstone quality. *Higher Education Research & Development, 37*(4), 730–743. https://doi.org/10.1080/07294360.2018.1453787

Hurtado, S., Eagan, K., Pryor, J. H., Whang, H., & Tran, S. (2012). *Undergraduate teaching faculty: The 2010–2011 HERI faculty survey.* Higher Education Research Institute: University of California, Los Angeles. https://www.heri.ucla.edu/monographs/HERI-FAC2011-Monograph-Expanded.pdf

Kezar, A., & Holcombe, E. (2017, March 3). *Support for high-impact practices: A new tool for administrators.* Association of American Colleges and Universities. https://www.aacu.org/liberaleducation/2017/winter/kezar_holcombe

Kuh, G. D. (2008). *High-impact educational practices: What they are, who has access to them, and why they matter.* Association of American Colleges and Universities.

Kuh, G. D., O'Donnell, K., Reed, S. D., Association of American Colleges and Universities, & Liberal Education and America's Promise (Program). (2013). *Ensuring quality and taking high-impact practices to scale.* AAC&U.

Laye, M. J., Boswell, C., Gresham, M., Smith-Sherwood, D., & Anderson, O. S. (2020) Multi-institutional survey of faculty experiences teaching capstones. *College Teaching, 68*(4), 201–213. https://doi.org/10.1080/87567555.2020.1786663

Lee, N., & Loton, D. (2019). Capstone purposes across disciplines. *Studies in Higher Education, 44*(1), 134–150. https://doi.org/10.1080/03075079.2017.1347155

Pierce, D., Zoeller, A., Wood, Z., Wendeln, K., Bishop, C., Engels, E., Powell, A., Poulsen, J., Brehl, N., & Nickolson, D. (2019). *Capstones: IUPUI high-impact practice taxonomy.* Indiana University–Purdue University Indianapolis. https://scholarworks.iupui.edu/handle/1805/21558

Pifer, M. J., Baker, V. L., & Lunsford, L. G. (2015). Academic departments as networks of informal learning: Faculty development at liberal arts colleges. *International Journal for Academic Development, 20*(2), 178–192. https://doi.org/10.1080/1360144X.2015.1028065

Reinholz, D. L., Corbo, J. C., Dancy, M. H., & Finkelstein, N. (2017). Departmental action teams: Supporting faculty learning through departmental change. *Learning Communities Journal, 9*(1). https://par.nsf.gov/servlets/purl/10181422

Roxå, T., & Mårtensson, K. (2009). Significant conversations and significant networks—Exploring the backstage of the teaching arena. *Studies in Higher Education, 34*(5), 547–559. https://doi.org/10.1080/03075070802597200

Thomson, K. (2015). Informal conversations about teaching and their relationship to a formal development program: Learning opportunities for novice and mid-career academics. *International Journal for Academic Development, 20*(2), 137–149. https://doi.org/10.1080/1360144X.2015.1028066

Thomson, K. E., & Trigwell, K. R. (2018). The role of informal conversations in developing university teaching? *Studies in Higher Education, 43*(9), 1536–1547. https://doi.org/10.1080/03075079.2016.1265498

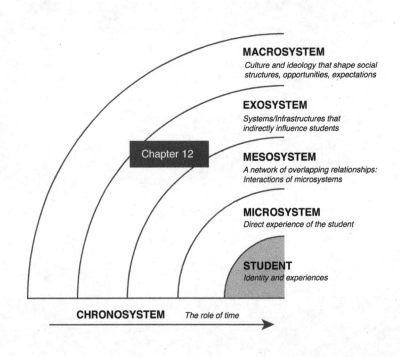

MACROSYSTEM
Culture and ideology that shape social structures, opportunities, expectations

EXOSYSTEM
Systems/Infrastructures that indirectly influence students

Chapter 12

MESOSYSTEM
A network of overlapping relationships: Interactions of microsystems

MICROSYSTEM
Direct experience of the student

STUDENT
Identity and experiences

CHRONOSYSTEM   *The role of time*

THE DEVELOPMENT OF CAPSTONE ASSIGNMENTS USING A FACULTY COMMUNITY OF PRACTICE MODEL

Silvia Reyes, Nelson Nunez Rodriguez, and Sarah Brennan

Our story begins with the birth of a capstone course, which led to the expansion of capstone learning at our institution. This chapter explores the shift of traditional definitions of capstone learning gleaned from capstone courses offered at the master's and bachelor's degree levels to reflect the different ways in which capstone experiences can be enacted in the classroom. We further discuss the implementation of a semester-long faculty professional development seminar as a coherent structure to engage faculty in an interdisciplinary and collegial environment for sharing, critiquing, and reflecting on pedagogical plans collectively and individually. In particular, we show how reassigned time in the form of release time provided faculty from dissimilar pedagogical preparation backgrounds and different levels of expertise the opportunity to come together to share resources for learning and building a community of practice. We also show how the transformation of a liberal arts curriculum now requires students to complete a capstone course, and how the faculty professional development seminar impacted a wide range of other academic degree programs by helping faculty infuse higher order skills and synthesized content into the curriculum. Lastly, we identify challenges related to the capstone initiative and offer a framework for the continued expansion of capstone learning into courses across the disciplines. This faculty community of practice also represents a model for institutions seeking to implement capstone experiences that document student accomplishment of academic program learning outcomes.

Defining Capstone in a Community College Setting

Hostos Community College, an urban community college located in Bronx, New York, is the smallest member institution of the City University of New York. In 2014, the college received a Title V grant focused on developing initiatives to promote student academic success. The funding allowed for the creation of student peer-tutoring opportunities, fostered undergraduate research, and developed a faculty community of practice for designing capstone assignments. Prior to the grant, capstone learning was limited to a course in the liberal arts program; it is now a requirement for liberal arts degree–seeking students.

The implementation of the faculty seminar expanded capstone learning experiences for upper-level students across all degrees. As a result, the majority of Hostos students can now access capstone learning before they graduate. The faculty seminar helped to integrate capstone learning into 26 courses, which represent the majority of degree programs at the college. To make this a reality, the college had to address two issues: (a) defining capstone learning for associate degree programs, and (b) creating a safe, collegial, and interdisciplinary space where faculty could design, plan, and implement capstone assignments.

The term *capstone* is commonly used to describe culminating experiences for students who are nearing completion of bachelor's or master's degrees. This community college initiative adopted the following scope and definition of *capstone learning*: Capstone learning would be designed for students in 200-level courses and serve as an opportunity for students to integrate learned knowledge and skills and use abstract thinking to propose solutions to real-world issues, problems, or scenarios. This skill set had already been established at the college as part of the general education core competencies that students should develop or master by the time they graduate with an associate degree.

Planning and Implementation

In 2015, the authors crafted a faculty professional development seminar to expand the use of capstone assignments as a high-impact teaching practice. To prepare for the seminar, faculty completed a brief survey that included a short set of questions addressing instruction, student learning, and assessment to gauge faculty perception of capstone learning. Survey results suggested the need to develop a semester-long seminar, which would be offered to small groups of faculty members over a 5-year period. The objective for the seminar would be to provide a safe and collegial space for brainstorming, discussing, and designing capstone assignments that reflect an integrative approach to learning and employ active-learning teaching pedagogies. The seminar design also aimed to establish a framework that emphasized a sense of community whereby faculty shared their experiences, received feedback from each other, determined assessment tools and grading rubrics, and decided how to incorporate experiential learning activities into an existing course to improve students' learning experiences.

The seminar consisted of biweekly meetings that lasted 90 minutes. The initial faculty cohort included seven faculty representing different disciplines and degree programs. Each seminar meeting was organized around a topic of discussion that was clearly delineated in a syllabus, which had emerged, in part, from the work that began in 2014 of a group of faculty members who designed the college's first capstone course for liberal arts majors. As part of the agenda for each seminar session, participants were allocated 10 minutes to present their ideas about the topic being discussed that week. The seminar allowed participants to redesign course materials, including a new capstone assignment, in a course. Seven cohorts in total participated between 2015 and 2019. Figure 12.1 represents the seminar framework.

Professional Development Conceptual Framework

The implementation of new instructional practices requires time, incentives, and support (Harden & Crosby, 2000; Silverthorn et al., 2006). The Hostos seminar used Silverthorn's faculty-development model, which involves

Figure 12.1. The semester-long biweekly framework engaged faculty in a several-step process.

Seminars	Jan/Feb	Feb/Mar	Mar/Apr	Apr/May
Clarifying Expectations				
Defining Capstone				
Understanding Online Platform				
Identifying Learning Outcomes				
Developing Assignments				
Modifying Course Content				
Discussion With Seminar Participants				
Creating Assessment Tools				
Peer-Review Process				
Final Product				

creating opportunities for faculty to (a) regularly meet to discuss ideas and answer questions, (b) create a community for interaction with colleagues where everyone is treated with respect and trust, and (c) receive ongoing coaching and feedback from colleagues (Silverthorn et al., 2006). Along with this, the webinar Designing and Teaching a High-Impact Capstone Course (Jacoby, 2012) was key in constructing the capstone-related content and cementing the seminar objective to create capstone assignments within existing courses. The webinar not only helped identify essential components that defined a capstone project and how to create a capstone course or assignment but also provided effective suggestions for facilitating course redesign. The biweekly seminar sessions covered topics including (a) identifying measurable student learning objectives, (b) developing assignment guidelines and modifying other course content, (c) embedding opportunities for critical reflection, and (d) identifying assessment measures or tools. Overall, the seminar allowed participants to redesign course materials, with consideration for the new capstone assignment. All activities took place in a collegial peer network, rich with opportunities to give and receive constructive feedback and support during the semester-long seminar.

Faculty Support

Although short-term participation in professional development is a common practice at Hostos, introducing capstone assignments as a new pedagogical approach required a longer period of commitment. In light of this, it became clear that requiring faculty to make a long-term commitment could be a barrier to successful implementation of the seminar. Evidence shows that carving out time to reflect upon teaching and a lack of incentives are major obstacles to faculty pedagogical change (Brownell & Tanner, 2012; Henderson et al., 2011). The grant provided funding for faculty to spend a minimum of 3 hours per week on the development of a capstone assignment by offering reassigned time, equivalent to a 3-hour course release; thus, faculty had "dedicated time" to look critically at their course content and craft a thoughtful capstone assignment (Harden & Crosby, 2000). The reassigned time allowed faculty to form a sustained community of practice that met frequently in person to support each other in the process of making instructional changes to their courses. Offering reassigned time also attracted faculty who otherwise would not have been able to commit the time needed to participate.

The faculty support structure involved expanding the expertise of faculty by providing opportunities for making meaningful connections and sharing ideas in a small-group setting. Based on Silverthorn's suggestions, faculty convened regularly to engage in collaborative learning over several months (Wenger-Trayner & Wenger-Trayner, 2015); they engaged in in-depth discussions, shared expertise, and reflected on their teaching practices (Silverthorn et al., 2006). All of these imparted a sense of purpose and collaboration, and enabled faculty to learn with and from each other. This process also served as a tool for faculty to ask questions and share additional information as they attempted to incorporate learned strategies into their courses. A key aspect of the seminar was to expand access and understanding of capstone learning that did not require changes in course content.

As faculty worked toward revising their courses and developing more student-centered integrated learning practices, they brainstormed ideas for class activities and discussed assignment models and ways to evaluate them, while making minor adjustments to their curriculum. Additionally, faculty had the opportunity to adopt these new practices as a shared academic goal rather than an individual goal and to broaden their knowledge following the principles of integrative learning (Klein, 2005)—as a pedagogy that promotes active learning in which members of the community come together to talk, to learn, to question, and to offer support and feedback (Silverthorn et al., 2006). The seminar structure, initially intended as a working framework, became an outcome itself as it informed how faculty, with dissimilar pedagogical backgrounds, working together in a safe space, can lead to the adaptation of instructional practices that are significant in improving student learning.

Crafting the Assignment in 200-Level Courses

The faculty invited to participate in the seminar represented a wide range of disciplines. All were full-time faculty who had previously taught 200-level courses and held administrative positions at this college and in other institutions. Their experience included implementing assessment tools to document learning outcomes in courses; creating writing-intensive courses, honors courses, and service-learning courses; and engaging students in undergraduate research. Overall, this faculty community capitalized on a myriad of pedagogical expertise and nurtured a collaborative spirit among each cohort's participants. Indeed, as the seminar progressed over time, former seminar participants were invited to share their expertise in different pedagogical areas such as crafting meaningful reflection guidelines and developing assignment guidelines. The seminar brought together a total of 35 faculty across the years, some of whom, in addition to designing a capstone assignment, also oversaw the revision of the previously created capstone course or participated in the creation of a new capstone course.

Measurable Learning Outcomes

The development of learning outcomes was an essential component of the capstone assignment. Furthermore, crafted assignments and learning outcomes needed to match outcomes established by the course. To help faculty determine student learning outcomes for the assignment, authors drew from the institution's general education competencies, which are considered essential skills in undergraduate education. These competencies highlight four extensive categories: (a) skills, (b) subject-area knowledge, (c) synthesis and application, and (d) global citizenship. While each faculty member identified course learning outcomes, they chose additional common outcomes that would capture capstone learning.

These common outcomes were broad enough to be applicable across degree programs and provided sufficient opportunities for students to learn and develop communication skills, self-directed learning, and information synthesis. These outcomes helped determine the type of assignment that needed to be developed to achieve the desired objectives for the course. For example, a General Chemistry course redesigned in this project included the following learning outcomes for the capstone assignment: to enhance student ability to evaluate, reflect on, and self-assess their own work; to be able to apply learned skills in a new context; and to be able to create new experimental designs based on produced data. These learning outcomes were intended to develop student skills in this chemistry course that also included outcomes normally related to chemistry knowledge, problem-solving, and lab equipment manipulation.

Assignment Guidelines and Making Connections

Faculty established the level of complexity for each capstone assignment based on their expertise and discipline. The assignment needed to be feasible, viable, and consistent with already determined capstone outcomes. In particular, assignments were to help students draw on prior knowledge while integrating new information. This would ensure that students had the opportunity to apply important skills gained in previous courses and connect various disciplinary topics and experiences. The expectations for student learning were delineated in a written description of the assignment. Instructions and time frames for assignment completion were included in the syllabus. The syllabus also included expected outcomes for each deliverable as part of the larger capstone assignment and provided faculty with the opportunity of incorporating feedback for improvement on the final student work. By the end of the project, students would have used multiple skill sets and knowledge gained in previous courses. Typical assignments that were created included term papers, presentations, research projects, case studies, and both independent and group work. Faculty designed rubrics to help students understand guidelines for their assignments and to provide consistency in evaluating student work.

Embedding Opportunities for Critical Reflection

A critical component of capstone learning is metacognitive reflection exercises. One of the common essential learning outcomes selected for the capstone assignments required students to organize, analyze, evaluate, and treat information critically in order to use and present it in a cohesive and logical fashion, which describes the role that these skills have in helping students develop critical thinking skills (Lee & Ash, 2010). Providing feedback and designing reflective writing assignments for critical reflection were two methods faculty used to help students develop the individual thinking that goes beyond problem-solving and helps students make meaning of their experiences in capstone learning.

Identifying Assessment Measures

A combination of formative and summative assessment measures was selected by most faculty to assess student learning over time. Both types of assessment provided faculty with a wide range of options to document student progress (Maki, 2004). The use of rubrics to outline expectations for student performance and criteria for successful project completion also helped faculty provide clarity and consistency in the grading process. Faculty used student assessments and rubrics as sources of information to determine what worked well and what did not work well in order to modify the curriculum and to improve their teaching practices.

Outcomes

Faculty developed major projects for students to complete that integrated all of the seminar components. The following assignment from one course shows how students were able to demonstrate accumulated content knowledge and skills by the end of the course.

Embedding Technical Writing Skills in Science Disciplines

The embedding of technical writing skills in science courses such as biology, physics, and science capstone courses highlights the importance of introducing students to research paradigms. The General Chemistry course is a requirement for science and engineering majors and provides students with the opportunity to engage in inquiry and analysis of lab experimental data. Thus, one of the course outcomes is to develop student ability to organize scientific information and communicate it effectively using appropriate terminology graphing tools. Originally designed as a writing-intensive course, one of the major components of the General Chemistry course is writing and revising lab reports. Creating a capstone assignment as part of the course created an opportunity for students to enhance their technical writing skills and lab report revision process. The capstone assignment included guidelines for incorporating critical reflection that would allow students to (a) evaluate difficult areas of the assignment and the challenges and advantages of teamwork, (b) realize how they solve lab techniques and problems, and (c) understand the advantages of using appropriate tables and graphs to document lab-obtained results.

This 12-lab sequence course scheduled a different lab procedure every week. Presenting a different lab procedure each week offered students the opportunity to organize the content, design a scientific project, evaluate results, and ultimately consolidate developed skills and knowledge. The capstone required students to integrate content and skills from three different labs. The assignment also included a written reflection that allowed students to think about how they navigated the whole lab experience sequence.

The capstone experience was assessed using a final case scenario that required the integration of all previously developed knowledge and skills. This also helped faculty to document student academic progress over a 12-lab sequence rather than by a single lab practice. Keeping track of student progress after taking a General Chemistry I course provided information regarding their preparation for future chemistry courses. Indeed, a capstone assignment for General Chemistry II was subsequently developed as part of this faculty community of practice. The General Chemistry II capstone assignment used a similar assessment framework and intended to document student development in chemistry experimental procedures after taking two chemistry courses.

Impact on Faculty Professional Development and Institutional Culture

The collaborative nature of this seminar enriched the campus culture of faculty collaboration among different disciplines and expertise as it represented an opportunity to learn from each other beyond crafting meaningful capstone assignments. Some faculty had more experience using online tools, crafting reflection guidelines, or infusing general education competencies in the curriculum. This professional development provided a rare opportunity to reflect on individual pedagogies and teaching styles. Participants built understanding for different disciplinary identities and ways to define rigor and document student progress. These cross-pollinating opportunities enhanced faculty pedagogical skills and boosted their understanding of other disciplines, which is critical for community colleges and liberal arts institutions hiring faculty from different disciplines.

The seminar model has also reverberated across subsequent faculty initiatives such as the college revitalization of liberal arts programs. Some faculty involved in the liberal arts redesign had previously participated in the capstone initiative. Thus, they were able to bring this perspective to discussions aimed at improving the liberal arts curriculum with the creation of topic-based course options and clusters. The seminar legacy also has an imprint on current departmental work related to ways of assessing student and program learning outcomes.

The seminar provided a framework to organize and structure professional development for faculty from different disciplines. The introduction of planned activities and specific outcomes helped faculty refine and build their knowledge and skills of capstone learning and assessment tools, which served to enrich their teaching identities. Working together enabled faculty to create a sense of community, increasing their motivation, satisfaction, and appreciation for other disciplines. This collegial community of practice was integral in engaging faculty in the design and implementation of a variety of learning strategies that helped them boost their teaching repertoire and disciplinary teaching identity.

Implications

Improving student learning experiences requires refining the tools faculty use to foster student success. The seminar, as a community of practice, represented an important opportunity for faculty to develop their teaching identities rooted in students' needs. The seminar developed faculty ability to learn from each other while discovering meaningful ways to embed general education competencies in their courses. It also built appreciation for other disciplines, and an ability to align selected general education competencies with assignments and assessment tools appropriate to each discipline. The opportunity for creating assignments grounded in different disciplinary expertise also represented a pedagogical growth in mindset for participating faculty, as they were able to harmonize their teaching identities with their scholarly identities. The seed planted by this project germinates in current faculty ability to embrace the meaning of capstone assignments, course redesign, and course assessment.

This endeavor has also served to inform the implementation and assessment of Hostos CUNY Pathways Outcomes (CUNY, 2021), which has been the official general education curriculum for all CUNY institutions since 2013. Students enrolled in capstone-redesigned courses were able to synthesize and integrate knowledge as part of their assignments, providing them with the opportunity for self-reflection on their intellectual development. These improved outcomes show how effective these practices are in promoting faculty and student engagement. Encouraging faculty to apply effective and integrative teaching and assessment tools that address institution-wide assessment practices can help enhance students' learning experiences and outcomes.

Conclusion

Kuh (2008) stated that schools committed to improving students' skills and outcomes utilize a variety of different approaches that are intentionally and strategically designed to support students academically and socially. Thus, it is important that faculty expand knowledge of their own pedagogy to be able to implement new strategies to facilitate and improve students' learning.

This seminar showed effectiveness in engaging faculty in a long-term intellectual practice that produced meaningful curricular results. Faculty were engaged and able to build a learning community that facilitated the development of capstone projects, which served to shed light on the myriad ways in which community colleges can enact capstone learning. The seminar offered faculty the opportunity to discover and adapt various pedagogies that served to supplement student learning with activities that were active, challenging, and creative.

References

Brownell, S. E., & Tanner, K. D. (2012) Barriers to faculty pedagogical change: Lack of training, time, incentives, and tensions with professional identity. *Life Sciences Education, 11*(4), 339–346.

City University of New York. (2021). CUNY *General education requirements/Pathways*. https://www.cuny.edu/about/administration/offices/undergraduate-studies/pathways/gened/

Harden, R. M., & Crosby, J. (2000). The good teacher is more than a lecturer—The twelve roles of a teacher. *Medical Teacher, 22*(4), 334–347.

Henderson, C., Beach, A., & Finkelstein, N. (2011). Facilitating change in undergraduate STEM instructional practices: An analytic review of the literature. *Journal of Research in Science Teaching, 48*(8), 952–984.

Jacoby, B. (2012). *Designing and teaching a high-impact capstone course* [Webinar]. Barbara Jacoby Consulting. https://barbarajacobyconsulting.com

Klein, J. T. (2005). Integrative learning and interdisciplinary studies. *Peer Review, 7*(4), 8–10.

Kuh, G. D. (2008). *High-impact educational practices: What they are, who has access to them, and why they matter.* Association of American Colleges and Universities.

Lee, V. S., & Ash, S. (2010). Unifying the undergraduate curriculum through inquiry-guided learning. In C. M. Wehlburg (Ed.), *Integrated General Education* (New Directions for Teaching and Learning, no. 121, pp. 35–46). Wiley.

Maki, P. L. (2004). Developing an assessment plan to learn about student learning. In P. Hernon & R. E. Dugan (Eds.), *Outcomes assessment in higher education: Views and perspectives* (pp. 89–101). Libraries Unlimited.

Silverthorn, D. U., Thorn, P. M., & Svinicki, M. D. (2006). It's difficult to change the way we teach: Lessons from the integrative themes in physiology curriculum module project. *The American Physiological Society, 30*, 204–214.

Wenger-Trayner, E., & Wenger-Trayner B. (2015). Learning in a landscape of practice: A framework. In E. Wenger-Trayner, M. Fenton-O'Creevy, S. Hutchinson, C. Kubiak, & B. Wenger-Trayner (Eds.), *Learning in landscapes of practice: Boundaries, identity, and knowledgeability in practice-based learning* (pp. 13–30). Routledge.

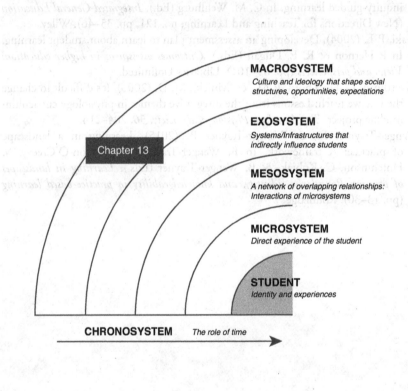

MACROSYSTEM
Culture and ideology that shape social structures, opportunities, expectations

EXOSYSTEM
Systems/Infrastructures that indirectly influence students

Chapter 13

MESOSYSTEM
A network of overlapping relationships: Interactions of microsystems

MICROSYSTEM
Direct experience of the student

STUDENT
Identity and experiences

CHRONOSYSTEM   *The role of time*

PEER REVIEWING TO SUPPORT QUALITY ASSURANCE OF CAPSTONE EXPERIENCES

A View From Australia

Michelle J. Eady and Simon B. Bedford

In the context of curriculum transformation work in Australia, capstone subjects are final year subjects that synthesize students' learning across all their years of study. In 2015, the External Referencing of Standards (ERoS) group was formed to meet the needs of the Australian universities that were going through reaccreditation with the government Tertiary Education Quality and Standards Agency (TEQSA) to meet new requirements contained in the Higher Education Standards Framework (2015). ERoS utilized a transparent and open process of collaboration that brought together academics from four distinct Australian institutions located thousands of kilometers apart (Figure 13.1) to share the issues that arose from aligning higher education standards with subject assessments and learning outcomes. This chapter describes the curriculum transformation project's design, objectives, and emergent outputs so that other institutions might adopt and apply a similar model to ensure quality learning outcomes for their capstone subjects.

Capstone experiences and tasks became a key element for consideration in the ERoS project, as they are an important part of curriculum transformation work and curriculum evaluation models (O'Donnell et al., 2015). The methodology underpinning the ERoS project enabled institutions to benchmark their whole-of-course learning outcomes and graduate attributes,

Figure 13.1. Map of universities involved.

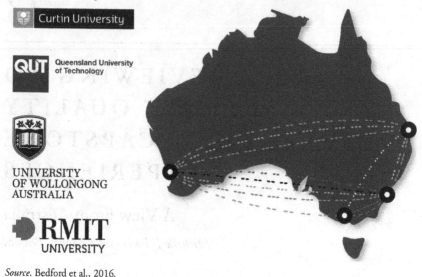

Source. Bedford et al., 2016.

primarily by focusing on assessment tasks within capstone subjects. This provided insights to enhance the quality of university tasks through the curriculum, and to explore ways in which these tasks can achieve quality outcomes for students.

Higher Education and Quality Standards

There is a global demand for universities to maintain and improve quality standards within teaching and curriculum (Verger et al., 2018). This demand is increasingly prevalent within organizations that govern institutions and educational bodies, and, as a result, quality standards are taking a crucial role in the higher education sector (Brøgger, 2019). As higher education develops to meet international and transnational demands and partnerships, global quality standards are needed to ensure consistent learning experiences and comparable outcomes for students. Typically, these global education standards are then embedded into a nation's tertiary education strategic plan, which then becomes the goal of every university to meet, with student achievements foregrounded as the outcomes to benchmark against the standards (Brøgger, 2019).

Australian universities are therefore required to uphold certain standards, to define best practices in order to improve the quality of the education for students (Universities Australia, 2020). TEQSA is Australia's independent regulatory body for quality assurance in higher education that ensures these

Figure 13.2. The higher educations standards framework as graphically summarized.

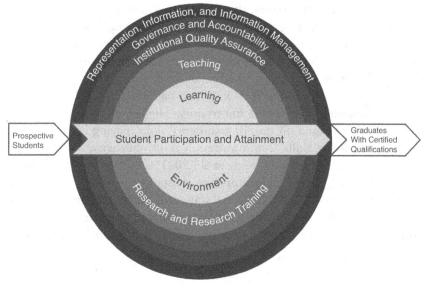

Source. TEQSA, 2015, para. 4.

standards are met. This body designed and implemented a framework that provides the set of requirements for tertiary education providers in Australia to monitor the quality of their education activities: The Higher Education Standards Framework (TEQSA, 2015). This framework (Figure 13.2) was created to focus on the progress of students from their initial year of study through to graduation.

All Australian universities, or established higher education providers, must apply for accreditation or renewal of each individual program of study (called *courses* in Australia) using the TEQSA principles (2015, Section 13)

- regulatory necessity
- reflecting risk
- proportionate regulation

Ultimately, the quality of a university, its teaching, and all infrastructure, systems, and support are evaluated by the success of the students and their graduate employability. While assessment for learning and the development of assessment literacy are important feedback indicators and milestones on the students' learning journey, it is the assurance of the program learning outcomes at its end point that determine the overall quality of a program of study and level of student-attainment. Thus, assessment of that learning and the skills and capabilities need to be evaluated and are in themselves clear quality indicators.

For Australian universities, there has been a growing level of competition in what is increasingly seen as a "market" for employable graduates. This competition has been heightened by the emergence of a political discourse in Australia that seeks to reposition the relationship of universities and society as one of individual financial benefit rather than of social good. This competition is in tension with a high level of regulation resulting in a language of risk and uncertainty. Higher education academics have therefore focused on fostering students' skills, paying keen attention to problem-solving skills, communication skills, creativity, and a general holistic approach to learning (Eady et al., 2021; Oliver & Jorre de St Jorre, 2018; Yan et al., 2019). Educators are constantly striving to refine and improve their craft. The credible assessment of outcomes is of interest to professional bodies around the world that provide competency standards programs of study in their regions need to address. One such assessment is the capstone experience.

Context of This Study

Four universities worked together to test a methodology and process of using capstone tasks for assessment purposes. Each of the identified university programs had embedded a capstone task within their subject. The purpose of being involved in this project was to improve the quality of their capstone experiences and tasks, resulting in successful outcomes for their students.

Project Processes

Academics in specific disciplines were matched with academics in other institutions who were teaching and assessing in similar subjects. While everyone on the research team had input, one university acted as the manager of the project to ensure consistency. The process of recruiting participants was a call for expression of interest moderated by the teaching and learning units at each university. This chapter provides an example of one section of the entire ERoS project, where academics from three universities volunteered to participate in "Triad 1" of the project.

The participants utilized an open and transparent process which allowed for discussions, delving deep into standards in the context of learning outcomes in their individual tertiary settings. The term *referencing* in this project was used to describe the activities related to assessing and reporting on a program of study and particular capstone task by a university staff member from one of the institutions. There was a seven-step process (Bedford et al., 2016) in this referencing work:

1. Initial matchmaking
2. Signing of participation agreements
3. Collection and exchange of the review materials
4. Redaction of student work samples
5. Setting up of online meetings, timetable and record keeping
6. Closing the loop on reporting processes and action planning
7. Feedback, evaluation e.g., timesheets and focus groups (p. 22)

Because of the distances involved in the collaborative work, due to the geographic location of the universities across Australia, Triad 1 met solely through online synchronous technology (Skype calls). The first of these meetings included introductions, discussing units, and alignment with learning outcomes. The chosen assessment item to benchmark against was examples of students' work (each team was asked to produce three samples), the documentation to be completed for the project, and creating a timeline moving forward. After the first meeting, it was agreed that the student material would be deidentified to protect student anonymity. The work samples and subject outline, including learning outcomes and assessment criteria, were shared via email between the three university participants. They were given 4 weeks to complete the first review of documentation and tracked the time spent reviewing each other's work samples and program documents. The participants provided each other with the students' grades as well as the corresponding rubrics. Each of the participants completed an ERoS project referencing report. All reports had been exchanged by all parties involved in the project within 5 weeks of the onset of the project. Subject outlines were explained and feedback given, with suggestions made within all of the referencing reports.

After the first review of the work samples and subject documents, Triad 1 met to discuss initial feedback. All participants were asked to finalize their comments and submit final reports together with a feedback survey. The report was made available to all academics who participated in the project.

Lessons Learned

This yearlong project provided valuable insights and recommendations for academics and institutions as a whole to improve their program designs (Bedford et al., 2016). For instance, one participant in the ERoS project stated, "I would love to work through the feedback and identify improvements. I do not want it to end here."

For larger programs, especially those that did not target capstone assessments, some participants suggested that it would have been useful to have all of the assessments to have a better idea of the program's context and how the various assessment pieces were evaluated (Sefcik et al., 2018). Participants also suggested that their time and effort in continuously changing and upgrading their subject and assessment content be reassessed: "As a pattern, we are being asked to do more and more of this sort of stuff, without getting any extra time to do it in."

The progressive steps of the study enabled participants to understand and feel supported throughout. They were provided with guidance and resources, and most utilized these to support their fuller understanding of both the process and template for the immediate referencing tasks. Concurrently, those involved gained both professional and personal development and built institutional capacity through the collaborative work, mentoring, and support networks provided by other university members (Bedford et al., 2016).

Participant Perspectives

The following section includes extracts from the reflective statements made by two participants.

Reflection 1

This reflection comes from the research project team member whose institution was in the state of New South Wales. The academic had been prior to this work in the United Kingdom, as a university director of teaching and an external examiner at several institutions there. He was involved in the creation and writing of several institutional assessment policies and procedures both in the United Kingdom and Australia. He has a passion and expertise for using curriculum transformation to make assessment *for* learning as valid as assessment *of* learning, and as a way of building assessment literacies in all students and staff through a shared experience. This is his self-reflection in being involved in the ERoS project:

> We are not good at making judgments on quality on our own without sound benchmarks, processes and methods in place. The ERoS project established a methodology to bring those elements together, and to do so in an open and collaborative way so as to share good practice and build both capacity and capabilities in staff that engage in this most important form of collegial peer review of our students' learning.
>
> For me in my experience there is no better challenge then to target the capstone task to determine if a course is delivering for its graduates. The

capstone represents the culmination of a learning journey for students, and also the considered application of a whole-of-course approach to curriculum design, something that is agreed to be a key determinant of success for capstones, but which can also represent enormous complexities and challenges for those making judgments on them.

I always make a point of seeking capstones out, be that in a new course proposal, a professional accreditation renewal or simply in an annual course review—they are the best way to determine the quality of the course and the graduates transitioning to the world of work from it.

Reflection 2

The second reflection was from a project participant from the East Coast of Australia. As a teacher educator, she approached teaching in an authentic and "hands-on" manner and gained a warm reputation for her connection with students, eagerness for continual self-improvement, and openness to trying new adventures in the scholarship of teaching and learning. Part of her self-reflection on being involved in the ERoS capstone Triad 1 follows:

> Being a lifelong learner is part of our teaching journey. While I can feel overwhelmed in the complexity of my job, there is something in the quote "practice what you preach" that nags for my attention. This was the case with the call out for the ERoS project.
>
> I was intrigued to see how other academics did capstone tasks in their education subjects. Capstones are an opportunity for professional and personal reflection and recognition of growth for each student. The tasks allows the student teachers to get creative and enjoy the process while seeing how much they had truly grown over the course of their 4-year degree.
>
> Giving my students opportunity to represent their knowledge and growth in education in their own creative ways leads to amazing assessment task products. Over the years I had storybooks, backpacks, tool kits, baked goods, quilts—yes, a student once made a quilt. I still have a capstone piece hanging in my office. The student had photos of all the significant milestones through her degree and the people who had helped her along the way. At the top there were photos of doors, her "doors of opportunity" and the whole piece was washed with black tea because, she explained, "without tea, I would not have survived my degree."
>
> I think the process of sharing our work with peers can be daunting and we tend to veer away from such vulnerable opportunities presented; however, in this case, it made a difference in my teaching and I know I helped the others improve their pedagogy. The time it took to review the other participants' subject outlines, rubrics and student examples was a learning experience for me as I was able to get a fresh view of how others create tasks and rubrics. It isn't always easy to give nor receive critical feedback from others but in the end, it helped everyone's learning.

The two perspectives shared here, one of a researcher and the other of an academic, raise some interesting yet important guidelines for other academics to think about when embarking on a similar evaluation of standards project.

Recommendations for Implementing Similar Projects

As institutions, standards, and expectations placed on universities change over time, the students then require these to be integrated into their programs and apply to their future education and professional lives (Becker et al., 2017).

The perspectives in the reflective statements offered by the project's researcher and participant highlight some points for other institutions to consider when moving forward in capstone assessment evaluations:

- Capstone tasks should be sought out in new programs, accreditation renewal, and program reviews as the gold standard of determining the quality of the learning that has occurred and how students transfer that learning into their careers.
- In order for capstones to be evaluated properly, institutions (if not at the level of state and territory) must create sound benchmarks for developing capstones and methods of assessing these tasks.
- Capstone tasks provide an opportunity to gauge the level of learning and quality of that learning both for students and institution academics.

The process of reviewing capstone experiences between universities is useful. This study demonstrated the effectiveness of collaborating together, drawing upon our expertise and our peers in other institutions to share good practice, support one another, and grow as universities.

From the perspective of the study participating in this case, there are four key points for other academics to consider when becoming involved in a sharing and evaluating approach such as this one:

1. *Dare to take risks.* Often, as university academics we become very comfortable in our style of teaching and learning including approaches to assessment. Trying something new is refreshing for both you and your students and keeps your practice relevant.
2. *Give new strategies time.* In our role as academics, we can unknowingly become automated in the way that we approach teaching. When we try something new, but do not give enough time for iterations to master new pedagogy, we often resort to giving up and going back to our "old ways."

3. *Drop your closed door policy.* Part of our role as academics is to grow and learn and to stay current in our discipline. Having constructive feedback, critical reflection, and collegial discussion with others who are attempting or have mastered an assessment such as a capstone can only add another perspective to what you are trying to achieve. Use the opportunity to share with others, as part of your career development plan moving forward.

4. *Be creative.* Think outside of the box and let your students create capstones that are meaningful to them and that help them reflect their own growth.

Interestingly, the four collaborating universities chosen to participate in ERoS were located in different Australian states. The rationale for this was that they were more open to collaboration as they were not in competition for local student enrollments. Additionally, it was noted that, when pairing up institutions to undertake external peer review during the pilots, few wished to undertake reciprocal external referencing with a near neighbor as this may have disclosed information about a competitive program of study.

After the completion of the collaborative work with the four universities, there has been an ongoing interest in both external referencing and benchmarking measures. The ERoS report (Wilson et al., 2019) has been used to inform the development of an Australian national peer review portal, as well as other national processes such as the UK external examiner review (Bedford et al., 2016). While the Australian peer review portal draws on the ERoS methodology, it uses a one-way, blind review approach that is akin to peer review of research articles—and has to be paid for. In this nonreciprocal approach, there is unfortunately no way to build staff capacity by developing an individual skill in collaborative evaluation work with peers, and also no way for a reviewer to get an in-depth view of the program related to the specific task they are evaluating. Ongoing data collected from the peer review portal and other systems such as QVS (Quality Verification System) and ACP (Academic Calibration Program) to evaluate their sustainability will be helpful moving forward in this area of study (Booth et al., 2016).

Overall, there are five good practice principles that underpin the ERoS model and foreground collaborative relationships:

- *Effective.* ERoS supports course and unit quality enhancement and quality assurance.
- *Efficient.* ERoS efficiently supports external referencing of assessment and grading of students' achievement of learning outcomes across comparable courses of study.

- *Transparent and open.* ERoS facilitates open dialogue between staff teaching analogous courses to support consensus-building around standards of students' attainment of learning outcomes.
- *Capability-building.* ERoS contributes to staff professional learning and enriches discipline communities of practice.
- *Sustainable.* ERoS provides a complete and sustainable process for external referencing that can be routinely enacted within higher education (Bedford et al., 2016).

Implications for Change

In the work of quality assuring capstones, prior learning is not always easy to evidence; as capstone subjects, experiences, or tasks come at the end of programs of study, they rely on a significant part of the program that has already occurred.

Nevertheless, the advantages of focusing quality assurance on capstones is very clear: Capstone outcomes are closest to the described program learning outcomes, and if students are not attaining these, it is a clear indicator to those who design and deliver programs to make changes.

The four universities who engaged with the pilot ERoS project and this evaluative study were receptive to the project's methodology that included sustained peer support and mentoring. The pilot concluded that the collaborative peer reviewing of capstone experiences and tasks was a valuable tool in the quality assurance process and curriculum enhancement initiatives to ensure that universities are attaining learning goals and preparing employable graduates. The methodology implemented by ERoS allows for fresh perspectives from disciplinary colleagues from cognate institutions. The authors encourage other universities to adopt and adapt this collaborative peer review methodology, with a focus on capstones.

Acknowledgment

We would like to thank Ruth G. C. Walker, University of Cambridge, for the editorial suggestions that she contributed to this work.

References

Becker, S. A., Cummins, M., Davis, A., Freeman, A., Glesinger Hall, C., & Ananthanarayanan, V. (2017). *NMC Horizon Report: 2017 higher education edition.* The New Media Consortium. https://www.nmc.org/publication/nmc-horizon-report-2017-higher-education-edition/

Bedford S. B., Czech, P., Sefcik, L. T., Smith, J., & Yorke, J. (2016). *External referencing of standards—ERoS Report: An example of a collaborative end-to-end peer review process for external referencing* [Final project report].

Booth, S., Beckett, J., & Saunders, C. (2016), Peer review of assessment network: Supporting comparability of standards. *Quality Assurance in Education, 24*(2), 194–210. https://doi.org/10.1108/QAE-01-2015-0003

Brøgger, K. (2019). *Governing through standards: The faceless masters of higher education.* Springer International.

Eady, M. J., Abrahamson, E., Green, C. A., Arcellana-Panlilio, M., Hatfield, L., & Namaste, N. (2021). Re-positioning SoTL toward the T-shaped Community. *Teaching and Learning Inquiry, 9*(1), 262–278. https://doi.org/10.20343/teachlearninqu.9.1.18

O'Donnell, M., Wallace, M., Melano, A., Lawson, R., & Leinonen, E. (2015). Putting transition at the centre of whole-of-curriculum transformation. *Student Success, 6*(2), 73–79. http://dx.doi.org/10.5204/ssj.v6i2.295

Oliver, B., & Jorre de St Jorre, T. (2018). Graduate attributes for 2020 and beyond: Recommendations for Australian higher education providers. *Higher Education Research & Development, 37*(4), 821–836. https://doi.org/10.1080/07294360.2018.1446415

Sefcik, L., Bedford, S. B., Czech, P., Smith, J., & Yorke, J. (2018). Embedding external referencing of standards into higher education: Collaborative relationships are the key. *Journal of Assessment and Evaluation in Higher Education, 43*(1), 45–57. http://dx.doi.org/10.1080/02602938.2017.1278584

Tertiary Education Quality and Standards Agency. (2015). *Higher Education Standards Framework (Threshold Standards) 2015—TEQSA contextual overview.* https://www.teqsa.gov.au/sites/default/files/hesf-2015-teqsa-contextual-overview-v1-1.pdf?acsf_files_redirect

Universities Australia. (2020). *How universities are funded.* https://www.universitiesaustralia.edu.au/policy-submissions/teaching-learning-funding/how-universities-are-funded/

Verger, A., Novelli, M., & Altinyelken, H. K. (2018). Global education policy and international development: A revisited introduction. In A. Verger, M. Novelli, & H. K. Altinyelken (Eds.), *Global education policy and international development: New agendas, issues and policies* (2nd ed., pp. 1–34). Bloomsbury.

Wilson, G., Bedford, S. B., & Readman, K. (2019). *External peer review of assessment: A guide to supporting the external referencing of academic standards* [Research report]. Council of Australasian University Leaders in Learning and Teaching. https://hdl.handle.net/1959.7/uws:53024

Yan, L., Yinghong, Y., Lui, S. M., Whiteside, M., & Tsey, K. (2019). Teaching "soft skills" to university students in China: The feasibility of an Australian approach. *Educational Studies, 45*(2), 242–258. https://doi.org/10.1080/03055698.2018.1446328

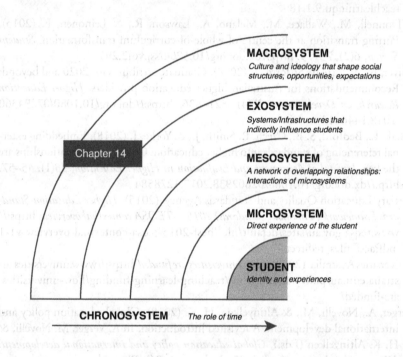

MACROSYSTEM
Culture and ideology that shape social structures; opportunities, expectations

EXOSYSTEM
Systems/Infrastructures that indirectly influence students

Chapter 14

MESOSYSTEM
A network of overlapping relationships: Interactions of microsystems

MICROSYSTEM
Direct experience of the student

STUDENT
Identity and experiences

CHRONOSYSTEM   *The role of time*

14

POSITIONALITY AND IDENTITY IN CAPSTONES

Renegotiating the Self Through Teaching and Learning

Moriah McSharry McGrath, Sarah Dyer, Joanna Rankin, and Trina Jorre de St Jorre

Fostering inclusive and transformative capstone experiences—where students learn and faculty advance their scholarship—requires understanding the interplay of identities and social positions in the learning context. In higher education, diversity is generally viewed as a characteristic of the student body or a state to be pursued, camouflaging the fact that social identities are a set of power relationships that both structure social interactions—such as capstone experiences—and which are themselves restructured through social interaction (Ahonen et al., 2013). Further, the conception of diversity in higher education functions in a White-centering logic (Mayorga-Gallo, 2019) that neglects the intersectionality (Crenshaw, 1989) of identities operating within and between individuals. "Diversity" is viewed as people and cultures who do not read as or conform to practices of White, able-bodied, cisgender norms. In our locations, this notion of "underrepresented" groups is conceived variously: people of color in the United States; Aboriginal people and people of color in Canada; and Black, Asian, and minority ethnic in the United Kingdom. Across our contexts, these racialized identities are foregrounded in discussions of diversity and social stratification in their multiplex natures. Our research moves the conversation further into the realm of power and intersectional identities, responding to McIlwaine and Bunge's (2019) call for "exploration of student" identities and agency, especially their "dutiful aspirational capital" alongside consideration of the "institutional habitus" that perpetuates existing power relations (p. 500).

Through analysis of capstone curricular documents and 10 in-depth team interviews with instructors and students engaged in different types of capstones (e.g., research, such as a thesis or dissertation; service, such as a program where students volunteer at a nonprofit organization; or professional practice, where students work as trainees under the mentorship of a senior professional in their field), we identified mechanisms through which capstone curricula perpetuate the hegemonic culture of academe despite far-reaching institutional commitments to diversity and inclusion. The programs we studied at Portland State University (U.S.), University of Alabama (U.S.), University of Calgary (Canada), and University of Exeter (U.K.) included both interdisciplinary curricula and capstone experiences that are explicitly grounded in one academic field or department. Our interviewees had a variety of personal backgrounds, although all were academics—either faculty or university graduates.

We analyzed our data through Bernstein's (2000) four lenses: the intended curriculum, that which is actually delivered, what is received or understood by students, and finally, the hidden or tacit curriculum. Our goal is to reconsider the idea of "barriers to learning" in favor of illuminating the ways that "more subtle aspects of higher education pedagogical cultures may themselves be creating conditions which make it difficult, or even impossible, for some students to learn" (Haggis, 2006, p. 521). We identified four mechanisms that normalize dominant culture in capstone experiences and discuss aspects of curriculum, instruction, and institutional culture that maintain power relationships. By mapping ways to better integrate diverse lived experiences as an asset to capstone experiences, we build on Matus and Infante's (2011) exploration of "the relations between the advancement of neutral discourses of difference and the value-free practices expressed in neoliberal educational agendas" (p. 293). We conclude that attention to positionality—for both faculty and students—is a key strategy for cultivating meaningful engagement in capstone learning, and we offer tools for fostering this reflective practice.

Exclusionary Capstones

In reviewing our interviews and institutional documents, we identified four mechanisms that perpetuate exclusionary capstone experiences. Capstones

- reproduce academics/professionals (what we call "reproducing ourselves")
- ignore and obscure students' identities
- make assumptions about learning happening in the field or "real world"
- are described as an endpoint

Each section is introduced with a quote from one of our interviewees that captures the essence of the mechanism being discussed. Throughout, we describe capstones *doing* things, as if they are a person with agency, since the capstone experience is a set of shared institutional and professional practices with a meaning and culture of its own created by the actions of a wide number of people.

Reproducing Ourselves

> [Our] model of the dissertation is pretty much the same across those institutions, across 25 years, and they're also pretty much the same as the version I did when I was an undergraduate. . . . And I think that goes back to longer traditions of essential field work. . . . So these days people might not necessarily be [doing] getting-their-feet-dirty field work, but it's that model of original research. (Wilson, faculty interviewee)

Capstones reproduce students in the image of what—or who—already exists, operating as a dialectic between student and faculty identities. Not only are capstones shaping students into a role, but for instructors themselves, the act of shaping students entails reproducing their own academic identities. Whatever the instructor's current identity and practice, it was forged within masculinist, ableist, and White supremacist research cultures—now passed along to the student.

Whether the capstone aims to reproduce an academic elite (research capstone) or a profession (practice), strikingly similar values and performances are valorized. Curriculum documents in the research capstone Wilson described heavily stressed independence and "originality," arguably unrealistic standards for novice researchers. Feminist scholars have critiqued this "heroic masculinity" in academic culture as a misrepresentation of the interconnections, relationships, dependencies, and vulnerabilities of doing research that harms researchers by devaluing many aspects of labor (Gill, 2009). In the practice capstone context, faculty discussed a similar "ableist" and "burnout" culture, where it is viewed as normal that students struggle through the experience and can only succeed by "pushing themselves to the limits."

Obscuring Student Identities

> We have a disproportionate representation of a certain kind of background as well, and so if you don't necessarily fit within that then I think you're probably going to feel all sorts of pressures. (James, faculty interviewee)

Both student and faculty identities are subsumed by the perpetuation—even through critique—of the idea that today's university students have economic and social privilege similar to that of earlier generations of students. As Haggis (2003) noted about the broader project of articulating curricula, "the statement of [learning] intentions is successful in creating a generalized description of the 'elite' goals and values of academic culture, but says surprisingly little about the majority of students in a mass system" (p. 89). Faculty's outmoded ideas of what students' lives are like inform how capstones are designed and taught—for example, in assuming that students do not work or provide care outside of school and therefore have flexible schedules for research visits or internships.

The assumed homogeneity of the student body relegates identity to something that is taught as an analytical frame rather than a lived experience (of education, research, or professional life). And as such, student identities are silenced or obscured within the capstone experience. Our faculty interviewees all discussed cases where lived identities came into sharp focus in ways that intruded on the capstone—for example, through students experiencing racism or sexism in a placement or being unable to fulfill capstone requirements because of outside responsibilities. But despite the frequency with which these "interruptions" to the idealized capstone occur, the recourse to address them is always outside the formal capstone program: a quiet word with a preceptor in a practice setting, counseling from a mental health practitioner, a waiver of academic requirements, or a supportive conversation with a peer.

The Unquestioned Logic of Field Research

> From the students' perspective, because they've been told that this practicum is going to be [a chance to apply theory to practice], and you're going to get all these things out of it, and they might be told to wash some dishes or clean up and do those kinds of tasks . . . so that's where there's been problems. (Renate, faculty interviewee)

The third mechanism we identified is an inured reliance on "the field" as learning environment. In all of our curricula, the capstone includes some notion that the student goes somewhere other than the typical learning environment to complete their integrative learning. Whether it's a research site, community service project, or professional practice setting, the field is presumed to offer an experience of difference that challenges students to apply their content-area knowledge. However, beyond this signaling of difference, the relationship between student and field goes largely unexamined by faculty.

The field is presented as a hallowed real-world crucible where learning is applied and the student transformed. There is an implicit assumption that students are from a dominant culture undertaking work in a "diverse" other context where student learning will be superior—regardless of the unique identities or experiences that the individual learner brings. Such practices align with the imperialist histories of universities, where members of the social elite traveled to "discover" new peoples or detail exotic practices.

We found it rare that the intended curriculum said much about the skills and approaches needed in the field, leaving it an unexamined concept. The relevant social skills (confidence and interpersonal communication) are left unarticulated, and students are expected to be able to undertake ethnographic research with little knowledge of the field site. In terms of relationships between the mechanisms we identified, only through obscuring student identity does it become possible to blithely frame the field as "out there," a notion of the field that operates across all three types of capstone we studied.

Capstone as Premature Ending

It's this kind of social process which, kind of, you become a graduate because you've endured and survived your dissertation. (Wilson, faculty interviewee)

The final mechanism is the overemphasis on the capstone as the end of a program of study, neglecting its role as a transition within the student's wider personal trajectory. As culminating experience, the capstone represents both the pinnacle of, as well as the cusp of transition beyond, students' university careers. This undertaking shapes students when they are asked to integrate learning from across the curriculum by applying it to authentic contexts in individualized ways. Thus, there is a profound irrelevance to capstones that serve solely as rite of passage, devoid of connection to current intellectual realities or students' personal futures.

The framing of capstone as ending and as a means of reproducing ourselves are mutually reinforcing. For example, despite the research capstone's emphasis on becoming an independent scholar, few students will stay in academe after graduation. However, acting as though students will become academics enables faculty to sidestep consideration of the impact of the capstone on students' personal, professional, and academic development.

Discussion: Repositioning the Capstone

The capstone experience demands reaching beyond disciplinary knowledge to a place of reflexivity about one's relationship to that knowledge and the world; this includes awareness of positionality and identities. The purposeful design of inclusive learning experiences therefore requires articulating the relationship between the classroom and the field and disentangling the skills used in advanced fieldwork (e.g., research techniques, intercultural negotiation, interpersonal skills). This clearer mapping of competencies and resources needed for capstone success enables better curriculum design and assessment.

However, looking beyond the capstone is necessary as well. Because teaching and learning are embedded in the larger university context, reforming the broader institutional culture is also a part of creating inclusive capstones. These practices operate at multiple levels, including the now-typical recruitment and retention programs for underrepresented groups. Yet universities in the era of "massification" require deeper interrogation of practices that privilege the White, male, elite roots of higher education over the cultivation of new practices grounded in the experiences of under-represented groups. McIlwaine and Bunge (2019) enumerated "diverse role models, curriculum change and targeted support practices that avoid the 'black deficit model'" (p. 500) as key mechanisms for dismantling exclu-sionary cultures, and here we focus on the second item in that list. Fostering inclusive excellence in the capstone also requires that faculty (instructors) and administrators (managers) consider what happens well before students reach their final year of coursework.

Implications for Faculty

In this section we discuss ways capstone instructors can address the issues identified in our analysis.

Reflection to Transform Instead of Reproduce

Our findings show how the logic of reproduction (of ourselves, our professions, and institutions) excludes people and preempts incipient possibilities. The drive for this reproduction is often deeply entrenched, not least because we (faculty) have likely invested a lot in finding a place within this commu-nity, and through this labor we have reified its practices.

The work needed to destabilize the reproductive logic (and its negative consequences) is largely reflective. To surface diversity among learners and instructors, faculty need to reckon with the ways that their own identities and experiences inform their teaching as well as how their own lived experi-ences are either overrepresented or underrepresented in the curriculum more broadly. While some of this reflection can be done alone, it is improved through dialogue.

Thinking about where students are headed and "de-elitizing" our professional culture requires directly confronting our assumptions about students and each other, including experiences and identities of race, class, ability, and beyond. Additionally, we must grapple with the changing nature of academic employment and the ramifications of a growing contingent faculty—such as the overrepresentation of people of color and women in this less resourced stratum of the faculty.

This reflection lays the groundwork for capstone design teams to interrogate ways the intended curriculum reproduces dominant cultures of scholarship (individualist, independent, carefree) and then find ways to better reflect multifaceted approaches to scholarship in the capstone program. Exercises A, B, and C in the supplemental resources for this chapter on the book website (https://www.centerforengagedlearning.org/books/cultivating-capstones/) could support this work.

Opening Up to Student Identities

Because student identities, in all their diversity and complexity, are central to capstone experiences, there's great potential to collaborate with students to develop projects with meaningful goals relevant to their personal purpose for attending a postsecondary institution. Faculty need to ask students who they are, encourage them to discuss the identities they bring to their academic work, and valorize these processes by scaffolding reflexivity and intercultural skills as learning outcomes for academic programs.

"Student" is not a homogeneous identity, and inclusive design requires the valuation rather than accommodation of difference. Additionally, students need space to discuss among themselves how identities operate within the group of learners. This identity work is central to intellectual engagement and academic success as identity formation is a crucial bridge between higher education and future employment (Tomlinson & Jackson, 2019). Exercises B and E in the supplemental materials serve as a starting point for opening up space for student identities in capstone experiences.

Questioning the Logic of the Field

Our analysis highlights the need for faculty to reevaluate the notion of "the field" or "the real world" in the capstone curriculum, and we suggest that faculty decouple research skills from intercultural skills when articulating a curriculum. The typical field encounter is far less tidy and edifying than the imagined capstone: a student conducting a sensitive and well-informed interview—with, for example, a houseless person—to develop some community-based recommendations for local policymakers. This idealized interaction presents an opportunity to practice in-person interviewing, communication across differences, and analysis of policy issues. In reality, these are usually, at best, awkward encounters where the student is underprepared to participate in an informed conversation with either the interviewee or policymaker. By specifying the skills used to do such work, we can better scaffold students' learning and reward the skills they bring into the experience. This also improves the ethical merit of the capstone by increasing the likelihood that students are appropriately skilled before seeking information or wading into the policy landscape.

We emphasize this preparation not just to improve student learning, but also to interrupt the history of exploitative university practices that have benefited academe at the expense of host communities that serve as field sites or offer research participants and other community partners. We warn against combining service capstones with student research, given the formulation of the host community being "in need" and therefore subordinated to the "serving" organization. Host communities generally provide free mentoring and training to students in these projects, yet the dynamics are viewed through a prism of gratitude for assistance that lends a coercive streak to community participation in student research. While students can learn from community-identified research projects, the complexity of "service" relationships makes them rocky terrain for unleashing novice researchers. Similarly, if students have limited experience working across race, class, gender, or ability differences, research on an "other" group should not be their first encounter. Given the potential harm to research participants and their communities that could be done by a new-comer researcher, building preliminary insight through archival and other secondary research is critical preparation for field research—particularly when conducted by people of dominant identities on people whose identities have been marginalized.

Exercises D and E in the supplemental resources support faculty in decoupling the field and cultural diversity.

Making Capstones a Beginning

Finally, it is necessary to rebalance the weight given to the capstone as a culmination versus a journey or "becoming." Instead, it is important to explicitly position capstones as a transition for students, rather than as a straightforward ending, by using assignments that ask students to address transition and creating spaces for dialogue about individual meaning that students make of capstone. We should support students to understand their work as part of a personal narrative, shifting from students seeing capstones as an assigned task to something more autonomous. Not only does this change the relationship between instructor and student but it also shifts the student's relationship to disciplinary expertise—moving from novice to someone who makes judgment about expertise.

Exercise B in the supplemental resources addresses this aspect of teaching inclusive capstones.

Implications for Administrators

Deans and department chairs retain important roles in the capstone landscape because of their responsibility to build infrastructure and manage university resources. They can either reward or constrain the practices that spark and sustain inclusive capstones.

Disrupting the "Reproductive" Process

As administrators ascend the university hierarchy, they are tacitly rewarded for successfully navigating academic culture. Therefore, they wield great power in renouncing or dismantling these same systems. In practice, this means articulating the value that "nontraditional" students and faculty bring to the educational endeavor and naming them for the intellectual and spiritual contributions that they are. (For an example of this praxis, see the work of the "Cite Black Women" movement throughout Twitter and at www .citeblackwomencollective.org.) Inclusive transformation also requires that administrators shift the reward structure for faculty to better align with institutions' stated values.

Additionally, administrators must be steadfast supporters and vocal advocates for faculty doing diversity, equity, and inclusion work and faculty members from underrepresented backgrounds. This includes getting them mentors; giving them money and course releases; and protecting them from the aggression (passive and otherwise) of colleagues, students, and members of the public whose feathers are ruffled by their work or mere existence.

Naming Identities

Similarly, administrators must reject totalizing discourses about the student body, including both presumptions that students are "traditional" and diversity narratives that celebrate a simple multiculturalism or "one big happy family" university culture when these narratives are not grounded in the specificity of the institution's history and context. Mere celebration of difference for difference's sake relies on the White-centered logic of othering, whereas a genuine discussion of the particulars is a generative act that surfaces locally grounded and personally embodied experiences. Administrators can help create a culture that values students' differences by naming both the compulsory student identity and the ways that the lived experiences of students, faculty, and administrators run counter to that of the imagined "typical" student.

Meaningful Partnerships

Administrators often cultivate and promote community partnerships, and for this reason they have an important role in supporting more robust—and less exploitative—field learning experiences. First, they must assure that faculty members are sufficiently skilled to supervise this work. Doctoral training rarely addresses the complex dynamics of field research; for these reasons we echo Martin and Strawser's (2017) perspective that "emphasizes the importance of faculty development and training as a means to prepare faculty to design the capstone course as a high-impact educational practice" (p. 25). Faculty also need emotional support and professional protection for innovations that go against the grain. As Castillo-Montoya (2020) reminded us, "equity-minded teaching entails intellectual and emotional labor that can create challenges and tensions for the instructors as well as the students" (p. 74). She noted that this work is usually conducted in institutions that give lip service to diversity but have yet to make any structural changes; as such, administrators must attend to the biases of teaching evaluations and promotion and tenure processes. Furthermore, it is a minority of faculty who will be leading this work, given that most are what Bensimon and Gray (2020) deemed "first-generation equity practitioners" and innovating in capstones will require simultaneously embracing and interrogating literature on "best" or "high-impact" practices given the racial illiteracy and other blind spots of mainstream faculty culture.

University as Springboard

Other research has shown that student perceptions of a curriculum's authenticity—including its relevance to their current and future selves—is a strong predictor of generic learning outcomes such as professional work readiness and self-efficacy (Smith & Worsfold, 2015). Administrators need to support faculty professional development that foregrounds capstones as meaningful for students as part of their own personal narratives. Importantly, administrators can redefine the culture of merit in university contexts beyond traditional academic skills and expectations to acknowledgment of other skills and knowledges (e.g., prior learning assessment and recognition).

Conclusions

Doing capstones differently truly requires swimming against the tide; instructors must work against "the way it's always been done," while higher education perpetuates the hegemonic order in so many ways: for example, in the United States, histories of racialized violence constrain access to higher education and the workforce does not reflect the student population (Espinosa & Mitchell, 2020). We call for a transformation that begins from looking inside and are therefore hopeful that the path to change is easily embarked upon despite the challenges. Revising capstones offers a lever for change that can have much wider impacts across universities. Given their role as a culminating experience, capstones reveal assumptions about what university learning is really about. Revealing these assumptions is critical to defining the true purpose of the capstone and enabling faculty to then "design backwards" to ensure students are prepared adequately.

Acknowledgments

We are grateful to our interviewees as well as the leaders and researchers of the Elon University Center for Engaged Learning Research Seminar on Capstone Experiences, especially to Caroline Ketcham for sharing in our group reflection process.

References

Ahonen, P., Tienari, J., Meriläinen, S., & Pullen, A. (2013). Hidden contexts and invisible power relations: A Foucauldian reading of diversity research. *Human Relations*, *67*(3), 263–286. https://doi.org/10.1177/0018726713491772

Bensimon, E. M., & Gray, J. (2020). First-generation equity practitioners: Are they part of the problem? *Change: The Magazine of Higher Learning*, *52*(2), 69–73. https://doi.org/10.1080/00091383.2020.1732790

Bernstein, B. B. (2000). *Pedagogy, symbolic control, and identity: Theory, research, critique* (Revised ed.). Rowman & Littlefield.

Castillo-Montoya, M. (2020). The challenges and tensions of equity-minded teaching. *Change: The Magazine of Higher Learning*, *52*(2), 74–78. https://doi.org/10.1080/00091383.2020.1732791

Crenshaw, K. (1989). Demarginalizing the intersection of race and sex: A Black feminist critique of antidiscrimination doctrine, feminist theory and antiracist politics. *University of Chicago Legal Forum*, *1989*, 139.

Espinosa, L. L., & Mitchell, T. (2020). The state of race and ethnicity in higher education. *Change: The Magazine of Higher Learning*, *52*(2), 27–31. https://doi.org/10.1080/00091383.2020.1732769

Gill, R. (2009). Breaking the silence: The hidden injuries of neo-liberal academia. In R. Ryan-Flood & R. Gill (Eds.), *Secrecy and silence in the research process: Feminist reflections* (pp. 228–244). Routledge.

Haggis, T. (2003). Constructing images of ourselves? A critical investigation into "approaches to learning" research in higher education. *British Educational Research Journal*, *29*(1), 89–104. https://doi.org/10.1080/0141192032000057401

Haggis, T. (2006). Pedagogies for diversity: Retaining critical challenge amidst fears of "dumbing down." *Studies in Higher Education*, *31*(5), 521–535.

Martin, J. M., & Strawser, M. G. (2017). Transforming the capstone: Transformative learning as a pedagogical framework and vehicle for ethical reflection in the capstone course. *The Journal of Faculty Development*, *31*(1), 25–34. https://doi.org/10.1080/03075070600922709

Matus, C., & Infante, M. (2011). Undoing diversity: Knowledge and neoliberal discourses in colleges of education. *Discourse: Studies in the Cultural Politics of Education*, *32*(3), 293–307. https://doi.org/10.1080/01596306.2011.573248

Mayorga-Gallo, S. (2019). The White-centering logic of diversity ideology. *American Behavioral Scientist*, *63*(13), 1789–1810. https://doi.org/10.1177/0002764219842619

McIlwaine, C., & Bunge, D. (2019). Placing diversity among undergraduate geography students in London: Reflections on attainment and progression. *Area*, *51*(3), 500–507. https://doi.org/10.1111/area.12506

Meyer, A., Rose, D. H., & Gordon, D. T. (2014). *Universal design for learning: Theory and practice*. CAST Professional Publishing.

Smith, C., & Worsfold, K. (2015). Unpacking the learning–work nexus: "Priming" as lever for high-quality learning outcomes in work-integrated learning curricula. *Studies in Higher Education*, *40*(1), 22–42. https://doi.org/10.1080/03075079.2013.806456

Tomlinson, M., & Jackson, D. (2019). Professional identity formation in contemporary higher education students. *Studies in Higher Education*, *46*(4), 885–900. https://doi.org/10.1080/03075079.2019.1659763

CONCLUSION

Committing to Equitable, High-Quality Capstone Experiences

Caroline J. Ketcham, Jessie L. Moore, and Anthony G. Weaver

As we looked at the capstone experiences research and practice landscape in the year leading up to the Center for Engaged Learning's 2018–2020 research seminar on capstones and took note of the range of pedagogies, learning experiences, and outcomes clustered under this high-impact educational experience, Tony and Caroline pondered what *capstone* signified:

> Is it a singular or multi-stoned cap to their [students'] college experience? Does this keystone experience help distribute the weight of their educational experiences to multiple stones in their lives or serve as the essential piece to their disciplinary experience? Or does it serve as a foundational cornerstone to their emerging professional life and require significant reflection, integration, and goal setting? (Weaver & Ketcham, 2017, para. 3)

As the chapters in Parts One and Two illustrate, each of these functions can lead to significant outcomes for students:

- Some *capstone* experiences allow students to demonstrate mastery in the context of an authentic learning experience (Devine et al., 2020; Lee & Loton, 2015).
- As *keystones*, students who participate in capstones are more likely to report gains in thinking critically, working with others, and solving complex problems than students who do not have the experience (Kinzie, 2013; Kuh, 2008; NSSE, 2018).
- As *cornerstones*, National Survey of Student Engagement results show that taking part in a culminating experience was positively related to seniors' perceptions of preparation for their postgraduation plans (NSSE, 2018).

Cornerstone experiences that connect professional dispositions and skills with content learning and knowledge help students understand and choose a profession that is a good personal and professional fit (Appleby et al., 2016; Chorazy & Klinedinst, 2019), facilitating their transition to postcollege careers.

Regardless of which of these intentions, combination of intentions, and corresponding outcomes programs and institutions pursue, this collection offers several takeaways that should inform the design, implementation, and ongoing assessment of high-quality capstone experiences.

Takeaway 1: Alignment in the Communication About Capstones Across Socioecological System Levels Matters

As the chapters in Parts One and Two demonstrate, higher education institutions vary substantially in how they implement capstone experiences and what goals they attempt to achieve. Given the varied assumptions students, their parents, faculty, administrators, policymakers, and others might bring to campus discussions about local capstones, consistent communication about the goals and value of capstones within the institution increases the likelihood that everyone involved reaches a shared understanding of the campus's unique culminating experience (see also Ketcham et al., 2022). Any single capstone design is unlikely to, or should, deliver all of the diverse goals described in Part One, so aligning institutional communication about local capstone experiences also helps institutions determine which learning outcomes they want to commit to and how they'll commit resources—including faculty time—to reaching those goals. This transparent alignment across the institution also helps faculty examine how well pathways leading to the capstone prepare students for their culminating experiences—and what broader curricular revisions might be necessary to support students' learning along these pathways. We envision the socioecological model helping institutions' ability to plan and articulate this alignment while considering direct and indirect impacts.

Takeaway 2: Capstone Experiences Lead to Meaningful Learning Outcomes, but Higher Education Still Needs to Attend to Equity in Experiences for Diverse Learners

Bean et al.'s analysis in chapter 1 suggests that less than a quarter of U.S. colleges and universities explicitly require capstone experiences. As a result, despite the range of exciting capstone designs reflected in Part Two, most students are not guaranteed this meaningful learning opportunity. Further, as McGrath et al. discuss in chapter 14, even the most thoughtfully designed capstone experiences might be perpetuating exclusive practices. Equitable learning experiences must embrace the diverse identities and experiences learners bring with them, rather than centering any one student identity as representative of a homogenous group.

Takeaway 3: High-Quality Capstone Experiences Require Ongoing Commitment to Faculty Development, Assessment, and Curricular Cohesion

Additionally, if programs use assessment data to "close the loop," high-quality capstone experiences also may necessitate curricular redesign, both in the capstone and in the pathways leading to the capstone. As the chapters in Part Three illustrate, this recursive design-and-assess process across socioecological levels requires thoughtful heuristics and substantial commitment from faculty and administrators, but exo- and macrolevel support (e.g., time and other resources for ongoing academic development and assessment) can foster significant learning outcomes for students. Of course, acknowledging the significant commitments faculty must make to teach high-quality capstones that provide equitable learning experiences for diverse learners also necessitates acknowledging that not all faculty are prepared to teach capstones. Furthermore, some faculty might never embrace the time commitment and mindset needed to develop—and routinely redevelop—equitable, high-quality capstones. Therefore, university policies at the ecosystem must navigate celebrating and supporting capstone faculty without requiring all faculty to step into this teaching role.

Capstone Experiences Post-COVID

As we write this conclusion in spring 2021, we're compelled to address how the global COVID-19 pandemic has altered the capstone landscape. Here are a few examples of changes that we find promising and hope will continue:

Opening Up New Opportunities for Collaboration and Communication

- As community and client partners have become less place-based, they also have been open to new types of collaborations with courses, extending opportunities that were not available with previous conceptions of site-based work. While remote work experiences are inherently different than in-person interactions, new remote partnerships have increased opportunities for capstone courses to include real-world applications.

- Faculty and staff have embraced the use of additional online communication tools, some of which allow for more frequent, timely, and constructive feedback—from faculty, staff, peers, and client or community partners—on students' work-in-progress.

- Similarly, increasing comfort with online communication platforms—both synchronous and asynchronous—has inspired long-distance connections and collaborations. Classes in the United States have partnered with classes in other countries. College classes have partnered with K–12 classes to support remote learners. And speakers seem a bit more willing to Zoom in for a class visit. While none of these activities are entirely new, they certainly are happening with more frequency.

An Increased Societal Awareness of Social Inequities

At the same time, many of the collection authors also live in countries grappling with social inequities that too often are perpetuated by higher education systems, and capstones should respond to the sociocultural context. Therefore, even as we embrace lessons learned from colleges' pivots to online or hybrid instruction during the pandemic, our concluding *charge to readers starts with a call for equity.*

Looking Forward

We challenge faculty, faculty developers, and other higher education leaders who are (re)designing capstones to:

- Focus on fostering equitable capstone experience. Equity starts with access, but it does not end there. *All* students should have access to high-quality capstones, which might necessitate making them a required part of the curriculum so that faculty, staff, and administrators can discuss intentional designs that allow students to have meaningful capstone experiences regardless of the other commitments in their academic and personal lives. Yes, equitable capstone designs also must *center students' diverse identities and experiences* in the implementation of culminating experiences. Capstones shouldn't be one-size-fits-some; whether they function as capstones, keystones, or cornerstones, they must genuinely embrace the diverse strengths and needs in the classroom.

- Commit to looking beyond the capstone experience to achieve that equity. What are the pathways diverse students take to the capstone, and do all of those pathways adequately prepare students for the capstone? What are the pipelines capstones support to careers and opportunities beyond? Equitable, high-quality capstone experiences attend to the pathways students have taken to the capstone and meet students where they are, rather than assuming prior knowledge that students haven't had opportunities to develop. Moreover, equitable capstone experiences might necessitate revising courses and other learning experiences in those pathways and pipelines, addressing inequities across the socioecological system.

- Allocate resources—including the resource of time—to professional development and to ongoing assessments that meaningfully inform (re) design of capstones and the pathways to them. As several chapters in this collection demonstrate, equitable, high-quality capstone experiences require ongoing, institutional commitment, but when colleges sufficiently invest in this high-impact practice, students demonstrate learning outcomes that prepare them not only for the workforce but also for responsible citizenship in a globally networked world.

Capstone experiences hold such promise for the future of higher education, and the socioecological contexts that impact students really matter. Our communities and societies are counting on future generations, and the promise of tomorrow relies on higher education connecting to social needs and providing 21st-century workforce skills. Capstone experiences support that promise modeling the missions institutions have for their place in creating greater good. This book gives readers resources and innovative ideas to engage in implementing positive change on their campuses; and collectively we can be a force for the greater good.

References

Appleby, K. M., Foster, E., & Kamusoko, S. (2016). Full speed ahead: Using a senior capstone course to facilitate students' professional transition. *JOPERD: The Journal of Physical Education, Recreation & Dance, 87*(3), 16–21. https://doi.org.proxyiub.uits.iu.edu/10.1080/07303084.2015.1131214

Chorazy, M. L., & Klinedinst, K. S. (2019, February 26). Learn by doing: A model for incorporating high-impact experiential learning into an undergraduate public health curriculum. *Frontiers in Public Health, 7.* https://doi.org/10.3389/fpubh.2019.00031

Devine, J. L., Bourgault, K. S., & Schwartz, R. N. (2020). Using the online capstone experience to support authentic learning. *TechTrends, 64,* 606–615. https://doi.org/10.1007/s11528-020-00516-1

Ketcham, C. J., Weaver, A. G., Moore, J. L., & Felten, P. (2022). Living up to the capstone promise: Improving quality, equity, and outcomes in culminating experiences. In J. Zilvinskis, J. Kinzie, J. Daday, K. O'Donnell, & C. Vande Zande (Eds.), *Delivering on the promise of high-impact practices: Research and models for achieving equity, fidelity, impact, and scale* (pp. 124–134). Stylus.

Kinzie, J. (2013). Taking stock of capstones and integrated learning. *Peer Review, 15*(4), 27–30.

Kuh, G. D. (2008). *High-impact educational practices: What they are, who has access to them, and why they matter.* Association of American Colleges and Universities.

Lee, N., & Loton, D. (2015). Integrating research and professional learning—Australian capstones. *Council on Undergraduate Research Quarterly, 35*(4), 28–35.

National Survey of Student Engagement. (2018). *Engagement insights: Survey findings on the quality of undergraduate education—Annual results 2018.* Indiana University Center for Postsecondary Research.

Weaver, T., & Ketcham, C. (2017). "Capstone" experience in higher education. [Blog Post]. *Elon University Center for Engaged Learning.* https://www.centerforengagedlearning.org/capstone-experience-in-higher-education/

EDITORS AND CONTRIBUTORS

Olivia S. Anderson is a clinical associate professor in the Nutritional Sciences Department at the University of Michigan (UM) School of Public Health. Anderson is interested in the scholarship of teaching and learning in public health education. Her research has a specific emphasis surrounding: (a) implications of the public health discipline to interprofessional education (IPE) and practice, (b) lactation education training aimed to reduce health disparities and promote population health, and (c) equitable teaching strategies for effective education especially in public health writing. Anderson teaches maternal child nutrition and professional development courses that foster public health writing and teaching skills.

Janet Bean is the director of the Institute for Teaching and Learning and an associate professor of English at the University of Akron (Ohio). She works with faculty development and curricular initiatives, including a revised general education program that includes capstones in the major. Her research interests include writing pedagogy, general education, and assessment of student learning.

Christina Beaudoin is a professor of Movement Science at Grand Valley State University in Allendale, MI. She teaches a major required capstone course within exercise science as well as a general education "Issues" capstone course. Christina is interested in examining the landscape of contemporary capstone experiences (CEs) and what will be important to the future of effective CEs. With a background in sport and exercise psychology, her exercise science research interests examine the impact of exercise and physical activity behaviors on health, fitness, and well-being.

Simon B. Bedford is the pro vice chancellor (Learning Futures) at Western Sydney University in Australia. He has helped to drive several national projects including Institutional External Referencing of Assessment Standards (ERoS), an interinstitutional collaboration; Assessment Standards in STEM, Assessing Assessments Against Threshhold Learning Outcomes, and a new Taxonomy for Credentialing Australasian University Educators (TCAUE). Professor Bedford leads the HERDSA assessment quality group, and is president of the Council of Australasian University Leaders in Learning and Teaching.

Sandra Bell is a professor in the Department of Humanities and Languages at University of New Brunswick, Saint John. She teaches 16th- and 17th-century literature and theatre courses, and has published on the writing of James VI of Scotland and his mother, Mary Stuart. She writes, directs, and acts for the local theatre scene. She is currently developing medical readers theatre scripts as educational tools in health care.

Caroline Boswell is a faculty development specialist in the Delphi Center for Teaching and Learning at the University of Louisville where she designs, facilitates, and evaluates faculty development programming and serves on the Quality Enhancement Plan staff team. Her research interests include teaching with archives, faculty equity orientation and student success outcomes, capstone experiences, and the social history of politics in revolutionary England.

Sarah Brennan codesigned and cofacilitated a Title V capstone seminar and undergraduate research initiative at Hostos Community College. She has more than a decade of experience working with faculty development initiatives and has presented both nationally and regionally on capstone learning, faculty development, and assessment. She earned master's degrees in public administration from CUNY Baruch College and student personnel administration from Buffalo State College. Brennan serves as the executive associate to the acting provost/VP for academic affairs.

Sarah Dyer is an associate professor of human geography at the University of Exeter in the United Kingdom. She teaches across the undergraduate program and is BA program director in the department. Sarah is also module convenor for the university's postgraduate academic practice module "Creating Effective Learning in Higher Education." This role provides her with insights from peers into the challenges of teaching in different disciplines across the university. Sarah is the director of the university's Education Incubator, an initiative for developing and spreading innovative and effective educational practice.

Michelle J. Eady is an associate professor in the School of Education at the University of Wollongong, Australia. Michelle is the president elect (2022–2024) of the International Society for the Scholarship of Teaching and Learning (ISSOTL). She is both an ISSOTL and HERDSA Fellow, a senior Fellow of the HEA, and holds a national teaching citation for her work in quality teacher preparation. Her research interests include SoTL, WIL, synchronous technologies, Indigenous studies, work integrated learning (WIL), and other current issues in education. Michelle has had the pleasure of speaking at conferences worldwide and looks forward to collaborations with colleagues who have a similar passion for SoTL.

Frederick T. Evers is a professor emeritus in the Department of Sociology and Anthropology at the University of Guelph. Evers has received the University of Guelph-Humber Medal of Merit in 2012, the 3M Teaching Fellowship in 2001, and the University of Guelph President's Distinguished Professor Award in 2001. *The Bases of Competence: Skills for Lifelong Learning and Employability*, by Evers, James Rush, and Iris Berdrow was published by Jossey-Bass in 1998.

Morgan Gresham is an associate professor at the University of South Florida St. Petersburg, where she serves as the area director of the MA/PhD in rhetoric and composition and the professional and technical communication major. Her scholarship brings together feminism, computers and composition, and writing program administration. She is particularly interested in the role of capstones for the assessment of upper-division general education requirements.

Paul Hansen joined the faculty of Bard High School Early College Cleveland in 2017. He teaches English courses in the high school program, seminar courses in the college program, and electives focused on contemporary American fiction. Hansen earned an AA from Bard College at Simon's Rock, a BA in English and photography from Oberlin College, and a PhD in English from the University of Wisconsin. He is always happy to answer questions about the Bard Early Colleges.

Trina Jorre de St Jorre is a senior lecturer in Deakin Learning Futures and the Centre for Research in Assessment in Digital Learning at Deakin University. She leads research and implements strategies focused on enhancing student achievement, employability, and graduate outcomes. She is an advocate for inclusive pedagogical approaches that incentivize and recognize distinct achievement, and partnerships that empower students, graduates, and educators to learn and impact change.

Caroline J. Ketcham is professor of exercise science at Elon University. She co-led the Center for Engaged Learning's (CEL) research seminar on capstone experiences and is currently the CEL scholar focusing on equity and access to high-impact practices for neurodivergent and physically disabled students. Caroline's expertise is in movement neuroscience and she serves as codirector of Elon BrainCARE Research Institute. Caroline has won university-wide awards for mentoring, scholarship, teaching, and service.

Jillian Kinzie is associate director of the Center for Postsecondary Research and the National Survey of Student Engagement Institute at the Indiana University School of Education. She conducts research and leads project activities on effective use of student engagement data to improve educational quality. She is coauthor of *Delivering on the Promise of High-Impact Practices: Research and Models for Achieving Equity, Fidelity, Impact, and Scale* (Stylus, 2022), *Using Evidence of Student Learning to Improve Higher Education* (Jossey-Bass, 2015), and *Student Success in College* (Jossey-Bass, 2005/2010).

Russell Kirkscey is assistant professor of English and technical and professional writing at Penn State Harrisburg. His research focuses on health and medical communication and the scholarship of teaching and learning. He teaches technical editing, document design, rhetorical analysis, and advanced writing for students in scientific and technical disciplines.

Matthew J. Laye is an associate professor of the Idaho College of Osteopathic Medicine. He teaches physiology and research methods to first- and second-year medical students. Previously he taught at the College of Idaho and was chair of the Health and Human Performance Department. He is interested in faculty motivation and previously studied the effects of physical activity on disease prevention and health promotion.

David I. Lewis is an associate professor in pharmacology and bioethics at the University of Leeds (UK). He creates innovative educational interventions that give learners ownership of their learning, promoting learner personal and professional development: capstone experiences, public engagement schemes, educational internships, and professional education in research animal sciences and ethics. Dave splits his time between the United Kingdom, European Union, India, and Africa. He has received multiple prestigious educational prizes from Advance HE, UK Physiological Society, British Pharmacological Society, and UK Biochemical Society.

Nicholas V. Longo is a professor of global studies and codirector of the Dialogue, Inclusion, and Democracy Lab at Providence College. He is also a faculty mentor and board member at College Unbound and faculty consultant on the AAC&U Civic Prompts in the Major Institutes. His recent coedited books include *Creating Space for Democracy: A Primer on Dialogue and Deliberation in Higher Education* (Stylus, 2019) and *Publicly Engaged Scholars: Next Generation Engagement and the Future of Higher Education* (Stylus, 2016).

Moriah McSharry McGrath is senior instructor of urban studies and planning at Portland State University (U.S.), where she focuses on teaching in the area of community development. She is an interdisciplinary social scientist cross-trained in urban planning and public health and her research centers on understanding how health inequities are rooted in space.

Caryn McTighe Musil, a national leader for diversity, democracy, equity, global learning, and women's issues, is distinguished fellow at the Association of American Colleges and Universities, having served in senior-level positions there for 3 decades. She is the lead author of *A Crucible Moment: College Learning and Democracy's Future* (AAC&U, 2012) and most recently was director of the Civic Prompts in the Major: Social Responsibility and the Public Good institute. Her BA is from Duke University and MA and PhD from Northwestern University.

Jessie L. Moore is director of the Center for Engaged Learning and professor of English in professional writing and rhetoric at Elon University. She leads the center's multi-institutional research seminars. She coedits the Stylus Publishing/Center for Engaged Learning Series on Engaged Learning and Teaching and the Center for Engaged Learning Open Access Book Series. Her professional service was recognized with the 2019 International Society for the Scholarship of Teaching and Learning Distinguished Service Award.

Shannon Murray is a professor and 3M National Teaching Fellow (2001), teaching early modern and children's literature at the University of Prince Edward Island. She gives workshops and talks on Active Learning, Capstone Courses, Learning Communities, and Teaching Dossiers, including since 2002 for the UPEI Faculty Development Summer Institute on Active Learning. Her book *Shakespeare's Guide to Hope, Life, and Learning*, with Lisa Dickson and Jessica Riddell, is forthcoming with the University of Toronto Press.

Nelson Nunez Rodriguez is professor of chemistry and former unit coordinator and director of the Center for Teaching and Learning at Hostos Community College, and Fulbright specialist on STEM education. He is a subaward principal investigator for an NIH-IRACDA program and cochair for the institution Middle States Accreditation Self-Study. He received a biology degree from Havana University, a PhD in chemistry from University of Cordoba, and developed a postdoctoral training at Mount Sinai School of Medicine, New York.

Matthew Park joined the faculty of Bard High School Early College (BHSEC) Newark in 2013 as a professor of African history and global social sciences. His PhD is in African history from Michigan State University and his BA is in history and secondary education from the College of New Jersey. He is currently the program chair for Second Year Seminar for the Bard Early College network and he teaches courses in African history, literature, and film at BHSEC Newark.

Andrew J. Pearl serves as the director of community engagement research and publications at the University of Alabama's Center for Community-Based Partnerships. His research interests include motivations for and the impacts of community engagement of students, faculty members, and institutions. He earned his PhD from the University of Georgia's Louise McBee Institute of Higher Education.

Joanna C. Rankin is the program director and an associate professor (teaching) in the community rehabilitation and disability studies program in the Cumming School of Medicine at the University of Calgary, in Alberta, Canada. Her work is centered around the role of equity, diversity, and inclusion in higher education; working with students as partners; and developing innovative mental health supports in collaboration with mental health service users.

Rico R. Reed serves as assistant director for communications and partnerships with the National Resource Center for the First-Year Experience and Students in Transition. He is responsible for developing, marketing, and promoting a consistent, positive, and accurate image of the center to internal and external publics. His duties also include coordinating the center's efforts to develop and share pertinent resources, products, and events with constituents. Rico has a background in public relations, graphic design, and journalism.

Silvia Reyes serves as the director of special projects and student engagement at Hostos. She is committed to student success, and her work has focused on designing and implementing a wide array of initiatives to improve students' college experiences and academic achievement. he received a BA in psychology from Hunter College, an MSW from Yeshiva University, and an EdD from St. John's University.

Cindy Koenig Richards is a professor at Willamette University, where she is the founding chair of the Civic Communication and Media Department and the director of Ringe Media Lab. A national leader for civic learning, she is a faculty consultant on the AAC&U Civic Prompts in the Major Institutes and a recipient of the National Communication Association Ecroyd Award for Outstanding Teaching in Higher Education.

Guy Risko joined Bard High School Early College (BHSEC) Cleveland as a founding faculty member in 2014 as a professor of English literature. He is currently the dean of collegiate studies at BHSEC Cleveland where he continues to teach electives focused on 20th- and 21st-century American literature and film.

Tracy L. Skipper is an editor, writer, and student success scholar focusing on college student development, first-year initiatives, and high-impact practices. She is the senior thesis director and academic advisor in the South Carolina Honors College at the University of South Carolina. Tracy has served as a student affairs administrator, taught writing at the college level, designed faculty development workshops on senior capstone experiences, and led workshops and online courses on applying student development theory to curricular and cocurricular contexts. She holds degrees in psychology, higher education, American literature, and rhetoric and composition.

Margaret Anne Smith is the president and a professor of English literature at St. Stephen's University, a small liberal arts university in St. Stephen, New Brunswick, Canada. She has worked in faculty development, and teaches and writes in the fields of American and environmental literature, and arts education.

Dawn Smith-Sherwood is professor of Spanish in the Department of Foreign Languages at Indiana University of Pennsylvania (IUP), where she also previously served as a faculty living-learning partner to the Global Awareness Living-Learning Community and a member of the IUP Living-Learning Executive Team. Currently, she is IUP's director of liberal studies.

Julie Vale received her PhD in electrical engineering from the University of Waterloo. She is an associate professor at the University of Guelph, where she teaches a wide range of first-year to graduate-level engineering courses. Her current research aims to improve the design and delivery of engineering courses and assessments with the goal of helping students achieve desired program outcomes ranging from problem-solving to equity-based approaches to engineering design.

Carol Van Zile-Tamsen is the associate vice provost for curriculum, assessment, and teaching transformation at the University at Buffalo. Her primary focus involves student learning sssessment, psychometrics, and using data for improvement efforts. She teaches pedagogy and psychometric theory for graduate students from across the university, as well as first-year seminars for incoming freshmen and transfer students. She is an alumni of UB, earning her doctorate in educational psychology in 1996.

Tania von der Heidt teaches marketing and management subjects at undergraduate and graduate levels, both in Australia and throughout Asia. Tania's scholarship of learning and teaching focuses on capstone experiences, education for sustainability in business, and creative problem-solving in marketing education. Her research portfolio also includes regulation of tourism accommodation in the sharing economy and consumer behavior related to sustainable products. In her PhD Tania investigated collaborative product innovation in Australian manufacturing.

Joshua Walker teaches Latin American history, history of the environment, and college seminar at Bard High School Early College, Cleveland. He studied history at the Ohio State University (BA) and the University of Maryland, College Park (MA and PhD).

Anthony G. Weaver is associate dean of the School of Communications and professor of sport management at Elon University. He co-led the Center for Engaged Learning's 2018–2020 research seminar on capstone experiences. His application of high-impact practices has led to several mentored capstone experiences including undergraduate research projects, internships, and the creation of student leadership opportunities.

Dallin George Young is an assistant professor in the College Student Affairs Administration and Student Affairs Leadership graduate programs at the University of Georgia. He is an affiliate scholar for the National Resource Center for the First-Year Experience and Students in Transition. His research focuses on a line of inquiry that investigates how novices are trained, socialized, and educated as they move from the periphery to full participation in academic communities of practice.

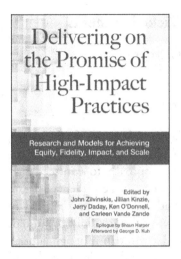

Delivering on the Promise of High-Impact Practices

Research and Models for Achieving Equity, Fidelity, Impact, and Scale

Edited by John Zilvinskis, Jillian Kinzie, Jerry Daday, Ken O'Donnell, and Carleen Vande Zande

Epilogue by Shaun Harper

Afterword by George D. Kuh

Research shows that enriching learning experiences such as learning communities, service-learning, undergraduate research, internships, and senior culminating experiences—collectively known as high-impact practices (HIPs)—are positively associated with student engagement; deep, and integrated learning; and personal and educational gains for all students—particularly for historically underserved students, including first-generation students and racially minoritized populations.

The goal of *Delivering on the Promise of High-Impact Practices* is to provide examples from around the country of the ways educators are advancing equity, promoting fidelity, achieving scale, and strengthening assessment of their own local high-impact practices. Its chapters bring together the best current scholarship, methodologies, and evidence-based practices within the HIPs field, illustrating new approaches to faculty professional development, culture and coalition building, research and assessment, and continuous improvement that help institutions understand and extend practices with a demonstrated high impact.

Creating Wicked Students

Designing Courses for a Complex World

Paul Hanstedt

"From its playful title to its final chapter, *Creating Wicked Students* offers a thought-provoking new approach to course design focused on helping college students develop the abilities and self-authorship needed to work—and live—meaningfully. Hanstedt guides the reader through a design process for courses where students learn skills and content, but more significantly, develop 'the ability to step into a complex, messy world and interact with that world in thoughtful and productive ways'."—***Deandra Little**, Director, Center for the Advancement of Teaching and Learning and Professor of English, Elon University*

"*Creating Wicked Students* is one of the best books I have read in the last decade. I am a midcareer teacher educator and scholar in an English department, and I wish I had read this book when I was a doctoral student. Nevertheless, this outstanding text has a lot to offer for all scholars trying to adapt to changing technologies and learner populations, providing innovative and practical strategies for course design."—***Teachers College Record***

Infusing Critical Thinking Into Your Course

A Concrete, Practical Approach

Linda B. Nilson

"This book should be read and used by every faculty member. Improved critical thinking is an essential outcome for all courses and for research training in any field. Nilson has drawn on her long experience as an outstanding faculty developer to make it easier for any of us to foster advanced critical thinking. She clearly explains the underlying rationale and provides powerful ways to engage students. She includes: (a) a quick and accurate review of major alternative frameworks, (b) extensively developed examples of ways to implement each of them with students, and (c) multiple approaches to assess students' thinking while fostering further sophistication. I would have been a much more effective teacher if I had had this foundation to build on."—*Craig E. Nelson, Professor Emeritus, Biology, Indiana University*

"The ability to think critically is vital to our capacity to 'routinely confront dishonesty' in Linda Nilson's words. In this lively and accessible book, Nilson reviews how students can be helped to investigate claims made across a wide range of disciplines. She provides numerous examples of classroom exercises and assessment formats for college teachers seeking practical guidance on how to infuse critical thinking across the curriculum."—*Stephen D. Brookfield, Distinguished Scholar, Antioch University*

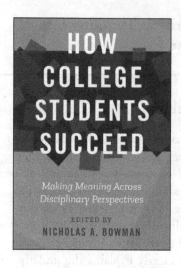

How College Students Succeed

Making Meaning Across Disciplinary Perspectives

Edited by Nicholas A. Bowman

"Nick Bowman is probably the nation's leading scholar on student success in college. He has pulled together a talented group of authors to focus on the different dimensions of student success. The result is a work that should be required reading for all faculty and administrators concerned about students and the impact of college."—***Ernest T. Pascarella***, *Professor Emeritus of Higher Education and Student Affairs, University of Iowa*

"Essential. Timely. Requisite reading. This interdisciplinary compendium not only provides a theoretical framework to advance our knowledge of college student success, but also serves as an indispensable guide for higher education institutions to anticipate the postpandemic needs of our students and eliminate the institutional barriers that inhibit their success. How College Students Succeed will help inform practice for years to come." —***Doneka R. Scott***, *Vice Chancellor and Dean for the Division of Academic and Student Affairs, North Carolina State University*

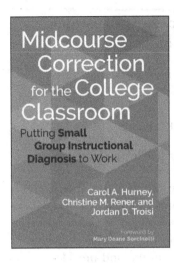

Midcourse Correction for the College Classroom

Putting Small Group Instructional Diagnosis to Work

Carol A. Hurney, Christine M. Rener, and Jordan D. Troisi

Foreword by Mary Deane Sorcinelli

Midcourse Correction for the College Classroom

Putting Small Group instructional Diagnosis to Work

Carol A. Hurney,
Christine M. Rener, and
Jordan D. Torisi

Foreword by Mary Dean Sorcinelli

This book is about using the small group instructional diagnosis (SGID) method to make improvements to the educational experience midcourse. The idea is to use this structured interview process to involve students in helping faculty improve a course while they are in it, potentially making a difference for themselves as well as for future students. Faculty gain the opportunity to work on a course before it ends, and can see what changes work without waiting for the next time the course is offered, or the end of semester student evaluations.

SGID is a consultation method developed to collect midsemester feedback from students using structured small and large group conversations, involving four conversations between students, a learned colleague the authors refer to as the SGID consultant, and the instructor. First, student talk with each other in small groups about the learning happening in a course, under the guidance of a consultant (SGID Conversation #1—Student & Students). Then the SGID consultant engages the students in a conversation about how the feedback provided impacts the *learning* in the course (SGID Conversation #2—Students & Consultant). Then there is a conversation between the consultant and the instructor, where they discuss how the feedback provided by the students can best inform the pedagogical approaches and strategies used by the instructor (SGID Conversation #3—Consultant & Instructor). Finally, the instructor closes the feedback loop with a conversation with their students about what they learned and how best to move forward (SGID Conversation #4—Instructor & Students).

The New Science of Learning, Third Edition

How to Learn in Harmony With Your Brain

Todd D. Zakrajsek

Foreword by John N. Gardner

"This book masterfully weaves together leading brain research and practical examples to show students 'how to learn'. It addresses common pitfalls that students encounter in their learning journey, and provides a clear roadmap of research-based strategies that can enhance comprehension, long-term retention, and the overall learning experience (such as spaced practice, metacognitive strategies, and yes, sleep). This book is a must-read for students who want the tools to succeed in college and beyond!"—*Tolulope (Tolu) Noah, Instructional Learning Spaces Coordinator, California State University, Long Beach*

"An instant classic when first published in 2013, this updated third edition of *The New Science of Learning* should be required reading for every college student. It is an invaluable resource for educators searching for concrete, evidence-based ways to help students build academic skills, agency, and self-efficacy. It is a truly empowering book for students and instructors alike." —*Jessamyn Neuhaus, Director, SUNY Plattsburgh Center for Teaching Excellence, author of Geeky Pedagogy: A Guide for Intellectuals, Introverts, and Nerds Who Want to be Effective Teachers*

Mind the Gap

Global Learning at Home and Abroad

Edited by Nina Namaste and Amanda Sturgill

With Neal W. Sobania and Michael Vande Berg

Series Foreword by Jessie L. Moore and Peter Felten

Part of the Series on Engaged Learning and Teaching

There is growing awareness that global learning is not confined to university, credit-bearing off-campus international programs, and that institutions of higher learning have, up until now, conceived of global education too narrowly. Global learning through study abroad and off-campus domestic study fits into a larger context of students' educational experiences. You can find global learning as part of other high-impact practices; domestic off-campus programs, undergraduate research, and service- or community-based learning all can be global learning opportunities. On-campus global learning can occur in the disciplines and in the core curriculum as well. Language and culture, anthropology, sociology, and other departments, multicultural centers, and diversity and inclusivity offices, to name a few, also teach students to be global learners. Global learning pertains to the many staff and faculty educators who intentionally encourage students to engage with and successfully navigate difference. Thus, there is a growing need for bridging across disciplinary and administrative silos; silos that are culturally bound within academia. The gaps between these silos matter as students seek to integrate off- and on-campus learning.

Higher education needs a new, holistic assessment of global learning. This book investigates not just student learning, but also faculty experiences, program structures, and pathways that impact global learning, and expands the context of global learning to show its antecedents and impacts as a part of the larger higher education experience. Chapters look at recent developments such as short-term, off-campus, international study and certificate/medallion programs, as well as blended learning environments and undergraduate research, all in the context of multi-institutional comparisons. Global learning is also situated in a larger university context.

Promoting Equity and Justice Through Pedagogical Partnership

Alise de Bie, Elizabeth Marquis, Alison Cook-Sather, and Leslie Patricia Luqueño

Foreword by Alexis Giron

Series Foreword by Jessie L. Moore and Peter Felten

Part of the Series on Engaged Learning and Teaching

"This is the book we have been waiting for. It provides a paradigmatic shift in understanding the relationships between partnership and equity and justice. From the moving account in the preface of the healing experienced by one Afro-Latino student during the course of her engagement in a partnership program; through the development and application of a powerful conceptual framework for understanding the violences and resulting harms that marginalized students face in higher education; to the insightful case studies, reflections, and recommendations focused on how pedagogical partnership can redress the harms equity-seeking groups experience; this book carries the reader forward with passion and care."—**Ruth and Mick Healey**, *Healey HE Consultants, UK*

"There are urgent and specific forms of violence faced by students from equity-seeking groups, practices that have led to harms that we, as educators and practitioners, are called on to redress. By synthesizing the literature on partnerships and postsecondary student equity, this essential text offers an invitation to reimagine how higher education can provide a collaborative space of engagement in which justice can be pursued."—**Steven Volk**, *Codirector, Great Lakes Colleges Association Consortium for Teaching and Learning; Professor of History Emeritus, Oberlin College*

Also available from Stylus

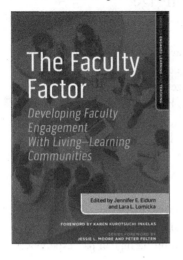

The Faculty Factor

Developing Faculty Engagement With Living–Learning Communities

Edited by Jennifer E. Eidum and Lara L. Lomicka

Foreword by Karen Kurotsuchi Inkelas

Series Foreword by Jessie L. Moore and Peter Felten

Part of the Series on Engaged Learning and Teaching

This practical resource examines how colleges and universities foster sustainable faculty involvement in living learning communities (LLCs). This volume delivers evidence-based research as well as practical examples and voices from the field, to guide and support faculty serving in different capacities in LLCs, to serve as a resource for student affairs practitioners collaborating with faculty in residential environments, and to offer guidance to administrators developing new and revising existing LLC programs.

This book demonstrates that faculty are key to creating equitable, engaging, and sustainable LLCs in diverse higher education settings. Chapters delve into both the microlevel experiences of individual faculty—and their families, as in the vignettes at the beginning of each chapter—and the macrolevel campus-wide planning that positions LLCs as meaningful learning experiences for students.

ELON UNIVERSITY | CENTER FOR Engaged Learning

The Center for Engaged Learning at Elon University (www .CenterForEngagedLearning.org) brings together international leaders in higher education to develop and to synthesize rigorous research on central questions about student learning. Researchers have identified "high-impact" educational practices—undergraduate research, internships, service-learning, writing-intensive courses, study abroad, living-learning communities, and so on. While we know *what* these practices are, we could know much more about three essential issues:

1. *how* to do these practices well and in diverse contexts,
2. how to *scale* these practices equitably to all students, and
3. how students *integrate* their learning across multiple high impact experiences.

The Center for Engaged Learning fosters investigations of these and related questions, principally by hosting multi-institutional research and practice-based initiatives, conferences, and seminars. To date, the Center's events have focused on topics like civic engagement, mentoring undergraduate research, global learning, residential learning, capstone experiences, and preparing students for writing beyond the university.

The Center also develops open-access resources on engaged learning practices and research for faculty and educational developers. Visit www .CenterForEngagedLearning.org to access supplemental resources for books in this series, as well as weekly blog posts, hundreds of videos, and introductory resource pages on specific engaged learning topics and on strategies for pursuing scholarship of teaching and learning.

Jessie L. Moore
Director
jmoore28@elon.edu

Peter Felten
Executive Director
pfelten@elon.edu

Sty/us

22883 Quicksilver Drive
Sterling, VA 20166-2019   Subscribe to our email alerts: www.Styluspub.com